Study Guide

for

Kendall's

Sociology in Our Times

Fifth Edition

Study Guide

for

Kendall's

Sociology in Our Times

Fifth Edition

Kathryn Sinast Mueller
Baylor University

Diana Kendall
Baylor University

THOMSON

WADSWORTH

Australia • Canada • Mexico • Singapore • Spain • United Kingdom • United States

Printed in the United States of America
1 2 3 4 5 6 7 07 06 05 04

Printer: Thomson West

0-534-62691-2

For more information about our products, contact us at:
**Thomson Learning Academic Resource Center
1-800-423-0563**

For permission to use material from this text or product, submit a request online at
http://www.thomsonrights.com
Any additional questions about permissions can be submitted at
thomsonrights@thomson.com

Thomson Wadsworth
10 Davis Drive
Belmont, CA 94002-3098
USA

Asia
Thomson Learning
5 Shenton Way #01-01
UIC Building
Singapore 068808

Australia/New Zealand
Thomson Learning
102 Dodds Street
Southbank, Victoria 3006
Australia

Canada
Nelson
1120 Birchmount Road
Toronto, Ontario M1K 5G4
Canada

Europe/Middle East/South Africa
Thomson Learning
High Holborn House
50/51 Bedford Row
London WC1R 4LR
United Kingdom

Latin America
Thomson Learning
Seneca, 53
Colonia Polanco
11560 Mexico D.F.
Mexico

Spain/Portugal
Paraninfo
Calle/Magallanes, 25
28015 Madrid, Spain

Table of Contents

From Students to Students about the Study Guide

Dear students,

With the aid of this study guide that Professor Mueller has tediously prepared, the information presented in the text book is concisely accessible for additional studying. I find that the study guide presents a less overwhelming teaching tool for the introduction of sociology and I appreciate all the work that Professor Mueller put into the study guide in order to give students a highlight of the text book material. This book is a great source for studying beyond the text.

Hillary Jacobson
Baylor University, Class of 2004

Dear students,

I have known Professor Mueller for years now, and she is my mentor, counselor, sounding-board, and friend. Being her teaching assistant has been one of the most rewarding jobs of my life. She has taught me more about sociology than any book has, and Professor Mueller has channeled her plethora of knowledge into this study guide. This study guide will steer you into the path of the sociological imagination. Pay attention because the information is applicable to almost every aspect of your lives.

Rachel E. Lovell, M.A.
Baylor University, Class of 2001
Ohio State, PhD. Student 2004

Dear students,

An enormous amount of labor and caring went into making this study guide. I have watched Professor Mueller, and her assistants all huddled over mounds of paper with post-it notes everywhere. Read, study, and remember the words of Sir Winston Churchill, "Never, never, never, give up."

Donna Grelle
Departmental Administrator and student
Baylor University, 2004

Dear Students,

I highly suggest reading this study guide in addition to the textbook. Professor Mueller has put a tredemenous amount of work into creating this book. You can learn a great deal of interesting facts from this guide. Both the text and the study guide are excellent sources for diverse and mind boggling concepts.

Belinda Ann May
Baylor University, Class of 2004

DEDICATED

to

Kenneth Ray Mueller, the wind beneath my wings!

Wonderful children: Kristy Mueller Suelflow & Jerry Suelflow,
Kirby Ray & Lisa Meyer Mueller, Keary Kal & Amy Hvasta Mueller

Wonderful grandchildren: Jeremy Allen, Joshua Ray, Kristyn MaryKathryn, Caitlin
Virginia, Delaney Rae, and Timothy Patrick

And Mom Beulah Mueller

And a special thanks to my assistant, Hillary Jacobson

YOU ARE ALL THE BEST!!! AND YOU ARE LOVED!!!

Preface

Welcome to the study of *Sociology in Our Times*, 5th Edition. The text, written by my colleague, Diana Kendall, is innovative, issue-oriented, interesting, globally conscious, and informative. It's good! You won't want to miss it! This study guide is written to assist your mastering the material in your text and enhancing your grade on your instructor's tests. Do not use it as a replacement for the text; it does not contain all of the passages from the text, nor does it depict all of the major topics illustrating the sociological concepts --your text does that! Each chapter in the Study Guide corresponds with the same chapter in *Sociology in Our Times* and has the following components:

Components of the Study Guide

Brief Chapter Outline
Chapter Summary
Learning Objectives
Key Terms
Key People
Chapter Outline
Practice Tests including:
- 25-30 Multiple Choice questions
- 10-15 True/False questions
- 8-10 Fill-in-the-Blank questions
Short Answer and Essay Questions
Student Class Projects and Activities
Internet Activites
InfoTrac College Edition Exercises

How To Use This Study Guide

- Before reading each chapter, look over the Brief Chapter Outline and Chapter Summary to get an overview of the topics in each chapter.

- As you read, use the Learning Objectives, Key Terms, and Key People as a guide for taking notes. (You may wish to start a sociology notebook with concise responses for study purposes.)

- Look for recurring themes in each chapter and between chapters. For example, how do functionalist, conflict, and symbolic interactionist perspectives view each of the topics being examined? Outline the key components of each theory in your notebook.

- Look at the topics and issues presented through the lenses of race, class, gender, age, and (where applicable) ability/disability.

- After you have read the chapter, take the practice test under actual testing situations (i.e., "closed book," sitting at a table, and timing yourself). Grade your practice test using the answers listed in the questions. Use the page numbers indicated on the practice test and in the answers to revisit the text for your information on each item you missed. (You may wish to save the practice tests to use as a self-test before you take an in-class examination.)

- <u>Study</u> the short answer and essay questions as a way to develop critical thinking skills and to synthesize information in a logical manner. These questions could also be used to assist your participation in class discussion.

- The student class projects, activities, and Internet and InfoTrac exercises are designed to involve you actively in the learning process and to help you recognize the relevance of sociology to your life and to our global society. Some of these projects may be assigned as a part of the course requirements.

Best wishes as you explore the text Sociology *in Our Times*, 5th Edition, and as you use this study guide. May you experience and enjoy the sociological imagination! I invite your questions, comments or suggestions. You may contact me at this address:

Kathryn Sinast Mueller
Baylor University
P.O. Box 97326
Waco, Texas 76798-7326
e-mail address: Kathryn_Mueller@Baylor.edu

Chapter 1

THE SOCIOLOGICAL PERSPECTIVE

BRIEF CHAPTER OUTLINE

Putting Social Life into Perspective

- Why Study Sociology?
- The Sociological Imagination

The Importance of a Global Sociological Imagination

The Origins of Sociological Thinking

- Sociology and the Age of Enlightenment
- Sociology and the Age of Revolution, Industrialization, and Urbanization

The Development of Modern Sociology

- Early Thinkers: A Concern with Social Order and Stability
- Differing Views on the Status Quo: Stability versus Change
- The Beginnings of Sociology in the United States

Contemporary Theoretical Perspectives

- Functionalist Perspectives
- Conflict Perspectives
- Symbolic Interactionist Perspectives
- Postmodern Perspectives

Comparing Sociology with Other Social Sciences

- Anthropology
- Psychology
- Economics
- Political Science
- In Sum

CHAPTER SUMMARY

Sociology is the systematic study of human society and social interaction. Sociology enables us to see how individual behavior is largely shaped by the groups to which we belong and the **society** in which we live. The **sociological imagination** helps us to understand how seemingly personal troubles actually are related to larger social forces including those that are related to **global interdependence**, a relationship in which the lives of all people are intertwined closely

1

and any one nation's problems are part of a larger global problem. The first systematic analysis of society is found in the philosophies of early Greek thinkers, such as Plato and Aristotle. With the onset of scientific revolution, social thinkers sought to develop a scientific understanding of social life. The origins of contemporary social thinking can be traced to the scientific revolution of the late seventeenth and mid-eighteenth centuries and to the Age of Enlightenment, where emphasis was placed on the individuals possession of critical reasoning and experience, coupled with a widespread skepticism of the primacy of religion as a source of knowledge, and a strong opposition to traditional authority. Sociology emerged out of the social upheaval produced by **urbanization** and **industrialization** during the nineteenth and early twentieth centuries. Some early social thinkers -- including **Auguste Comte**, **Harriet Martineau**, **Herbert Spencer**, and **Emile Durkheim** -- emphasized social order and stability; others -- including **Karl Marx**, **Max Weber**, and **Georg Simmel** -- focused on conflict and social change. From its origins in Europe, sociology spread to the United States in the 1890s when departments of sociology were established at the University of Chicago and Atlanta University. Sociologists use four major contemporary sociological perspectives to examine social life: (1) **functionalist perspectives** assume that society is a stable, orderly system; (2) **conflict perspectives** assume that society is a continuous power struggle among competing groups, often based on **class**, **race**, **ethnicity**, or **gender**; (3) **symbolic interactionist perspectives** focus on how people make sense of their everyday social interactions; and (4) **postmodern perspectives** examine the efforts of postindustrialization consumerism and global communications in explaining social life in contemporary societies. The areas of interest and research in the social sciences, such as Sociology, Anthropology, Psychology, Economics, and Political Science, overlap in that the goal of scholars, teachers, and students is to learn more about human behavior and its causes and consequences.

LEARNING OBJECTIVES

After reading Chapter 1, you should be able to:

1. Describe the sociological imagination and explain its importance in understanding people's behavior.

2. Explain what C. Wright Mills meant by the sociological imagination and why it requires us to include many points of view and diverse experiences in our own thinking.

3. Define race, ethnicity, class, sex, and gender, and explain why these terms are important to the development of our sociological imagination.

4. Explain how industrialization and urbanization contributed to the development of sociological thinking.

5. Identify Auguste Comte, Harriet Martineau, and Herbert Spencer, and explain their unique contributions to early sociology.

6. Contrast Emile Durkheim's and Karl Marx's perspectives on society and social conflict.

7. Explain what Max Weber meant by value free sociology and *Verstehen*. What part do these terms play in the sociological imagination?

8. Discuss the contributions of Georg Simmel to the discipline of sociology.

9. Describe the origins of sociology in the United States and discuss the role of women in early departments of sociology and social work.

10. State the major assumptions of functionalism, conflict theory, symbolic interactionism, and postmodernism. Identify the major contributors to each perspective.

11. Describe the views of Max Weber, and C. Wright Mills on power and who holds it.

12. Distinguish between microlevel and macrolevel analyses and state which level of analysis is utilized by each of the major theoretical perspectives.

13. State the key assumptions of the interactionist perspective.

14. Explain the major assumptions of social life from the postmodern perspective.

15. Differentiate among the four major theoretical perspectives in explaining the social processes of shopping and consumption.

16. Explain the positions of the early thinkers who were concerned with social order and stability.

17. Identify the later social thinkers who were concerned with social change

18. Compare and contract Sociology with other social sciences.

KEY TERMS

(defined at page number shown and in glossary)

KEY PEOPLE
(identified at page number shown)

Jane Addams 25

Herbert Bloomer 26

Auguste Comte 14

Charles Horten Cooley 31

W.E.B DuBois 25

Emile Durkheim 17

Erving Goffman 29

Harriet Martineau 15

Karl Marx 18

George Herbert Mead 24

Robert K. Merton 26

C. Wright Mills 5

Robert E. Park 24

Talcott Parsons 26

George Ritzer 7

Henri de Saint-Simon 14

Juliet B. Schor 5

Georg Simmel 23

Herbert Spencer 16

Max Weber 18

CHAPTER OUTLINE

I.   PUTTING SOCIAL LIFE INTO PERSPECTIVE

    A.   Sociology is the systematic study of human society and social interaction.

    B.   Why Study Sociology?

        1.   **Sociology** helps us see the complex connections between our own lives and the larger, recurring patterns of the society and world in which we live.

            a.   A **society** is a large social grouping that shares the same geographical territory and is subject to the same political authority and dominant cultural expectations.

            b.   When we examine the world order, we become aware of *global interdependence* -- a relationship in which the lives of all people are intertwined closely and any one nation's problems are part of a larger global problem.

            c.   Sociological research often reveals the limitations of myths associated with commonsense knowledge that guides ordinary conduct in everyday life.

    C.   The Sociological Imagination

        1.   According to sociologist **C. Wright Mills**, the **sociological imagination** enables us to distinguish between personal troubles and public issues.

II. IMPORTANCE OF GLOBAL SOCIOLOGICAL IMAGINATION

    A.   A *global sociological imagination* enables us to distinguish between the world's **high income**, **middle income** and **low-income countries**.

    B.   Developing a personal sociological imagination requires that we take into account perspectives of people

        1.   People in today's world differ by *race* -- a term used by many people to specify groups of people distinguished by physical characteristics such as skin color -- and *ethnicity* -- cultural heritage or identity of a group, based on factors such as language or country of origin.

2.   They also differ by *class* -- the relative location of a person or group within a larger society, based on wealth, power, prestige, or other valued resources -- and by *gender* -- the meanings, beliefs, and practices associated with sex differences referred to as femininity and masculinity.

III.   THE ORIGINS OF SOCIOLOGICAL THINKING

    A.   Sociology and the Age of Enlightenment

        1.   In this European time period, critical reasoning and experience is emphasized; religion is viewed with skepticism.

        2.   The individual's pursuit of enlightened self-interest is conducive to the welfare of society as a whole; new forms of political and economic organizations, such as democracy and capitalism, emerge.

    B.   Sociology and the Age of Revolution, Industrialization, and Urbanization

        1.   The Enlightenment produces an *intellectual revolution*; political and economic revolutions in America and then France follow.

        2.   **Industrialization** -- the process by which societies are transformed from dependence on agriculture and handmade products to an emphasis on manufacturing and related industries -- and **urbanization** -- the process by which an increasing proportion of a population lives in cities rather than rural areas -- contributed to the development of sociological thinking.

IV.   THE DEVELOPMENT OF MODERN SOCIOLOGY

    A.   Early Thinkers: A concern with social order and stability

        1.   **Auguste Comte** coined the term sociology and stressed the importance of **positivism** -- a belief that the world can best be understood through scientific inquiry. He developed the law of the three stages: the theological, metaphysical, and scientific (or positive). Some consider Comte to be the founder of sociology. Both Comte and his mentor, Saint-Simon, advocated the use of the methods of the natural sciences as models for the objective study of society.

        2.   **Harriet Martineau** translated and condensed Comte's works. Her most influential work was *Society in America* in which she paid special attention to diversity in the United States based on race, class, and gender. She advocated gender equality, enlightened reform, and creating a science of society.

        3.   **Herbert Spencer** used an evolutionary perspective to explain stability and change in societies. He coined the term "survival of the fittest", equating this process of *natural selection* with progress and success. His view of society is known as **social Darwinism**, the idea that those species of animals, including humans, best adapted to their environment survive and prosper, whereas the poorly adapted die out.

        4.   According to **Emile Durkheim**, societies are built upon **social facts** which are patterned ways of acting, thinking, and feeling that exist outside any one individual and exert social control over each person. **Anomie** is a condition in which social control becomes ineffective as a result of the loss of shared values and of a sense of purpose in society.

    B.   Differing Views on the Status Quo: Stability versus Change

        1.   **Karl Marx** believed that conflict -- especially *class conflict* -- is inevitable.

a. Class conflict is the struggle between members of the capitalist class, or *bourgeoisie* and the working class, or *proletariat*; conflict is necessary for producing social change and a better society.

b. Exploitation of workers by capitalists results in workers' alienation -- a feeling of powerlessness and estrangement from other people and from oneself. When workers overthrow capitalist, a free and classless society results, thus eliminating gender and class divisions.

2. **Max Weber**'s concern with the growth of large-scale organizations is reflected in his work on bureaucracy. According the Weber, *rational bureaucracy*, rather than class struggle, is the most significant factor in determining the social relations between people in industrial societies. By emphasizing the goal of value free inquiry and employing *verstehen*, sociologists could then understand how others see the world.

3. **Georg Simmel** emphasized that society is best seen as a web of patterned interactions among people. By analyzing how interaction patterns vary depending on the size of the social groups and the *forms* and the content of the social interaction, Simmel provided major insights into social life. He assessed the costs of industrialization on individuals and urbanization.

C. The Beginnings of Sociology in the United States

1. The first U.S. department of sociology was at the University of Chicago. **Robert E. Park** studied the disintegrating influence of urbanization on social life, such as the influence of increases in the crime rate and racial and class antagonisms.

2. **George H. Mead** founded the symbolic perspective.

3. **Jane Addams** wrote *Hull House Maps and Papers* which was used by other Chicago sociologists for the next forty years. She received a Nobel Prize for her assistance to the underprivileged.

4. **W.E.B. Du Bois** founded the second U.S. department of sociology at Atlanta University and wrote *The Philadelphia Negro: A Social Study*, examining Philadelphia's African American community.

V. CONTEMPORARY THEORETICAL PERSPECTIVES

A. A **theory** is a set of logically interrelated statements that attempts to describe, explain, and (occasionally) predict social events. Theories provide a framework or perspective - an overall approach or viewpoint toward some subject -- for examining various aspects of social life.

B. **Functionalist perspectives** are based on the assumption that society is a stable, orderly system characterized by societal consensus.

1. Societies develop social structures, or institutions, that persist because they play a part in helping society survive. These institutions include: the family, education, government, religion, and economy.

2. **Talcott Parsons** stressed that all societies must make provisions for meeting social needs in order to survive. For example, a division of labor (distinct, specialized functions) between husband and wife is essential for family stability and social order.

3. **Robert K. Merton** distinguished between intended and unintended functions of social institutions.

    a. **Manifest functions** are intended and/or overtly recognized by the participants in a social unit.

    b. **Latent functions** are unintended functions that are hidden and remain unacknowledged by participants.

    c. *Dysfunctions* are the undesirable consequences of any element of society. For example, a dysfunction of education in the United States is the perpetuation of gender, racial, and class inequalities.

C. According to **conflict perspectives**, groups in society are engaged in a continuous power struggle for control of scarce resources.

1. Along with **Karl Marx, Max Weber** believed that economic conditions were important in producing inequality and conflict in society; however, Weber also suggested that power and prestige are other sources of inequality.

2. **C. Wright Mills** believed that the most important decisions in the United States are made largely behind the scenes by the *power elite*, a small clique composed of the top corporate, political, and military officials. He contended that value-free sociology was impossible because social scientists must make value-related choices.

3. **Feminist perspectives** focus on patriarchy -- a system in which men dominate women. That which is considered masculine is more highly valued than that which is considered feminine.

D. Symbolic Interactionist Perspective

1. Functionalist and conflict perspectives focus primarily on **macrolevel analysis** -- an examination of whole societies, large scale social structures, and social systems. By contrast, symbolic interactionist approaches are based on a **microlevel analysis** -- an examination of everyday interactions in small groups rather than large scale social structures.

2. **Symbolic Interactionist perspectives** are based on the assumption that society is the sum of the interactions of individuals and groups. Symbols help people derive meanings from social situations.

    a. **George Herbert Mead**, a founder of this perspective, emphasized that a key feature distinguishing humans from other animals is the ability to communicate in symbols -- anything that meaningfully represents something else.

    b. Some interactionists focus on people's behavior while others focus on each person's interpretation or definition of a given situation.

    c. Others, such as **Erving Goffman**, utilize *dramaturgical analysis*, the idea that individual go through their life like actors performing on stage.

E. Postmodern Perspectives

1. According to **postmodern perspective**, existing theories have been unsuccessful in explaining social life in contemporary societies that are characterized by postindustrialization, consumerism, and global communications.

2.   Postmodern societies are characterized by an *information explosion*, the rise of a *consumer society*, and the emergence of a *global village* in which people around the world communicate with each other by electronic technologies.

3.   Social life is not an objective reality waiting for us to discover how it works, but rather, is how we think about it.

F.   All four of these perspectives will be used in this textbook as lenses through which to view our social world

VI.   COMPARING SOCIOLOGY WITH OTHER SOCIAL SCIENCES

A.   Anthropology is the study of human existence over geographic space and evolutionary time; it is divided into four main subfields: sociocultural, linguistic, archaeological, and biological anthropology.

B.   Psychology is the systematic study of behavior and mental processes—what occurs in the mind.

C.   Economics is the study of how the limited resources of a society are allocated among competing demands and is divided into two branches: macroeconomics and microeconomics.

D.   Political Science is the study of power relations, and how power is distributed, and political institutions such as the state, government, and political parties.

E.   In sum, the areas of interest and research in the social sciences overlap, the goal is to learn more about human behavior.

PRACTICE TESTS

MULTIPLE CHOICE QUESTIONS

Select the response that best answers the question or completes the statement:

1.   Sociology is the systematic study of:

a.   intuition and commonsense knowledge.

b.   human society and social interaction.

c.   the production, distribution, and consumption of goods and services in a society.

d.   personality and human development.

2.   All of the following are reasons to study sociology, **except**:

a.   Sociology helps us gain a better understanding of ourselves and our social world.

b.   Sociology utilizes scientific standards to study society.

c.   Sociology confirms the accuracy of common sense knowledge

d.   Sociology helps us look beyond our personal experiences and gain insights into society.

3. According to C. Wright Mills, the sociological imagination refers to the ability to:
    a. distinguish between personal troubles and public issues.
    b. see the relationship between preliterate and literate societies.
    c. be completely objective in examining social life.
    d. seek out one specific cause for a social problem such as suicide.

4. The ability to provide theory and research beyond one's own country enveloping countries all over the world is known as a _____ approach.
    a. global
    b. developed nation
    c. developing nation
    d. personal awareness

5. Brazil and Mexico are examples of _____ countries.
    a. high-income
    b. high middle-income
    c. middle-income
    d. low-income

6. Femininity and masculinity are _____-related terms.
    a. sex
    b. gender
    c. biology
    d. anatomically

7. Ethnicity can be based upon the _____ of the group.
    a. cultural heritage
    b. cultural identity
    c. native language
    d. all of the above can be used to identify ethnicity

8. The first systematic analysis of society is found in the _____.
    a. work of Auguste Comte
    b. philosophies of the Age of Reason
    c. work of the eighteenth century social philosophers
    d. philosophies of early Greek philosophers

9. In eighteenth century France, _____ provided a place for women and men in early France to discuss ideas and opinions.
    a. the Christian church
    b. salons
    c. the Parliament
    d. city hall

10. In France, the Enlightenment is also referred to as the _____.
    a. industrial revolution
    b. French Revolution
    c. Age of Discord
    d. Age of Reason

11. Two historical factors that contributed to the development of sociological thinking were:
    a. industrialization and urbanization.
    b. industrialization and immigration.
    c. urbanization and centralization.
    d. urbanization and immigration.

12. Each of the following people made an important contribution to early sociology, **except**:
    a. Auguste Comte.
    b. Harriet Martineau.
    c. Adam Smith.
    d. Herbert Spencer.

13. Comte's works were made more accessible to scholars through the efforts of _____.
    a. Marianne Weber
    b. Harriet Martineau
    c. Jane Addams
    d. Max Weber

14. _____ argued that conflict -- especially class conflict -- is necessary in order to produce social change and a better society.
    a. Auguste Comte
    b. Emile Durkheim
    c. Karl Marx
    d. Harriet Martineau

15. One of Simmel's most exciting studies, _____ analyzes consumerism.
    a. *The Protestant Ethic and the Spirit of Capitalism*
    b. *The Philosophy of Money*
    c. *Society in America*
    d. *The Rules of Sociological Method*

16. The first U.S. department of sociology was established at _____ , where _____ was one of the best known women in the field.
    a. University of Chicago - Jane Addams
    b. Harvard University - Harriet Martineau
    c. University of California - Arlie Hochschild
    d. Princeton University - Sara McLanahan

17. Social theorist _____ observed that rapid social change can lead to a breakdown in traditional values and an increase in _____.
    a. DuBois; subjectivity
    b. Weber; alienation
    c. Durkheim; anomie
    d. Comte; positivism

18. The word that Max Weber used to stress the need for sociologists to take into account other peoples feelings, viewpoints, or attitudes was:
    a. anomie
    b. *verstehen*
    c. rationalization
    d. *gesundheit*

19. The credit card industry has contributed to the _____ process by the efficiency with which it makes loans and deals with consumers.
    a. ritualization
    b. formalization
    c. procenduralization
    d. rationalization

20. W. E. B. Du Bois referred to the identity conflict of being a black and an American as:
    a. group consciousness.
    b. the American dilemma.
    c. false consciousness.
    d. double-consciousness.

21. _____ perspectives are based on the assumption that society is a stable, orderly system.
    a. Functionalist
    b. Interactionist
    c. Conflict
    d. Feminist

22. _____ perspectives are based on the assumption that groups are engaged in a continuous power struggle for control of scarce resources.
    a. Functionalist
    b. Interactionist
    c. Conflict
    d. Feminist

23. That students meet their spouses on a university campus would likely be viewed as a _____.
    a. latent function of education
    b. latent dysfunction of education
    c. manifest function of education
    d. manifest dysfunction of education

24. According to your text, all of the following are conflict theorists, **except**:

    a. Max Weber.

    b. Talcott Parsons.

    c. Georg Simmel.

    d. C. Wright Mills.

25. The _____ approach directs attention to women's experiences and the importance of gender as an element of social structure.

    a. functionalist

    b. interactionist

    c. conflict

    d. feminist

26. Goffman's dramaturgical analysis represents the _____ perspective.

    a. conflict

    b. functionalist

    c. symbolic interactionist

    d. postmodern

27. Which sociological perspective would focus on the fact that "participation in volunteer activities contributes to the emergence of friendship networks that can permeate everyday life"?

    a. functionalist perspective

    b. conflict perspective

    c. interactionist perspective

    d. postmodern perspective

28. Signs, gestures, written language, and shared values are all examples of:

    a. symbols.

    b. psychological defense mechanisms.

    c. norms.

    d. roles.

29. Which one of the following statements reflects the views of a conflict theorist?

    a. A small clique of corporate leaders controls the U.S.A. political process.

    b. Wealthy capitalist employers benefit from poverty because the poor serve as a cheap source of labor.

    c. Women often have difficulty moving up the corporate ladder because some male managers resent female employees.

    d. All of the above reflect the views of the conflict theorist.

30. The theory that best explains consumerism, global communications, and postindustrial social life is the _____ perspective.
    a. postmodern
    b. functionalist
    c. conflict
    d. symbolic interactionist

TRUE FALSE QUESTIONS

1. Global interdependence affects the lives of all people
    True or False

2. All sociologists attempt to discover patterns or commonalties in human behavior.
    True or False

3. Industrialization first occurred in France between 1700 and 1850.
    True or False

4. The writings of Mary Wollstonecraft strongly influenced the ideas of human equality.
    True or False

5. Auguste Comte is considered by some to be the "founder of sociology."
    True or False

6. Herbert Spencer coined the term "survival of the fittest."
    True or False

7. Count Henri de Saint-Simon, as a mentor to Comte, was primarily interested in social reform.
    True or False

8. In the Marxian framework, class conflict is the struggle between the capitalist class and the working class.
    True or False

9. According to Marx, the "fetishism of commodities" describes the situation wherein the proletariat recognize that their labor gives he commodity its value.
    True or False

10. The first U.S. departments of sociology were located at the University of Chicago and at Harvard University.
    True or False

11. From a functionalist perspective, leadership, decision making, and employment outside the home to support the family, all constitute expressive tasks.
    True or False

12. According to Robert K. Merton, latent functions are intended and/or overtly recognized by the participants in a social unit.
    True or False

13. The conflict perspective is one unified theory using the branches of neo-Marxism and feminism.
    True or False

14. Interactionist perspectives are based on a macrolevel analysis of society.
    True or False

15. Sociology, Psychology, Economics and Political Science are all examples of social sciences.
    True or False

FILL IN THE BLANK QUESTIONS

1. _____ translated Comte's work; sociologist in own right
2. _____ suggested that societies are built upon social facts.
3. _____ is considered the founder of sociology.
4. _____ studied the rationalization of society
5. _____ coined the term "survival of the fittest."
6. _____ analyzed how social actions vary according to group size.
7. _____ coined the term "double-consciousness."
8. According to Marx the _____ are exploited by the _____
9. The _____ analysis focuses on small groups.
10. The _____ perspective examines the emergence of a global village.

SHORT ANSWER/ESSAY QUESTIONS

1. How might the sociological imagination help the individual personally and professionally?

2. Why were the early social thinkers concerned with social stability? Why did so many analyze society from the perspectives of the biological and physical sciences?

3. How do race, class, and gender affect and how are they affected by shopping and consumption?

4. How did the Age of Enlightenment and the Industrial Revolution contribute to the emergence of sociology in Europe?

5. What are the major tenets of the social sciences discussed in the text?

STUDENT CLASS PROJECTS AND ACTIVITIES

1. Research the origins of the social sciences, other than Sociology, mentioned in this chapter. Provide answers to the following: (a) describe the development of each: how, why, and when did they develop; (b) identify the early founders or early thinkers in each discipline and describe their contributions and influence on each social science; (c) identify the major contemporary theorists in each of these social sciences and explain their contributions to each; (d) explain how most theorists define the term "social science" today. Submit your research to your professor on the due date, following any instructions given to you.

2. As discussed in your text, C. Wright Mills distinguishes between "personal troubles" and "public issues." You are to compose a list of ten personal troubles that you have recently experienced—for example, money problems, problems in a specific course, problems in interpersonal relationships, maintaining a decent grade point average, inability to find a part-time job, parental pressures, etc. You are to be specific in your listing. This information will be kept strictly confidential by your professor. Next, you are to write a paragraph about an analysis of the problems. Of these, select five from the list of ten that could possibly extend beyond your personal problems and could be considered a public issue. You are to specifically provide information that would indicate how these five do have their roots in social causes. Next, choose one of the "public problems" and briefly research that specific problem, providing some statistical data that would verify that indeed this specific problem is a social issue. (Hint: a recent divorce in your family). You certainly can find research indicating that this one problem is certainly not only a private issue, but a public issue as well. You must provide a bibliographical reference for the one specific problem that you choose to briefly research. Submit your paper to your instructor following any other directions given to you in the writing of the paper.

3. Choose ten specific cartoons from various sources that illustrate some sociological concepts or ideas or any ideas of interest to sociologists as discussed in Chapter 1. Provide a copy of each of the cartoons in your paper. Type at least a paragraph per each cartoon describing what concept or idea or area of sociology the cartoon is illustrating, as well how it illustrates that concept, and why you believe it can be of interest to sociologists. Provide any other additional commentary of each cartoon. Finally, evaluate not only the cartoons, but the value/worth of this project. Submit your paper to your instructor following any other directions your instructor may have given you in the writing of the paper. Be certain to submit your paper on the correct date!

4. Select a specific historical or contemporary well-known sociological theorist. Your instructor may provide a list for your selection. In this project you are to: (1) investigate the background of the theorist, (2) the life-style of the theorist, and (3) provide any other important bibliographic information on that theorist. (4) Include in your paper the major works and ideas of your particular theorist and (5) evaluate the contribution that your theorist makes to the field of sociology. (6) Briefly evaluate the value of this project and (7) submit your paper to your instructor on the due date.

INTERNET ACTIVITIES

1. To get a better grip on what sociology is all about, explore the *American Sociological Association's* web site. Explore the three major sections of the main page; (1) sociologists, (2) students and, (3) public. Bring to class a piece of information that you discovered from exploring the site. www.asanet.org

2. In order to introduce to the broad field of sociology explore the *SOCIOSITE*. From this page you can access dozens of subject areas within the discipline. The web site has hundreds of resources organized within these subject areas. www.pscw.uva.nl/sociosite/topics/index.html

3. *A Sociological Tour Through Cyberspace* is a web site created by Professor Michael C. Kearl. There are loads of information resources on this site. Read the essay on credit cards found on the site. www.trinity.edu/~mkearl/index.html#in

4. As Chapter 1 points out, social thought has a very long history. Learn more about the historical development of key ideas as well as biographical information about a range of social thinkers and sociologists by going to *A Sociology Timeline from 1600*. Locate on the time line social thinkers covered in chapter one then explore the historical context in which they lived. www.wwu.edu/~stephan/timeline.html

5. Anyone wishing to study sociological theory on the Internet must access the *Dead Sociologists Society* for a comprehensive archive of information on social thinkers and theories. From this site you can conduct a more extensive analysis of one or more of the social thinkers introduced in this chapter. http://www2.pfeiffer.edu/~lridener/DSS/DEADSOC.HTML

INFOTRAC EXERCISES

1. Conduct a keyword search for **American Consumerism.** Using the resources found on InfoTrac, write an essay on the global impact of American culture.

2. Under the subject search for **Credit Cards** there are a number of subdivisions. Go to the *Usage* subdivision where you will find 45 articles. Select a number of articles to bring to class and work in groups to synthesize information with reading from the text and class presentations.

3. Put together a subject search for the term **Sociology**. There are dozens of categories and over a hundred articles. Explore the discipline and bring back to class information of interest that was not presented neither in class nor in the assigned readings.

Solutions

MULTIPLE CHOICE QUESTIONS

1. B p. 4
2. C pp. 4
3. A p. 5
4. A p. 9
5. C p. 9
6. B p. 2
7. D p. 2
8. D p. 12
9. B p. 13
10. D p. 12
11. A p. 13
12. C p. 15
13. B p. 15
14. C p. 18
15. B p. 23
16. A p. 25
17. C p. 17
18. B p. 22
19. D p. 12
20. D p. 25
21. A p. 26
22. C p. 28
23. A p. 26
24. B p. 28
25. D p. 28
26. C p. 28
27. C p. 32
28. A p. 32
29. D p. 28
30. A p. 33

TRUE FALSE QUESTIONS

1. T p. 4
2. T p. 5
3. F p. 13
4. T p. 13
5. T p. 15
6. T p. 16
7. T p. 14
8. T p. 18
9. F p. 19
10. F p. 24
11. F p. 26
12. F p. 26
13. F p. 28
14. F p. 29
15. T p. 34

FILL IN THE BLANK QUESTIONS

1. Harriet Matineau
2. Emile Durkheim
3. Auguste Comte
4. Max Weber
5. Herbert Spencer
6. Georg Simmel
7. W.E.B. DuBois
8. proletariats (workers), Bourgeoisie (owners).
9. microlevel
10. postmodern

Chapter 2

SOCIOLOGICAL RESEARCH METHODS

BRIEF CHAPTER OUTLINE

Why is Sociological Research Necessary?

- Common Sense and Sociological Research
- Sociology and Scientific Research
- The Theory and Research Cycle

The Sociological Research Process

- The "Conventional" Research Model
- The Qualitative Research Model

Research Methods

- Survey Research
- Secondary Analysis of Existing Data
- Field Research
- Experiments
- Multiple Methods: Triangulation

Ethical Issues in Sociological Research

- The ASA Code of Ethics
- The Zellner research
- The Humphreys Research
- The Scarce Research

CHAPTER SUMMARY

Social research is a key part of sociology. The sociological perspective incorporates theory and research to arrive at a more accurate understanding of society and provide a factual and objective counterpoint to commonsense knowledge and ill-informed sources of information. Sociological research involves *debunking* and utilizes approaches that answer questions through the **empirical approach**, an approach that attempts to answer questions through the systematic collection and analysis of data. Theory and research form a continuous cycle that encompasses both deductive and *inductive approaches*. Many sociologists engage in *quantitative* research, which focuses on data that can be measured numerically. Other research is *qualitative*, based upon interpretive description rather than statistics. Research models are tailored to the specific problem being investigated and the focus of the researcher, which may be quantitative or qualitative. The following are steps in the conventional quantitative research: (1) select and define the research problem, (2) review previous research, (3) formulate the hypothesis, (4) develop the research design, (5) collect and analyze the data, (6) draw conclusions and report the findings. Although the qualitative approach follows the conventional research approach, which is to: (1) formulate the problem to be studied instead of creating a hypothesis, (2) collect and analyze the data and (3) report the results, it also has several unique features. These features are: (1) the research begins with a general approach rather than a highly developed plan, (2) the researcher decides when the literature review and theory application should take place, (3) the study presents a detailed view of the topic, (4) the researcher must have access to people or other resources that can provide the necessary data is crucial, and (5) the researcher uses appropriate methods for acquiring useful qualitative data. **Research methods**—systematic techniques for conducting research—include **survey research**, **secondary analysis of existing data**, **field research**, and **experiments**. Many sociologists use *triangulation*-multiple methods-in a single study in order to gain a wider scope of data and points of view. Studying human behavior raises important ethical issues for sociologists, such as the research of Zellner, Humphreys, and Scarce. The challenge for social research today is to find new ways to integrate knowledge, action, and all people in the research process, in order to fill in the gaps of existing knowledge about social life.

LEARNING OBJECTIVES

After reading Chapter 2, you should be able to:

1. Explain the difference between commonsense and sociological research

2. Describe the difference between the normative approach and the empirical approach.

3. Differentiate between descriptive and explanatory studies.

4. Explain the theory and research cycle.

5. Contrast the inductive and deductive approaches for collecting data.

6. Know how sociologists build theories.

7. Differentiate between quantitative and qualitative research and give examples of each.

8. Describe the six steps in the conventional research process, which focuses on quantitative research.

9. Indicate the relationship between dependent and independent variable in a hypothesis.

10. Distinguish between a representative sample and a random sample and explain why sampling is an integral part of quantitative research.

11. Explain why validity and reliability are important considerations in sociological research.

12. Describe the key steps in conducting qualitative research.

13. Describe the major types of surveys and indicate their major strengths and weaknesses

14. State the major strengths and weaknesses of secondary analysis of existing data.

15. Describe the major methods of field research and indicate when researchers are most likely to utilize each of them.

16. Explain how and why experiments are conducted.

17. Define and explain why triangulation is important in sociological research.

18. Describe the major ethical concerns in sociological research, and provide examples of controversial research.

KEY TERMS

(defined at page number shown and in glossary)

content analysis 58
control group 65
correlation 66
dependant variable 47
experimental group 65
ethnography 62
experiment 65
field research 61
Hawthorne effect 67
hypothesis 46
independent variable 47
interview 56

participant observation 61
probability sampling 50
questionnaire 55
random sample 50
reliability 50
research methods 53
respondents 53
secondary analysis 58
survey 53
unstructured interview 63
validity 50

KEY PEOPLE

(identified at page number shown)

Elijah Anderson 63
Leon Anderson 67
Arruro Biblarz 65
Silvia Canetto 51
Emile Durkheim 40
Kevin Earley 55
Laud Humphreys 70

Elliot Liebow 62
Robert and Helen Lynd 62
Rik Scarce 70
David Snow 67
Steve Taylor 61
William F. Whyte 63
William Zellner 69

CHAPTER OUTLINE

I. WHY IS SOCIOLOGICAL RESEARCH NESSESARY?

    A. Common sense and sociological research

        1. Sociologists obtain knowledge of human behavior through research, which results in a body of information that helps to move beyond guesswork and common sense in understanding society.

    B. Sociology and scientific evidence

        1. Sociology involves *debunking*—the unmasking of fallacies—in everyday and official interpretations of society.

        2. Two approaches—the *normative*, which uses religion, customs, habits, and traditions—and the *empirical approach*, which uses systematic collection and analysis of data in attempt to answer questions concerning social life.

        3.   The empirical approach is referred to as the conventional model, or scientific method; it utilizes two types of empirical studies: *descriptive* which provide social facts or describe social reality and *explanatory studies*, which attempt to explain cause and effect relationships.

    C.   The theory and research cycle

        1.   A theory is a set of logically interrelated statements that attempts to describe, explain, and (occasionally) predict social events.

        2.   Research is the process of systematically collecting information for the purposes of testing an existing theory or generating a new one.

        3.   The theory and research cycle consists of the *deductive approach* and *inductive approach*.

        4.   Theory gives meaning to research; research helps support theory.

II.   THE SOCIOLOGICAL RESEARCH PROCESS

    A.   The "conventional" research model

        1.   *Quantitative research* is based on the goal of scientific objectivity and focuses on data that can be measured in numbers while *qualitative research* uses interpretive descriptions (words) rather than statistics (numbers) to analyze underlying meanings and patterns of social relationships.

        2.   The steps in the conventional research method include:

             a.   Selecting and defining the research problem;

             b.   Reviewing previous research;

             c.   Formulating hypothesis (if applicable);

             d.   Developing research design selecting either *cross-sectional* or *longitudinal* time frames;

             e.   Collecting and analyzing data; and

             f.   Drawing conclusions and reporting the findings.

        3.   Important concepts in the research process

             a.   A **hypothesis** is a statement of the relationship between two or more concepts.

             b.   **Variables** are concepts with measurable traits or characteristics that can change or vary from one person, time, situation, or society to another.

             c.   The **independent variable** is presumed to cause or determine a dependant variable.

             d.   The **dependant variable** is assumed to depend on or be caused by the independent variable(s).

             e.   To use a variable, sociologists create an *operational definition*—an explanation of an abstract concept in terms of observable features that are specific enough to measure the variable.

        4.   Important concepts in collecting and analyzing data:

             a.   A **random sample** is chosen by chance: every member of an entire population being studied has the same chance of being selected.

             b.   In **probability sampling**, participants are deliberately chosen because they have specific characteristics, such as age, race, and ethnicity.

        c.   **Validity** is the extent to which a study or research instrument accurately measures what it is supposed to measure.

        d.   **Reliability** is the extent to which a study or research instrument yields consistent results.

B.   A qualitative research model

    1.   Qualitative research differs from quantitative research in several ways:

        a.   Qualitative research is often used when the research question does not lend itself to numbers and statistical methods.

        b.   They may engage in *problem formulation* instead of creating a hypothesis.

        c.   This type of research is often built on a collaborative approach in which the "subjects" are active participants in the design process, not just passive objects to be studied.

        d.   Researchers tend to gather data in natural settings, such as where the person lives or works, rather than in a laboratory or other research setting.

        e.   Data collection and analysis frequently occur concurrently, and the analysis draws heavily on the language of the persons studied, not the researcher.

    2.   Qualitative research follows the conventional research approach, but has several unique features:

        a.   The researcher begins with a general approach rather than a highly detailed plan.

        b.   The researcher has to decide when the literature review and theory application should take place.

        c.   The study presents a detailed view of the topic.

        d.   Access to people or other resources that can provide the necessary data is crucial.

        e.   Appropriate research methods are important for acquiring useful qualitative data.

III.   **RESEARCH METHODS**

    A.   **Research methods** are strategies or techniques for systematically conducting research.

    B.   A **survey** is a poll in which researchers gather facts or attempt to determine the relationship between facts. Survey data are collected by using self-administered questionnaires, personal interviews, and/or telephone surveys.

        1.   **Respondents** are persons who provide data for analysis through interviews or questionnaires.

        2.   A **questionnaire** is a printed research instrument containing a series of items for the subjects' response. Questionnaires may be self-administered by respondents or administered by interviewers in face-to-face encounters or by telephone.

        3.   An **interview** is a data-collection encounter in which an interviewer asks the respondent questions and records the answers. Survey research often uses structured interviews, in which the interviewer asks questions from a standardized questionnaire.

C. In **secondary analysis of data**, researchers use existing material and analyze data that originally was collected by others.

   1. Existing data sources include public record, official reports of organizations or government agencies, surveys taken by researchers in universities and private corporations, books, magazines, newspapers, radio, television, and personal documents.

   2. **Content analysis** is the systematic examination of cultural artifacts or various forms of communication to extract thematic data and draw conclusions about social life.

D. **Field research** is the study of social life in its natural setting: observing and interviewing people where they live, work, or play.

   1. In **participant observation**, researchers collect systematic observations while being part of the activities of the groups they are studying.

   2. A *case study* is an in-depth, multi-faceted investigation of a single event, person, or social grouping.

   3. An **ethnography** is a detailed study of the life and activities of a group of people by researchers who may live with that group over a period of years.

   4. An **unstructured interview** is an extended, open-ended interaction between an interviewer and an interviewee.

E. **Experiments** – carefully designed situations in which the researcher studies the impact of certain variables on subjects' attitudes or behavior – typically require that subjects be divided into two groups:

   1. The **experimental group** contains the subjects who are exposed to the independent variable (the experimental condition) to study its effect on them.

   2. The **control group** contains the subjects who are not exposed to the independent variable.

   3. At the conclusion of the research, the experiment and control groups are compared to see if they differ in relation to the dependant variable, and the hypothesis about the relationship of the two variables is confirmed or rejected. **Correlation** exists when two variables in an experiment are associated more frequently than could be expected by chance.

   4. Researchers acknowledge that experiments may have a problem known as the **Hawthorne effect** – changes in the subject's behavior caused by the researcher's presence or by the subject's awareness of being studied.

F. Multiple Methods: Triangulation

   1. Many sociologists utilize *triangulation* – the use of multiple approaches in a single study.

   2. Triangulation refers to both multiple research methods and multiple data sources.

IV. ETHICAL ISSUESS IN SOCIOLOGICAL RESEARCH

A. The ASA Code of Ethics

   1. The American Sociological Society (ASA) has a Code of Ethics that sets forth certain basic standards sociologists must follow in conducting research.

2. Sociologists are committed to adhering to this code and to protecting research participants; however, many ethical issues arise that cannot be resolved easily.

B. The Zellner Research

1. The research sought to determine if some automobile accidents were actually suicides.

2. To recruit respondents, he misrepresented the reasons for his study.

C. The Humphreys Research

1. This research studied homosexual acts in public restrooms in parks.

2. Humphreys did not ask permission of his subjects, nor did he inform them that they were being studied. His subsequent personal interviews with them were held under false pretenses.

D. The Scarce Research

1. As a graduate student, Ric Scarce was jailed because he refused to breach guarantee of confidentiality he made with his subjects.

2. These examples demonstrate the difficulties of resolving ethical issues in research.

PRACTICE TESTS

MULTIPLE CHOICE QUESTIONS

Select the response that best answers the question or completes the statement:

1. The _____ approach involves gathering evidence to answer questions through systematic collection and analysis of data.

    a. empirical
    b. descriptive
    c. normative
    d. evaluative

2. A type of research which describes social reality or provides facts about the social world is:

    a. explanatory.
    b. descriptive.
    c. evaluative.
    d. observational.

3. In the _____ approach, the researcher begins with a theory and uses research to test the theory:

    a. inductive.
    b. deductive.
    c. model.
    d. command.

4. The first step in the conventional research process is:
    a. reviewing the literature.
    b. selecting a research model.
    c. formulating the hypothesis.
    d. selecting and defining the research problem.

5. When concepts have two or more degrees or values, they are referred to as _____
    a. hypotheses.
    b. triangulation.
    c. variables.
    d. theories.

6. Which of the following can serve as a variable in a study?
    a. age.
    b. sex.
    c. ethnic background.
    d. all of the above.

7. In Emile Durkheim's study of suicide, the degree of social integration was the:
    a. operational definition.
    b. dependant variable.
    c. independent variable.
    d. spurious correlation.

8. In a medical study, lung cancer could be the _____ variable, while smoking could be the _____ variable.
    a. dependant, independent
    b. independent, dependant
    c. valid, reliable
    d. reliable, valid

9. In creating an operational definition, a sociologist:
    a. duplicates research in a precise manner.
    b. analyzes the findings of a research.
    c. makes a concept or variable measurable.
    d. conducts field research.

10. Suppose we are investigating the primary causes of suicide in the late 1990s. Upon looking into recent cases of suicide, we find out that a number of the people had lost their jobs; that they had been unemployed off and on for the past ten years; that they had no religious affiliation; and that a number of them had been divorced within the past five years. The analysis reflects what the text terms:

    a. singular determination
    b. multivariate involvement
    c. plural association
    d. multiple causation

11. A _____ sample refers to a situation in which every member of an entire population has the same chance of being selected for a study.

    a. selective
    b. random
    c. representative
    d. longitudinal

12. _____ is the extent to which a study or research instrument accurately measures what it is supposed to measure; _____ is the extent to which a study or research instrument yields consistent results.

    a. Validity - replication
    b. Replication – validity
    c. Validity – reliability
    d. Reliability – validity

13. The national census is an example of _____

    a. survey research.
    b. a field experiment.
    c. secondary analysis.
    d. participant observation research.

14. Research involving more than two independent variables is known as:

    a. multivariate analysis.
    b. secondary analysis.
    c. random sampling.
    d. field analysis.

15. Researchers who use existing material and analyze data that originally was collected by others are engaged in:

    a. unethical conduct.
    b. primary analysis.
    c. secondary analysis.
    d. survey analysis.

16. Observation, ethnography, and case studies are examples of:
    a. survey research.
    b. experiments.
    c. secondary analysis of existing data.
    d. field research.

17. In an experiment, the subjects in the control group:
    a. are exposed to the independent variable.
    b. are not exposed to the independent variable.
    c. are exposed to the dependant variable.
    d. are not exposed to the dependant variable.

18. A sports sociologist finds that body temperature increases as the "pumping iron" increases. In this example, body temperature would be the:
    a. dummy variable.
    b. null hypothesis.
    c. dependant variable.
    d. independent variable.

19. _____ exists when two variables change together in a predictable direction.
    a. correlation
    b. triangulation
    c. multiple causation
    d. quantification

20. According to your text, important ethical concerns were raised by all of the following researchers, **except**:
    a. Elijah Anderson
    b. William Zellner
    c. Ric Scarce
    d. Laud Humphreys

TRUE FALSE QUESTIONS

1. Emile Durkheim was one of the first sociologists to challenge the commonsense view of suicide.
   True or False

2. The normative approach answers questions through systematic collection and analysis of data.
   True or False

3. Theory gives meaning to research; research helps support theory.
   True or False

4. In the deductive approach the researcher collects data and then generates theories from the analysis of that data.
   True or False

5. With qualitative research, the focus is on data that can be measured numerically.
   True or False

6. The first step in the conventional research model is to formulate the hypothesis.
   True or False

7. Cross-sectional studies study what has happened over a period of time.
   True or False

8. In random sampling, each member of a population has an equal chance of being selected.
   True or False

9. Validity is when a study gives consistent results to different research over time.
   True or False

10. Altruistic suicide occurs when individuals are excessively integrated into society.
    True or False

11. The research method determines how the data will be collected.
    True or False

12. In survey research, every person of that population must be interviewed.
    True or False

13. Content analysis provides objective coding procedure for analyzing written material.
    True or False

14. Participant observation is a quantitative research method.
    True or False

15. The Hawthorne effect refers to changes in the subject's behavior caused by the researcher's presence or by the subject's awareness of being studied.
    True or False

FILL IN THE BLANK QUESTIONS

1. Sociology involves _____ which challenges false or mistaken ideas or opinions.

2. A _____ is a statement of the relationship between two or more concepts.

3. _____ studies compare data over a period of time.

4. In _____ sampling, participants are deliberately chosen because they have specific characteristics.

5. According to Durkheim, _____ suicide results from a lack of shared values or purpose.

6. Specific strategies for systematically conducting research are known as _____ .

7. Persons who provide data for analysis through interviews or questions are called _____ .

8. Researchers use _____ research to study social life in its natural setting.

9. In a classic study, sociologist _____ conducting long term participant observation studies in Boston's low-income Italian neighborhoods.

10. The controversial research of _____ examined "tearoom trade."

SHORT ANSWER/ESSAY QUESTIONS

1. What is the difference between qualitative and quantitative research? Give an example of each.

2. What is the relationship between theory and research?

3. What are the steps in the conventional research process?

4. List and describe the five basic types of research methods.

5. Identify four ethical concerns which must be considered when conducting research, and give three examples of controversial research discussed in your textbook.

STUDENT CLASS PROJECTS AND ACTIVITIES

1. Collect, over a period of two or three weeks, five articles from newspapers or magazines reporting the results of a public opinion poll. (Examples: NEW YORK TIMES, GALLUP, CNN, etc.). Evaluate the polls and respond in writing to these questions: (1) were the questions fully reported? (2) What is the size of the sample, its composition (i.e., gender, age, race, nationality, region of country), and the method of selecting the sample (i.e., was it random, stratified, etc.) (3) How was the data collected (telephone, mail, etc.)? (4) What was the wording of the questions asked in the poll? (5) Summarize the findings of the poll. (6) Did you find any problems of the poll? Was it scientifically designed? (7) Include any other information in your paper appropriate to this assignment. (8) Provide bibliographic reference for the polls you have selected. (9) Evaluate this project. Follow the directions of the writing of this project given to you by your instructor. Submit your paper on the due date.

2. Conduct a survey of any 20 people and ask these questions: (1) what is sociology? (2) What do sociologists do? (3) What is your opinion of sociologists? (4) Have you had a course in sociology? If so, where? (5) Have you had a course in a social science? (6) Do you know a sociologist? If so, who? (7) Include any other kind of information you may want to obtain from your subjects. (8) Include the names, gender, the ages, and, if students, the college majors of your subjects. (9) Provide a summary and an evaluation of this project in the writing of your paper. Submit your paper to your instructor following any other directions your instructor may have given you in the writing of this project. (10) Submit your paper on the correct date.

3. A recent *Parade Magazine* published a poll of the top ten issues frustrating to Americans. The top 10 recorded in this poll were: (1) the faltering economy; (2) government misconduct and mismanagement; (3) the medical care crisis; (4) crime; (5) the abortion issue; (6) the tax burden; (7) government waste; (8) the crumbling infrastructure; (9) the learning decline; and (10) free trade. You are to conduct an informal poll, collecting data from 10 to 20 students enrolled in your institution. (1) You are to have your subjects list and briefly explain their top 10 frustrations. (2) Summarize your findings and list the top ten frustrations according to your subjects. (3) Compare

and contrast this list with that of your subjects. (4) Provide an analysis of this comparison. (5) Provide the names, ages, and gender of your subjects in your written paper. (6) Provide a conclusion and an evaluation of this project in your paper. Submit your paper to your instructor following any other directions your instructor may have given you in the writing of this paper.

INTERNET ACTIVITIES

1. Access the U.S. Census website. www.census.gov/main/www/cen2000.html
   The best starting point is the *American FactFinder*. This is a more user-friendly entry point to see reports that are being generated from data collected during the 2000 Census.

2. More students are using Internet sources for their class research projects. Before you join the herd, access the *Guide for Citing Electronic Information* provided by the William Paterson University (New Jersey). www.wpunj.edu/wpcpages/library/citing.htm
   The site contains guidelines for citing everything from e-mails to online journal articles. Also included are links to other related web pages.

3. The *National Opinion Research Center* at the University of Chicago is one of the largest survey research organizations. www.norc.uchicago.edu/projects/gensoc.asp
   On this site you can access information about the General Social Survey. First, go to the FAQ link on this site and bring to class a basic description of the GSS.

4. Some research organizations openly admit that their research is guided by a particular set of political values. One such example is the *Cato Institute*, a politically conservative research organization guided by Libertarian Principles. www.cato.org
   Go to their home page and click on daily commentaries and then select a topic that interests you. Can you find examples of research that is guided by conservative principles? How does this compare with the standards of objectivity that are discussed in the text?

5. When you start thinking about the difficulties of researching highly subjective social phenomena you should consider accessing the *World Database of Happiness*. www.eur.nl/fsw/research/happiness/
   This site is an ongoing register of scientific research related to subjective appreciation of life. Can you find out which nation is most happy?

INFOTRAC EXERCISES

1. Look up the keywords **Suicide Research** on InfoTrac. Among the articles you find should be those that address social factors. Bring articles to class and be prepared to discuss them in small group and determine what kinds of research methods were used in each study.

2. The **Hawthorne Effect** is a phenomenon that you may hear referenced in other courses and reading assignments. A recent re-examination of the phenomenon and the original research contains some new surprises. Use InfoTrac to look up the keywords **Hawthorne Effect** (be sure of the spelling) and read the article. Please construct a list of new facts contained in the report and bring to class.

3. Why are surveys chosen over other methods of collecting data? Research the keyword **Survey** and select a survey study to examine. Read the research report and then try to determine why a survey was used.

Solutions

MULTIPLE CHOICE QUESTIONS

1. A p. 41

2. B p. 42

3. B p. 43

4. D p. 45

5. C p. 47

6. D p. 47

7. C p. 47

8. A p. 47

9. C p. 47

10. D p. 48

11. B p. 50

12. C pp. 50

13. A p. 53

14. A p. 58

15. C p. 58

16. D pp. 61

17. B p. 65

18. C pp. 66

19. A p. 67

20. A pp. 69-70

TRUE FALSE QUESTIONS

1. T p. 40

2. F p. 41

3. T p. 43

4. F p. 43

5. F p. 45

6. F p. 45

7. F p. 49

8. T p. 50

9. F p. 50

10. T p. 51

11. T p. 52

12. F p.53

13. T p. 60

14. F p. 61

15. T p. 67

FILL IN THE BLANK QUESTIONS

1. debunking

2. hypothesis

3. Longitudinal

4. probability

5. anomic

6. research methods

7. respondents

8. field.

9. William F. Whyte

10. Laud Humphreys

Chapter 3

CULTURE

BRIEF CHAPTER OUTLINE

Culture and Society in a Changing World
- The Importance of Culture
- Material Culture and Nonmaterial Culture
- Cultural Universals

Components of Culture
- Symbols
- Language
- Values
- Norms

Technology, Cultural Change, and Diversity
- Cultural Change
- Cultural Diversity
- Culture Shock
- Ethnocentrism and Cultural Relativism

A Global Popular Culture?
- High Culture and Popular Culture
- Forms of Popular Culture

Sociological Analysis of Culture
- Functionalist Perspectives
- Conflict Perspectives
- Symbolic Interactionist Perspectives
- Postmodernist Perspectives

Culture in the Future

CHAPTER SUMMARY

Culture is the knowledge, language, values, customs, and material objects that are passed from person to person and from one generation to the next. At the macrolevel, culture can be a stabilizing force or a source of discord, conflict, and even violence. At the microlevel, culture is essential for individual survival. Sociologists distinguish between **material culture** -- the physical creations of society -- and **nonmaterial culture** -- the abstract or intangible human creations of society (such as **symbols**, **language**, **values**, and **norms**). According to the **Sapir-Whorf hypothesis**, language shapes our perception of reality. For example, language may create and reinforce inaccurate perceptions based on gender, race, ethnicity, or other human attributes. Cultural change and diversity are intertwined. In the United States, diversity is reflected through race, ethnicity, age, sexual orientation, religion, occupation, and so forth. **Culture shock** refers to the anxiety people experience when they encounter cultures radically different from their own. **Ethnocentrism** -- a belief based on the assumption that one's own culture is superior to others -- is counterbalanced by **cultural relativism** -- the belief that the behaviors and customs of a society must be examined within the context of its own culture. While it is assumed that **high culture** appeals primarily to elite audiences, **popular culture** is believed to appeal to members of the middle and working classes. Political and religious leaders in some cultures fear and oppose **cultural imperialism**, the extensive infusion of one nation's cultures into other cultures, while others point to numerous cross-cultural influences. Sociologists regard culture as a central ingredient in human behavior and share a similar purpose; however, they typically use different theoretical perspectives in their research of culture. A functional analysis of culture assumes that a common language and shared values help produce consensus and harmony. According to some conflict theorists, culture may be used by certain groups to maintain their privilege and exclude others from society's benefits. Symbolic interactionists suggest that people create, maintain, and modify their culture as they go about their everyday activities. Postmodern theorists suggest that there are many cultures within the United States alone. In order to grasp a better understanding of how popular culture may simulate reality rather than being reality, postmodernists believe that we need a new way of conceptualizing culture and society. As we look toward even more diverse and global cultural patterns in the future, it is important to apply the sociological imagination not only to our society, but to the entire world as well.

LEARNING OBJECTIVES

After reading Chapter 3, you should be able to:

1. Explain what culture is and describe how it can be both a stabilizing force and a source of conflict in societies.

2. Describe the importance of culture in determining how people think and act on a daily basis.

3. Describe the importance of language and explain the Sapir-Whorf hypothesis.

4. List and briefly explain ten core values in U.S. society.

5. Contrast ideal and real culture and give examples of each.

6. State the definition of norms and distinguish between folkways, mores, and laws.

7. Distinguish between discovery, invention, and diffusion as means of cultural change. Explain why the rate of cultural change is uneven.

8. Describe subcultures and countercultures; give examples of each.

9. Explain how cultural diversity is reflected in a society.

10. State the definitions for culture shock, ethnocentrism, and cultural relativism, and explain the relationship between these three concepts.

11. Distinguish between high culture and popular culture and between fads and fashion, and explain their effects on culture.

12. State the functionalist and conflict perspectives on popular culture.

13. Describe the functionalist, conflict, symbolic interactionist, and the postmodernist perspectives on culture.

14. Discuss some probable changes of culture in the future.

KEY TERMS

(defined at page number shown and in glossary)

counterculture 95

cultural imperialism 98

cultural lag 90

cultural relativism 96

cultural universals 80

culture 75

culture shock 95

diffusion 91

discovery 91

ethnocentrism 96

folkways 89

invention 91

language 83

laws 90

material culture 79

mores 90

nonmaterial culture 79

norms 89

popular culture 96

sanctions 89

Sapir-Whorf hypothesis 83

subculture 93

symbol 81

taboos 90

technology 90

values 87

KEY PEOPLE

(identified at page number shown)

Jean Baudrillard 103

Pierre Bourdieu 101

Napoleon Chagnon 95

Stephen M. Fjellman 103

Marvin Harris 96

Bronislaw Malinowski 98

George Murdock 79

William F. Ogburn 90

Edward Sapir and Benjamin Whorf 83

Georg Simmel 102

Ann Swidler 78

Robin M. Williams 87

CHAPTER OUTLINE

I.   CULTURE AND SOCIETY IN A CHANGING WORLD

    A.   **Culture** is the knowledge, language, values, customs, and material objects that are passed from person to person and from one generation to the next in a human group or society.

    B.   Culture is essential for our individual survival and for our communication with other people.

C.   As our society becomes more diverse and communication among members of international cultures more frequent, the need to appreciate diversity and to understand how people in other cultures view their world increases.

D.   **Material culture** consists of the physical or tangible creations that members of a society make, use, and share while **nonmaterial culture** consists of the abstract or intangible human creations of society that influence people's behavior.

E.   According to anthropologist George Murdock, **cultural universals** are customs and practices that occur across all societies. Examples include appearance, activities, social institutions, and customary practices.

II.   COMPONENTS OF CULTURE

     A.   A **symbol** is anything that meaningfully represents something else.

     B.   **Language** is defined as a set of symbols that express ideas and enable people to think and communicate with one another.

         1.   Language and social reality

             a.   According to the **Sapir-Whorf hypothesis**, language shapes the view of reality of the speaker.

             b.   Most sociologists contend that language may *influence* but does not *determine* social reality.

         2.   Language and gender

             a.   Examples of situations in which the English language ignores women include using the masculine gender to refer to human beings in general, and nouns that show the gender of the person we expect in a particular occupation.

             b.   Words have positive connotations when relating to male power, prestige, and leadership; when related to women, they convey negative overtones of weakness, inferiority, and immaturity.

         3.   Language, race, and ethnicity

             a.   Language may create and reinforce our perceptions about race and ethnicity by transmitting preconceived ideas about the superiority of one category of people over another.

             b.   The "voice" of verbs may devalue contributions of members of some racial-ethnic groups.

             c.   Adjectives can have different meanings when used in certain contexts.

     C.   **Values** are collective ideas about what is right or wrong, good or bad, and desirable or undesirable in a particular culture.

         1.   Ten U.S. core values are:

             a.   Individualism;

             b.   Achievement and success;

             c.   Activity and work;

             d.   Science and technology;

             e.   Progress and material comfort;

             f.   Efficiency and practicality;

             g.   Equality;

        h.   Morality and humanitarianism;

        i.   Freedom and liberty; and

        j.   Racism and group superiority.

2.   *Value contradictions* are values that conflict with one another or are mutually exclusive (achieving one makes it difficult to achieve another).

3.   *Ideal culture* refers to the values and standards of behavior that people in a society profess to hold; *real culture* refers to the values and standards of behavior that people actually follow.

D.   **Norms** are established rules of behavior or standards of conduct.

1.   **Folkways** are everyday customs that may be violated without serious consequences within a particular culture.

2.   Mores are strongly held norms that may not be violated without serious consequences within a particular culture. **Taboos** are mores so strong that their violation is considered to be extremely offensive.

3.   **Laws** are formal, standardized norms that have been enacted by legislatures and are enforced by formal sanctions.

III.   TECNOLOGY, CULTURAL CHANGE, AND DIVERSITY

A.   Cultural change is continual in societies, and these changes are often set in motion by these processes:

1.   **Technology** refers to the knowledge, techniques, and tools that allow people to transform resources into a usable form and the knowledge and skills required to use what is required.

2.   **Cultural lag** is a gap between the technical development (material culture) of a society and its moral and legal institutions (nonmaterial culture).

3.   **Discovery** is the process of learning about something previously unknown or unrecognized.

4.   **Invention** is the process of combining existing cultural items into a new form.

5.   **Diffusion** is the transmission of cultural items or social practices from one group or society to another.

B.   Cultural diversity

1.   *Cultural diversity* refers to the wide range of cultural differences found between and within nations.

        a.   Homogeneous societies include people having a common culture.

        b.   Heterogeneous societies include people who are dissimilar.

2.   A **subculture** is a group of people who share a distinctive set of cultural beliefs and behaviors that differ in some significant way from that of the larger society. Examples include Old Order Amish and Chinatowns.

3.   A **counterculture** is a group that strongly rejects dominant societal values and norms and seeks alternative lifestyles. Examples include skinheads and members of some paramilitary militias.

    C.   **Culture shock** is the disruption that people feel when they encounter cultures radically different from their own, and they believe they cannot depend on their own taken-for-granted assumptions about life.

    D.   **Ethnocentrism** is the assumption that one's own culture and way of life are superior to all others. **Cultural relativism** is the belief that the behaviors and customs of a society must be viewed and analyzed within the context of its own culture.

IV.   A GLOBAL POPULAR CULTURE?

    A.   *High culture* consists of activities usually patronized by elite audiences while **popular culture** consists of activities, products, and services which are assumed to appeal primarily to members of the middle and working class.

    B.   *Culture capital theory* is based on the assumption that high culture is a device used by the dominant class to exclude the subordinate classes.

    C.   Forms of popular culture

        1.   A *fad* is a temporary but widely copied activity followed enthusiastically by large numbers of people.

        2.   A *fashion* is a currently valued style of behavior, thinking, or appearance that is longer lasting and more widespread than a fad.

        3.   **Cultural imperialism** is the extensive intrusion of one nation's culture into other nations, and is viewed as a threat with many countries becoming westernized.

        4.   Others argue that if a global culture comes into existence it will include many components from many societies and cultures.

V.   SOCIOLOGICAL ANALYSIS OF CULTURE

    A.   According to functionalist theorists, societies where people share a common language and core values are more likely to have consensus and harmony.

    B.   Conflict theorists suggest that values and norms help create and sustain the privileged position of the powerful in society. According to Karl Marx, ideas are *cultural relations* of a society's most powerful members who use *ideology* to maintain their positions of dominance.

    C.   According to symbolic interactionist theorists, people create, maintain, and modify culture as they go about their everyday activities; symbols make communication with others possible by providing shared meanings.

    D.   According to postmodern theorists, no single perspective can grasp the complexity and diversity of the social world; we should speak of *cultures* rather than *culture*. Reality may not be what it seems to be; we should therefore deconstruct existing beliefs and theories about culture in hopes of gaining new insights.

VI.   CULTURE IN THE FUTURE

    A.   In future decades, the issue of cultural diversity will increase in importance.

    B.   Some of the most important changes in cultural patterns may include: (1) television and radio, films and videos, and electronic communications including computers and cyberspace will continue to accelerate the flow of information; however, (2) most of the world's population will not participate in this technological revolution.

C.   The study of culture helps us understand not only our own "tool kit" of symbols, stories, rituals, and world views, but to expand our insights to include those of other people of the world who also seek strategies for enhancing their own quantity and quality of life.

PRACTICE TESTS

MULTIPLE CHOICE QUESTIONS

Select the response that best answers the question or completes the statement:

1.   _____ consists of knowledge, language, values, customs, and material objects.

   a.   Social structure

   b.   Society

   c.   Culture

   d.   Social organization

2.   All of the following statements regarding culture are true, **except**:

   a.   culture is essential for our survival.

   b.   culture is essential for our communications with other people.

   c.   culture is fundamental for the survival of societies.

   d.   culture is always a stabilizing force for societies.

3.   According to the functionalist perspective, cultural universals are:

   a.   useful because they ensure the smooth and continued operation of society.

   b.   the result of attempts by a dominant group to impose its will on a subordinate group.

   c.   independent from functional necessities.

   d.   very similar in form from one group to another and from one time to another within the same group.

4.   How a person is dressed demonstrates:

   a.   the use of language to construct social reality.

   b.   how symbols affect our thoughts about class.

   c.   cultural universals.

   d.   ideal cultural norms.

5.   Regarding the relationship between language and gender, the text points out that:

   a.   the pronouns he and she are seldom used in everyday conversation by most people.

   b.   the English language largely has been purged of sexist connotations.

   c.   the English language ignores women by using the masculine form to refer to human beings in general.

   d.   words in the English language typically have positive connotations when relating to female power, prestige, and leadership.

6. From a _____ perspective, a shared language is essential to a common culture.

    a. functionalist

    b. conflict

    c. feminist

    d. interactionist

7. The most frequently spoken language in U.S. homes other than English is:

    a. Italian.

    b. Spanish.

    c. French.

    d. German.

8. Which of the following hypothetical statements does **not** express a core U.S. value?

    a. "How well does it work?"

    b. "Is this a realistic thing to do?"

    c. "My freedom is important to me."

    d. "It is good to be lazy."

9. All of the following are examples of U.S. folkways, **except**:

    a. using underarm deodorant.

    b. brushing our teeth.

    c. avoiding sexual relationships with siblings.

    d. wearing appropriate clothing for specific occasions.

10. The most common type of formal norms is:

    a. folkways.

    b. mores.

    c. sanctions.

    d. laws.

11. Laws that deal with public safety and well-being are classified as:

    a. criminal law.

    b. civil law.

    c. state ways.

    d. federal law.

12. When one part of a culture changes at a faster pace than another_____ occurs.

    a. cultural diffusion

    b. cultural lag

    c. cultural shock

    d. cultural diversity

13. _____ is the process of reshaping existing cultural items into a new form.
    a. Discovery
    b. Diffusion
    c. Invention
    d. Restoration

14. According to the text, all of the following are examples of countercultures, **except**:
    a. the Old Order Amish.
    b. neo-Nazi skinheads.
    c. beatniks and flower children.
    d. the Nation of Islam.

15. The disorientation that people feel when they encounter cultures radically different from their own is referred as:
    a. cultural diffusion.
    b. cultural relativism.
    c. cultural disorientation.
    d. cultural shock.

16. National anthems, pledges to a flag, and nationalism:
    a. ethnocentrism.
    b. cultural relativism.
    c. cultural diffusion.
    d. cultural indifference.

17. Anthropologist Marvin Harris has pointed out that the Hindu taboo against killing cattle is very important to the economic system in India. This exemplifies:
    a. ethnocentrism.
    b. cultural relativism.
    c. cultural diffusion.
    d. cultural indifference.

18. Some view the widespread infusion of the English language into non-English speaking countries as a form of:
    a. cultural relativism.
    b. cultural imperialism.
    c. cultural diversity.
    d. cultural lag.

19. Which theoretical perspective suggests that ideas are used by agents of the ruling class to maintain their positions of dominance in a society?
    a. symbolic interactionist
    b. postmodernist
    c. conflict
    d. structural functionalism

20. Which theoretical perspective suggests that reality in a culture may not be what it seems?
    a. symbolic interaction
    b. postmodernist
    c. conflict
    d. structural functionalism

TRUE FALSE QUESTIONS

1. Culture is composed of people, whereas a society is composed of ideas.
   True or False

2. The U.S. Constitution designates the official language of the United States.
   True or False

3. Humans have a number of basic instincts.
   True or False

4. As the United States is increasing in diversity, most dominant group members are becoming more tolerant of social and cultural diversities.
   True or False

5. The subject matter of jokes is thought to be a cultural universal.
   True or False

6. As a result of their symbolic significance, flags can be a source of discord and strife among people.
   True or False

7. According to the Sapir-Whorf hypothesis, language shapes the view of reality of its speakers.
   True or False

8. Functionalist theorists view language as a source of power and social control that perpetuates inequalities in society.
   True or False

9. According to sociologist Robin M. Williams, racism and group superiority is a core value in the United States.
   True or False

10. Unlike folkways, mores have strong moral and ethical connotations that may not be violated without serious consequences.
    True or False

11. Popular culture is the U.S.A.'s second largest export to other countries.
    True or False

12. Fads tend to be longer lasting and more widespread than fashions.
    True or False

13. An example of cultural imperialism would be if most world cultures became westernized.
    True or False

14. Chinatowns and other ethnic subcultures help first generation immigrants adapt to abrupt cultural change.
    True or False

15. When Napoleon Chagnon visited the Yanomamo, he found that they live in a culture very similar to that of the United States.
    True or False

FILL IN THE BLANK QUESTIONS

1. The physical or tangible creations that members of a society make, use, and share are examples of _____ .

2. A _____ is anything that meaningfully represents something else.

3. The _____ hypothesis argues that language shapes the view of reality of its speakers.

4. Collective ideas about what is right or wrong, good or bad are known as _____ .

5. _____ culture refers to the values that people profess to hold, while _____ culture refers to values and standards that people actually follow.

6. _____ sanctions are rewards for appropriate behavior.

7. Mores so strong that their violation is considered to be extremely offensive are known as _____ .

8. Societies wherein people are dissimilar in " social characteristics" such as religion, income, or race/ethnicity are referred to as _____ societies.

9. A group that strongly rejects dominant societal values within a culture are known as a _____ .

10. A _____ includes clothing, behavior, thinking, or appearance that is longer lasting and more wide spread than a fad.

SHORT ANSWER/ESSAY QUESTIONS

1. What are the major types of norms in our society? Give an example of each.

2. Define the concept and then explain how the following could reflect diversity within our society: (1) counterculture; (2) subculture; (3) non-material culture; (4) fads; (5) fashions; and (6) symbols.

3. Explain the relationship between: (a) language and social reality; (b) language and gender; and (c) language, race, and ethnicity.

4. What is culture? How do sociologists distinguish between "culture" and "society"?

5. Which values of those discussed in this chapter seems to be the most important and enduring in our society today? Which would seem to be the most important in the future?

STUDENT CLASS PROJECTS AND EXERCISES

1. Examine the lyrics to ten popular contemporary songs that have to do with identity and the problems of teenagers in America. Country-western, rock, folk, rap, and Christian rock movement are some possible sources. Write your response to the following: (1) Analyze the content of the lyrics in terms of culture; (2) Examine the norms that the lyrics promote; (3) What are the suggestions made by the lyrics; (4) What are the themes of the lyrics? (5) What type of music accompanies the lyrics, and what are some of the impacts of the musical sounds? Write up your paper according to any given instructions and submit your paper at the appropriate time.

2. Write a paper on this issue: "Are non-industrial cultures an 'endangered species' in the world today?" In this paper, discuss the localizing and globalizing forces of all cultures today. Examine why, in previous obscure cultures, the native cultures appear to be eroding and becoming "acculturated" into the norms of the industrialized world. Is this globalizing force welcomed by the few remaining aboriginal cultures today? Why? Why not ? Is it functional for them? Why? Why not? Select a specific culture where this process may or may not be occurring. For example, you could research the Australian aborigine; the Tanomamo; some of the native groups in Venezuela and other South American cultures; the Mayan Indians of Mexico; the Bushmen in Africa; the Zulu in South Africa; the IK in Uganda, Kenya and the Sudan; the Wajos, Bugis, and Makassarese of Sulawesi, the Navaho or Hopi in the United States, etc. Provide bibliographic references for your data and any other information that you may find relevant to your topic. In your paper, provide a conclusion and a personal evaluation of this project. Be sure to submit your paper on the proper due date!

3. Write a paper on one event that is considered to be the top ten most important cultural events worldwide in the history of humankind. You can choose from one of the top ten of the following list, or you may choose another event, if you prefer. The top ten, according to the staff of TIME MAGAZINE: (1) the Crusades; (2) the signing of the Magna Carta; (3) the Black Death; (4) the Renaissance; (5) the discovery of the Americas; (6) the Reformation; (7) the Industrial Revolution; (8) American and French Revolutions; (9) World War II; and (10) the Rise and Fall of Communism. Explain why you chose a specific event, and fully describe, discuss and evaluate that event. You must provide in your paper a historical background to that specific event. You must include in your discussion why this specific event was most influential in worldwide history. In your writing of this project, you must include bibliographic references and an evaluation of this project. Submit your paper according to specifications of your instructor on the assigned due date.

4. Since the 9-11-01 terrorist attacks in the United States, the word "Jihad" has sparked debates all over the world. Research the origin of the word, the definition of the word, and various uses of the word. Explain how some acts of world terrorism are related to the term and specifically how/why terrorism is directed against the United States and the western world. Does the term evoke acts and thoughts of ethnocentrism? Explain. Next, conduct a survey of 20-25 people either

on your campus or in your community. Ask these questions: (1) what does Jihad mean to you? (2) what do you think this word means to most people in the United States? (3) what do you think this word means, or implies, to Muslims in the United States? to Muslims in the Middle East and in other various parts of the world? (4) summarize your results, following any directions given to you by your instructor.

INTERNET ACTIVITIES

1. *The Voice of the Shuttle* is one of the most extensive collections of cultural studies resources. http://vos.ucsb.edu/index-netscape.asp It's huge! "Cultural studies" on this page designates the intersection between cultural criticism/theory and selective resources in sociology, media studies, postcolonial studies, economics, literature, and other fields chosen to represent the alignments that now signify "culture" for the contemporary humanities. This is a great research site if you are interested in doing further study of cultural topics. The page will link you to a number of strictly sociology sites that might be useful for future studies.

2. Find out who lives in the *Global Village*. www.empowermentresources.com/info2/theglobalvillage.html It answers the question, "What would the world look like if it contained just 1000 people?" in very eye-opening ways.

3. This is the first site that you should surf if you think you might be interested in cultural studies. www.popcultures.com/ It's an academic site where you can find journals, articles, papers, bibliographies, reading lists, theorists and critics. This is a good site for resource material for papers and reports.

4. To read about etiquette on the Internet, go to the University of Michigan's Electronic Library and click on the *Netiquette* section. http://mel.lib.mi.us/internet/INET-netiquette.html Explore the emerging net culture.

INFOTRAC EXERCISES

1. Go to InfoTrac and look up the concept **social norms**. You should first view the encyclopedia excerpt. From the text of the definition, jump to the definition of other related concepts (blue colored links). Follow the related concepts and develop a string of at least five branching off of the social norms definition where you began. Cut and paste these encyclopedia definitions and create a single document that provides a broader perspective on social norms.

2. Discover the meaning of the concept **ethnocentrism** from reading its use in the periodical literature found on InfoTrac. Could you explain why this phenomenon develops to a group of sixth graders?

3. Look up the subject **technology culture** on InfoTrac. Scan several of the articles. Create a list of problems that appear to be related to technological aspects of culture

Solutions

MULTIPLE CHOICE QUESTIONS

1. C p. 75

2. D pp. 77-78

3. A p. 81

4. B p. 82

5. C p. 84

6. A p. 86

7. B p. 87

8. D pp. 87-88

9. C p. 90

10. D p. 91

11. A p. 90

12. B p. 90

13. C p. 91

14. A p. 93

15. D p. 95

16. A p. 96

17. B p. 96

18. B p. 98

19. C p. 101

20. B p. 103

TRUE FALSE QUESTIONS

1. F p. 75

2. F p. 77

3. F p. 77

4. F p. 77

5. F p. 80

6. T p. 80

7. T p. 83

8. F p. 87

9. T p. 88

10. T p. 90

11. T p. 98

12. F p. 97

13. T p. 98

14. T p. 95

15. F p. 95-96

FILL IN THE BLANK QUESTIONS

1. material culture

2. symbol

3. Sapir-Whorf

4. values

5. Ideal, real

6. Positive

7. taboos

8. heterogeneous

9. counter culture

10. fashion

Chapter 4

SOCIALIZATION

BRIEF CHAPTER OUTLINE

Why Is Socialization Important Around the Globe?

- Human Development: Biology and Society

- Problems Associated with Social Isolation and Maltreatment

Social Psychological Theories of Human Development

- Freud and the Psychoanalytic Perspective

- Erikson and Psychosocial Development

- Piaget and Cognitive Development

- Kohlberg and the States of Moral Development

- Gilligan's View on Gender and Moral Development

Sociological Theories of Human Development

- Cooley, Mead, and Symbolic Interactionist Perspectives

- Recent Symbolic Interactionist Perspectives

- Ecological Perspectives

Agents of Socialization

- The Family

- The School

- Peer Groups

- Mass Media

Gender and Racial Ethnic Socialization

Socialization Through the Life Course

- Infancy and Childhood

- Adolescence

- Adulthood

Resocialization

- Voluntary Resocialization

- Involuntary Resocialization

Socialization in the Future

CHAPTER SUMMARY

Socialization is the lifelong process through which individuals acquire a self identity and the physical, mental, and social skills needed for survival in society. Socialization is essential for the individual's survival and for human development; it also is essential for the survival and stability of society. People are a product of two forces: heredity and social environment. Most sociologists agree that while biology dictates our physical makeup, the social environment largely determines how we develop and behave. Humans need social contact to develop properly. Cases of isolated children have shown that people who are isolated during their formative years fail to develop their full emotional and intellectual capacities and that social contact is essential in developing a self. A variety of psychological and sociological theories have been developed to explain child abuse but also to describe how a positive process of socialization occurs. Psychological theories focus primarily on how the individual personality develops. Sigmund Freud developed the psychoanalytic perspective, while Erik Erikson, drawing from Freud's theory, identified eight psychosocial stages of development. Jean Piaget pioneered the field of cognitive development, which emphasizes the intellectual development of children. The stages of moral development were developed by Lawrence Kohlberg and later criticized and corrected by Carol Gilligan. Sociological perspectives examine how people develop an awareness of self and learn about their culture. This **self-concept** is not present at birth; it arises in the process of social experience. Charles Horton Cooley developed the image of the **looking glass self** to explain how people see themselves through the perceptions of others. George Herbert Mead linked the idea of self concept to **role taking** and to learning the rules of social interaction. Ecological perspectives emphasize cultural or environmental influences on human development. When children do not have a positive environment in which to develop a self concept, it becomes difficult to form a healthy social self. According to sociologists, **agents of socialization** -- including families, schools, peer groups, and mass media -- teach us what we need to know in order to participate in society. Gender, racial-ethnic, and social class are all determining factors in the life long socialization process. **Anticipatory socialization**—the process by which knowledge and skills are learned for future roles—often occurs before achieving a new status. **Resocialization** -- the process of learning new attitudes, values, and behaviors, either voluntarily or involuntarily -- sometimes takes place in **total institutions**. In today's global society, because of the rapid pace of technological change, we must learn how to anticipate and consider the consequences of the future.

LEARNING OBJECTIVES

After reading Chapter 4, you should be able to:

1. Define socialization and explain why this process is essential for the individual and society.

2. Distinguish between sociological and sociobiological perspectives on the development of human behavior.

3. Explain why cases of isolated children are important to our understanding of the socialization process.

4. Explain Freud's views on the conflict between individual desires and the demands of society.

5. Present the stages of psychosocial development proposed by Erik H. Erikson and note the major strengths and weaknesses of his approach.

6. Outline the stages of cognitive development as set forth by Jean Piaget.

7. Compare and contrast the moral development theories of Lawrence Kohlberg and Carol Gilligan.

8. Explain the key components of the human development theories of Charles Horton Cooley and George Herbert Mead and evaluate the contribution of each to our understanding of the socialization process.

9. Describe Mead's concept of the generalized other and explain why socialization is a two way process.

10. Discuss the major approaches of ecological perspectives on human development.

11. State the major agents of socialization and describe their effects on children's development.

12. Explain what is meant by gender socialization and racial socialization.

13. Outline the stages of the life course and explain how each stage varies based on gender, race/ethnicity, class, and positive or negative treatment.

14. Describe the process of resocialization and explain why it often takes place in a total institution.

KEY TERMS

(defined at page number shown and in glossary)

KEY PEOPLE

(identified at page number shown)

CHAPTER OUTLINE

I. WHY IS SOCIALIZATION IMPORTANT AROUND THE GLOBE?

    A.   **Socialization** is the lifelong process of social interaction through which individuals acquire a self-identity and the physical, mental, and social skills needed for survival in society.

    B.   Human Development: Biology and Society

        1.   Every human being is a product of biology, society, and personal experiences, or heredity and environment.

        2.   **Sociobiology** is the systematic study of how biology affects social behavior.

    C.   Problems Associated with Social Isolation and Maltreatment

        1.   Social environment is a crucial part of an individual's socialization; people need social contact with others in order to develop properly.

        2.   Researchers have attempted to demonstrate the effects of social isolation on nonhuman primates that are raised without contact with others of their own species.

        3.   Isolated children illustrate the importance of socialization.

        4.   The most frequent form of child maltreatment is child neglect.

II. SOCIAL PSYCHOLOGICAL THEORIES OF HUMAN DEVELOPMENT

    A.   Freud's Psychoanalytic Perspective suggested that human behavior and personality originate from unconscious forces within individuals.

        1.   The **id** is the component of personality that includes all of the individual's basic biological drives and needs that demand immediate gratification.

        2.   The **ego** is the rational, reality oriented component of personality that imposes restrictions on the innate pleasure seeking drives of the id.

        3.   The **superego** consists of the moral and ethical aspects of personality. When a person is well adjusted, the ego successfully manages the opposing forces of the id and the superego.

    B.   **Erik H. Erikson** identified eight psychosocial stages of development, each of which is accompanied by a crisis or potential crisis that involves transitions in social relationships:

        1.   Trust versus Mistrust (birth to age 1).

        2.   Autonomy versus Shame and Doubt (1 3 years).

        3.   Initiative versus Guilt (3 5 years).

        4.   Industry versus Inferiority (6 11 years).

        5.   Identity versus Role Confusion (12 18 years).

        6.   Intimacy versus Isolation (18 35 years).

        7.   Generativity versus Self absorption (35 55 years).

        8.   Integrity versus Despair (maturity and old age).

    C.   **Jean Piaget**'s theory of cognitive development is based on the assumption that there are four stages of cognitive development based on how children understand the world around them:

1.   Sensorimotor Stage (birth to age 2) -- children understand the world only though sensory contact and immediate action because they cannot engage in symbolic thought or use language.

2.   Preoperational Stage (ages 2 7) -- children begin to use words as mental symbols and to develop the ability to use mental images.

3.   Concrete Operational Stage (ages 7 11) -- children think in terms of tangible objects and actual events; they also can draw conclusions about the likely physical consequences of an action without always having to try it out.

4.   Formal Operational Stage (age 12 through adolescence) -- adolescents are able to engage in highly abstract thought and understand places, things, and events they have never seen. Beyond this point, changes in thinking are a matter of changes in degree rather than in the nature of their thinking.

D.   **Lawrence Kohlberg** classified moral reasoning into three sequential levels:

1.   Preconventional Level (ages 7 10) -- children give little consideration to the views of others.

2.   Conventional Level (age 10 through adulthood) -- children initially believe that behavior is right if it receives wide approval from significant others, including peers, and then a law and order orientation, based on how one conforms to rules and laws.

3.   Postconventional Level (few adults reach this stage) -- people view morality in terms of individual rights. At the final stage of moral development, "moral conduct" is judged by principles based on human rights that transcend government and laws.

E.   Gilligan's View on Gender and Moral Development

1.   One of the major critics of Kohlberg's work was psychologist **Carol Gilligan**, who noted that Kohlberg's model was based solely on male responses.

2.   Her research suggested that there are male-female differences regarding morality and identified three stages in female development.

III.   SOCIOLOGICAL THEORIES OF HUMAN DEVELOPMENT

A.   Cooley, Mead, and Symbolic Interactionist Perspectives

1.   Without social contact, we cannot form a **self-concept** -- the totality of our beliefs and feelings about ourselves.

2.   According to **Charles Horton Cooley's looking-glass self**, a person's sense of self is derived from the perceptions of others through a three step process:

a.   We imagine how our personality and appearance will look to other people.

b.   We imagine how other people judge the appearance and personality that we think we present.

c.   We develop a self concept.

3.   **George Herbert Mead** linked the idea of self concept to **role taking** -- the process by which a person mentally assumes the role of another person in order to understand the world from that person's point of view.

a.   **Significant others** are those persons whose care, affection, and approval are especially desired and who are most important in the development of the self; these individuals are extremely important in the socialization process.

b.   Mead divided the self into the "I" -- the subjective element of the self that represents the spontaneous and unique traits of each person -- and the "me" -- the objective element of the self, which is composed of the internalized attitudes and demands of other members of society and the individual's awareness of those demands.

c.   Mead outlined three stages of self development:

    i.   preparatory stage -- children largely imitate the people around them;

    ii.   play stage (from about age 3 to 5) -- children learn to use language and other symbols, thus making it possible for them to pretend to take the roles of specific people;

    iii. game stage -- children understand not only their own social position but also the positions of others around them. At this time, the child develops a **generalized other** -- an awareness of the demands and expectations of the society as a whole or of the child's subculture.

4.   Some recent symbolic interactionist research emphasize that socialization is a collective process in which *children* are active and creative agents, not passive recipients in the socialization process.

    a.   Children are capable of actively constructing their own shared meanings as they acquire language skills and accumulate interactive experiences.

    b.   Some researchers believe that the peer group is the most significant public realm for children.

5.   Ecological perspectives emphasize cultural or environmental influences on human development.

    a.   *Ecological systems theory* focuses on the interactions a child has with other people and situations.

    b.   The ecological systems are as follows: (1) the *microsystem*, (2) the *mesosystem*, (3) the *exosystem*, and (4) the *macrosystem*.

IV.   AGENTS OF SOCIALIZATION

A.   **Agents of socialization** are the persons, groups, or institutions that teach us what we need to know in order to participate in society. These are the most pervasive agents of socialization in childhood:

B.   The family is the most important agent of socialization in all societies.

    1.   Functionalists emphasize that families are the primary locus for the procreation and socialization of children, as well as the primary source of emotional support.

    2.   Conflict theorists stress that socialization reproduces the class structure in the next generation.

    3.   The social construction/symbolic interactionist perspective suggests that children affect their parents' lives and change the overall household environment.

C.   The school has played an increasingly important role in the socialization process as the amount of specialized technical and scientific knowledge has expanded rapidly.

1. Schools teach specific knowledge and skills; they also have a profound effect on a child's self image, beliefs, and values.

2. From a functionalist perspective, schools are responsible for: (1) socialization -- teaching students to be productive members of society; (2) transmission of culture; (3) social control and personal development; and (4) the selection, training, and placement of individuals on different rungs in the society.

3. According to conflict theorists such as Samuel Bowles and Herbert Gintis, much of what happens in school amounts to a hidden curriculum -- the process by which children from working class and lower income families learn to be neat, to be on time, to be quiet, to wait their turn, and to remain attentive to their work -- attributes that are important for later roles in the work force.

4. Symbolic interactionists might focus on how daily interactions and practices in school affect the construction of students' beliefs, practices, and values.

D. A **peer group** is a group of people who are linked by common interests, equal social position, and (usually) similar age.

1. Peer groups function as agents of socialization by contributing to our sense of "belonging" and our feelings of self worth.

2. Individuals must earn their acceptance with their peers by meeting the group's demands for a high level of conformity to its own norms, attitudes, speech, and dress codes.

E. The **mass media** is an agent of socialization that has a profound impact on both children and adults.

1. The media function as socializing agents in several ways: (1) they inform us about events; (2) they introduce us to a wide variety of people; (3) they provide an array of viewpoints on current issues; (4) they make us aware of products and services that, if we purchase them, supposedly will help us to be accepted by others; and (5) they entertain us by providing the opportunity to live vicariously (through other people's experiences).

2. Recent studies have shown that, on average, U.S. children spend more time per year in front of television sets, computers, and video games than they spend per year in school.

   a. Television has been praised for offering children numerous positive, educational, and prosocial experiences; but blamed for children having lower grades in school, reading fewer books, exercising less and becoming overweight.

   b. The influence of the Internet on young people continues to be a concern; young people make up the fastest- growing segment of Internet users.

   c. Cultural studies scholars and some postmodern theorists believe that "media culture" has in recent years dramatically changed the sociological process for very young children.

V. GENDER AND RACIAL-ETHNIC SOCIALIZATION

A. **Gender socialization** is the aspect of socialization that contains specific messages and practices concerning the nature of being female or male in a specific group or society.

1.   Families, schools, and sports tend to reinforce traditional roles through gender socialization.

2.   From an early age, media, including children's books, television programs, movies, and music provide subtle and not so subtle messages about masculine and feminine behavior.

B.   **Racial socialization** is the aspect of socialization that contains specific messages and practices concerning the nature of one's racial or ethnic status as it relates to: (1) personal and group identity; (2) intergroup and inter individual relationships, and (3) position in the social hierarchy.

VI.   SOCIALIZATION THROUGH THE LIFE COURSE

A.   Socialization is a lifelong process: each time we experience a change in status, we learn a new set of rules, roles, and relationships.

1.   Even before we enter a new status, we often participate in **anticipatory socialization** -- the process by which knowledge and skills are learned for future roles.

2.   The most common categories of age are infancy, childhood, adolescence, and adulthood (often subdivided into young adulthood, middle adulthood, and older adulthood).

B.   During infancy and early childhood, family support and guidance are crucial to a child's developing self concept; however, some families reflect the discrepancy between cultural ideals and reality -- children grow up in a setting characterized by fear, danger, and risks that are created by parental neglect, emotional maltreatment, or premature economic and sexual demands.

C.   Anticipatory socialization for adult roles often is associated with adolescence; however, some young people may plunge into adult responsibilities at this time.

D.   In early adulthood (usually until about age forty), people work toward their own goals of creating meaningful relationships with others, finding employment, and seeking personal fulfillment. Wilbert Moore divided workplace, or occupational, socialization into four phases:

1.   career choice;

2.   anticipatory socialization;

3.   conditioning and commitment; and

4.   continuous commitment.

E.   Between the ages of 40 and 65, people enter middle adulthood, and many begin to compare their accomplishments with their earlier expectations.

F.   In older adulthood, some people are quite happy and content; others are not. Difficult changes in adult attitudes and behavior may occur in the last years of life when people experience decreased physical ability and **social devaluation** -- when a person or group is considered to have less social value than other groups.

G.   It is important to note that everyone does not go through certain passages or stages of a life course at the same age and that life course patterns are strongly influenced by race, ethnicity, gender, and social class.

VII. RESOCIALIZATION

    A.   **Resocialization** is the process of learning a new and different set of attitudes, values, and behaviors from those in one's previous background and experience.

        1.   *Voluntary resocialization* occurs when we enter a new status of our own free will (e.g., medical or psychological treatment or religious conversion).

        2.   *Involuntary resocialization* occurs against a person's wishes and generally takes place within a **total institution** -- a place where people are isolated from the rest of society for a set period of time and come under the control of the officials who run the institution. Examples include military boot camps, prisons, concentration camps, and some mental hospitals.

VIII. SOCIALIZATION IN THE FUTURE

    A.   Families are likely to remain the institution that most fundamentally shapes and nurtures personal values and self identity.

    B.   However, parents increasingly may feel overburdened by this responsibility, especially without societal support -- such as high quality, affordable child care -- and more education in parenting skills.

    C.   A central issue facing parents and teachers as they socialize children is the growing dominance of the media and other forms of technology.

    D.   With the rapid pace of technological change in the socialization process, we must anticipate -- and consider the consequences of -- the future.

PRACTICE TESTS

MULTIPLE CHOICE QUESTIONS

Select the response that best answers the question or completes the statement:

1. _____ is the lifelong process of social interaction through which individuals acquire a self identity.

    a.   Human development

    b.   Socialization

    c.   Behavior modification

    d.   Imitation

2. The systematic study of how biology affects social behavior is known as:

    a.   sociophysiology.

    b.   sociobiology.

    c.   sociology.

    d.   social psychology.

3. Harry and Margaret Harlow's experiment with rhesus monkeys demonstrated that:
    a. food was more important to the monkeys than warmth, affection, and physical comfort.
    b. monkeys cannot distinguish between a nonliving "mother substitute" and their own mother.
    c. socialization is not important to rhesus monkeys; their behavior is purely instinctive.
    d. without socialization, young monkeys do not learn normal social or emotional behavior.

4. In discussing child maltreatment, the text points out that:
    a. many types of neglect constitute child maltreatment.
    b. the extent of this problem has been exaggerated by the media.
    c. most sexual abuse perpetrators are punished by imprisonment.
    d. most child maltreatment occurs in families living below the poverty line.

5. According to Sigmund Freud, the _____ consists of the moral and ethical aspects of personality.
    a. id
    b. ego
    c. super ego
    d. libido

6. Which of the following is **not** one of Jean Piaget's stages of cognitive development?
    a. preoperational
    b. concrete operational
    c. formal operational
    d. post operational

7. The stages of moral development were initially set forth by _____ and then criticized by _____.
    a. Charles Horton Cooley - George Herbert Mead
    b. Lawrence Kohlberg - Carol Gilligan
    c. Jean Piaget - Lawrence Kohlberg
    d. Erik Erikson - Jean Piaget

8. All of the following are components of the self concept, **except**:
    a. the physical self.
    b. the active self.
    c. the functional self.
    d. the psychological self.

9. The theories of Charles Horton Cooley and George Herbert Mead can best be classified as _____ perspectives.
    a. symbolic interactionist
    b. functionalist
    c. conflict
    d. feminist

10. According to Charles Horton Cooley, we base our perception of who we are on how we think other people see us and on whether this seems good or bad to us. He referred to this perspective as the:

    a. self-fulfilling prophecy.

    b. generalized other.

    c. looking-glass self.

    d. significant other.

11. All of the following are stages in Mead's theory of self development, **except** the:

    a. anticipatory stage.

    b. game stage.

    c. play stage.

    d. preparatory stage.

12. The _____ refers to the child's awareness of the demands and expectations of society as a whole or of the child's subculture.

    a. looking glass self

    b. id

    c. ego

    d. generalized other

13. All of the following are components of the ecological systems **except**:

    a. ecosystem.

    b. microsystem.

    c. mesosystem.

    d. exosystem.

14. Sociologist Melvin Kohn has suggested that _____ is one of the strongest influences on what and how parents teach their children.

    a. race/ethnicity

    b. religion

    c. social class

    d. age

15. Currently, about _____ percent of all U.S. preschool children are in day care of one kind or another.

    a. 15

    b. 25

    c. 60

    d. 75

16. As agents of socialization, peer groups are thought to "pressure" children and adolescents because:
    a. individualism is encouraged and rewarded in these groups.
    b. individuals must earn their acceptance with their peers by conforming to the group's norms.
    c. individuals are encouraged to put friendship above material possessions.
    d. individuals are discouraged from making long term friends in the peer group.

17. According to Patricia Hill Collins, _____ play an important role in the gender socialization and motivation of African-American children, especially girls:
    a. "other mothers"
    b. substitute mothers
    c. aunts
    d. siblings

18. The process by which knowledge and skills are learned for future roles is known as:
    a. resocialization.
    b. anticipatory socialization.
    c. cybersocialization.
    d. expectant socialization.

19. Social devaluation is most likely to be experienced during this stage of the life course:
    a. infancy and childhood.
    b. adolescence.
    c. early adulthood.
    d. older adulthood.

20. All of the following are examples of voluntary resocialization, **except**:
    a. becoming a student.
    b. going to prison.
    c. becoming a Buddhist.
    d. joining Alcoholics Anonymous.

TRUE FALSE QUESTIONS

1. Around the globe, the process of socialization is essential for the survival of both the society and the individual.
   True or False

2. After-school programs have greatly reduced the number of children who are home alone after school.
   True or False

3. Unlike humans, nonhuman primates such as monkeys and chimpanzees do not need social contact with others of their species in order to develop properly.
   True or False

4. Extensive therapy used in a program to socialize Genie proved to be highly successful.
   True or False

5. The cases of "Anna" and "Genie" make us aware of the importance of the socialization process because they show the detrimental effects of social isolation and neglect.
    True or False

6. Sigmund Freud theorized that our personalities are largely unconscious -- hidden away outside our normal awareness.
    True or False

7. Erik Erikson suggested that, if infants receive good care and nurturing from their parents, they will develop a sense of trust that is important to their future psychosocial development.
    True or False

8. According to George H. Mead, our looking glass self is based on our perception of how other people think of us.
    True or False

9. According to Cooley, the self develops only through contact with others.
    True or False

10. The family is the most important agent of socialization in all societies.
    True or False

11. Conflict theorists assert that students have different experiences in the school system, depending on their class, racial ethnic background, gender, and the neighborhood in which they live.
    True or False

12. Peer pressure does not affect preschool children.
    True or False

13. Gender socialization contributes to people's beliefs about what the "preferred" sex of a child should be and in influencing our beliefs about acceptable behaviors for males and females.
    True or False

14. Scholars have found that ethnic values begin to crystallize among children at about the age of adolescence.
    True or False

15. Occupational socialization tends to be most intense immediately after a person makes the transition from school to the workplace.
    True or False

FILL IN THE BLANK QUESTIONS

1. The life-long process of social interaction through which individuals acquire a self-identity is defines as _____ .

2. The systematic study of how biology affects social behavior is _____ .

3. According to Freud, the _____ consists of the moral and ethical aspects of personality.

4. The _____ is the totality of our beliefs and feelings about ourselves.

5. According to Cooley, the _____ refers to the way in which a person's sense of self is derived from the perceptions of others.

6. According to Mead, the _____ refers to the child's awareness of the demands and expressions of the society as a whole or of the child's subculture.

7. A _____ group is a group of people who are linked by common interest, equal social position and similar age.

8. Gender _____ is important in determining what we think the "preferred" sex of a child should be and our ideas about acceptable behaviors for females and males.

9. The process by which knowledge and skills are learned for future roles is termed _____ .

10. The process wherein a person or group is considered to have less social value than other persons or groups is known as _____ .

SHORT ANSWER/ESSAY QUESTIONS

1. What do the cases of isolated children suggest about socialization and human development?

2. What are the differences between the sociological theories of human development and the psychological theories of human development?

3. How do we develop a self-concept according to sociologists?

4. Why, according to Anne Kasper, are Mead's ideas about the social self more applicable to men than women?

5. What is Lawrence Kohlberg's perspective on moral development and what is Carol Gilligan's criticism of his perspective?

STUDENT CLASS PROJECTS AND ACTIVITIES

1. Think back to your childhood and list the 4 or 5 televisions programs that you watched most often. Next, list the 4 or 5 programs you watch most often today. Respond in writing to these questions: (1) What values were demonstrated in each of the respected programs--yesteryear and today? (2) Were there, or are there any stereotypes presented via the programs? If so, what were/are they? (3) Were there/are there any values presented that contradict your parents' values? If so, what were/are they? (4) How do you personally evaluate each of these television programs? Include any other information pertinent to this project. Submit your paper on the due date, following any other specific instructions provided by your professor.

2. Write a five to ten page biography of your life, with special emphasis upon your own socialization processes. Include responses to the following questions: (1) Identify the major agencies of

socialization in your life; (2) Who, specifically (by name and status) were the "significant others" in your life? (3) What type of values did your significant others advocate? (4) Who were/are the generalized others in your life? Why? What impact did they have? (5) In what way did any of the above shape your self-image and goals? Provide any additional information in the writing of your biography. Evaluate this project and submit your paper at the appropriate time, following any specific instructions provided by your instructor.

INTERNET ACTIVITIES

1. Michael Kearl's fabulous sociology web gateway addresses parents and children. www.trinity.edu/mkearl/fam-kids.html
    There are connections to pages that directly address socialization. This is an excellent resource when you are looking for more information for a paper/presentation or want to bring additional facts to a class discussion.

2. An enormous sociological gateway site, the SOCIOSITE has a topical index that will introduce you to dozens of subjects. www.pscw.uva.nl/sociosite/TOPICS/index.html
    Once you access this address use the topical index and search for sites in the social psychology category. Most of the websites in this category are actually resource or gateway sites. You can construct a *Social Psychology Web Site Fact Sheet*. Related web sites can be listed, categorized, and summarized paying special attention to those sites related to aspects of socialization.

3. You can read Charles Horton Cooley's introduction to the concept of the *Looking Glass Self*. http://www2.pfeiffer.edu/~lridener/DSS/Cooley/COOLWRK.HTML
    This is a good site to gain additional information for an expanded presentation on this social psychological perspective.

4. This web site contains information about the mass media and society. www.public.asu.edu/~zeyno217/365/notes1.html
    It is a wonderfully concise presentation of some of the most important concepts. A great resource for those interested in the media and popular culture.

INFOTRAC EXERCISES

1. Bring to class an article that addresses a subcategory of **socialization**.

Gender	Racial/Ethnic	Cross-cultural	Family	School
Media	Resocialization	Peers	Self concept	Role taking

1. You can use InfoTrac to conduct a search about **Carol Gilligan**, a pioneer in the field of feminist oriented developmental psychology. Articles include several reviews of her book, *Between Voice and Silence: Women and Girls, Race and Relationship*. Compare the reviews from a number of divergent sources.

2. It's possible, using InfoTrac, to locate biographical sketches of the major psychologists and sociologist introduced in this chapter. InfoTrac provides access to encyclopedia excerpts containing biographical information. Put together a one-page sketch of each thinker - portraits can be exported from the Internet and inserted in the document. If you are taking psychology and sociology courses in the future, a resource such as this might prove useful.

Solutions

MULTIPLE CHOICE QUESTIONS

1. B p. 103

2. B p. 104

3. D p. 106

4. A p. 106

5. C p. 107

6. D p. 109

7. B p. 110

8. C p. 111

9. A p. 112

10. C p. 112

11. A p. 114

12. D p. 114

13. A p. 115

14. C p. 116

15. C p. 117

16. B p. 118

17. A p. 121

18. B p. 123

19. D p. 125

20. B p. 125

TRUE FALSE QUESTIONS

1. T p. 103

2. F p. 104

3. F p. 106

4. F p. 106

5. T p. 106

6. T p. 107

7. T p. 107

8. F p. 112

9. T p. 113

10. T p. 115

11. T p. 117

12. F p. 118

13. T p. 122

14. F p. 123

15. T p. 124

FILL IN THE BLANK QUESTIONS

1. socialization

2. sociobiology

3. superego

4. self-concept

5. looking-glass self

6. generalized other

7. peer

8. socialization

9. anticipatory socialization

10. social devaluation

Chapter 5

SOCIETY, SOCIAL STRUCTURE, AND INTERACTION

BRIEF CHAPTER OUTLINE

Social Structure: The Macrolevel Perspective

Components of Social Structure

- Status
- Role
- Groups
- Social Institutions

Societies, Technology, and Sociocultural Change

- Horticultural and Pastoral Societies
- Agrarian Societies
- Industrial Societies
- Postindustrial Societies

Stability and Change in Societies

- Durkheim: Mechanical and Organic Solidarity
- Tonnies: *Gemeinschaft* and *Gesellschaft*
- Social Structure and Homelessness

Social Interaction: The Microlevel Perspective

- Social Interaction and Meaning
- The Social Construction of Reality
- Ethnomethodology
- Dramaturgical Analysis
- The Sociology of Emotions
- Nonverbal Communications

Future Changes in Society, Social Structure, and Interaction

CHAPTER SUMMARY

Social structure and interaction are critical components of everyday life. At the microlevel, **social interaction** -- the process by which people act toward or respond to other people -- is the foundation of meaningful relationships in society. At the macrolevel, **social structure** is the stable pattern of social relationships that exist within a particular group or society. This structure includes **status, roles, groups**, and **social institutions**. Social researchers have identified five types of societies based on various levels of subsistence technology: **hunting** and **gathering, horticultural** and **pastoral, agrarian, industrial**, and **postindustrial** societies. Changes in social structure may dramatically affect individuals and groups, as demonstrated by Durkheim's concepts of **mechanical** and **organic solidarity** and Tonnies' *Gemeinschaft* and *Gesellschaft*. In examining the relationship between social structure and homelessness, several suggestions for homelessness are offered; however the answers derived are often based upon perceptions of reality in a society. Social interaction within a society is guided by certain shared meanings across situations. The microlevel perspective focuses on the social interactions among individuals, especially face-to-face encounters. Not everyone interprets social interaction situations in the same way. Race/ethnicity, gender, and social class often influence perceptions of meaning. The **social construction of reality** refers to the process by which our perception of reality is shaped by the subjective meaning we give to an experience. **Ethnomethodology** is the study of the commonsense knowledge that people use to understand the situations in which they find themselves. **Dramaturgical analysis** is the study of social interaction that compares everyday life to a theatrical presentation. **Presentation of self** refers to efforts to present our own self to others in ways that are most favorable to our own interests or image. Feeling rules shape the appropriate emotions for a given role or specific situation. Social interaction also is marked by **nonverbal communication**, which is the transfer of information between people without the use of speech. In the future, macrolevel and microlevel analyses are essential in determining how our social structures should be shaped so that they can respond to pressing social needs.

LEARNING OBJECTIVES

After reading Chapter 5, you should be able to:

1. State the definition of social structure and explain why it is important for individuals and society.

2. State the definition of status and distinguish between ascribed and achieved statuses.

3. Explain what is meant by master status and give at least three examples.

4. Define and explain role expectation, role performance, role conflict, and role strain, and give an example of each.

5. Describe the process of role exiting.

6. Explain the difference in primary and secondary groups.

7. Define formal organization and explain why many contemporary organizations are known as "people-processing" organizations.

8. State the definition for social institution and list the major social institutions found in contemporary society.

9. Evaluate functionalist and conflict perspectives on the nature and purpose of social institutions.

10. Explain the basic characteristics of the five types of societies.

11. Know how societies maintain stability in times of social change.

12. Compare Emile Durkheim's typology of mechanical and organic solidarity with Ferdinand Tonnies' *Gemeinschaft* and *Gesellschaft*.

13. Explain what interactionists mean by the social construction of reality.

14. Describe ethnomethodology and note its strengths and weaknesses.

15. Describe Goffman's dramaturgical analysis and explain what he meant by presentation of self.

16. Explain what is meant by the sociology of emotions and describe sociologist Arlie Hochschild's contribution to this area of study.

17. Define nonverbal communication and personal space and explain how these concepts relate to our interactions with others.

18. Analyze the projected future changes in social structure in the United States and provide some possible reactions to those changes.

KEY TERMS
(defined at page number shown and in glossary)

achieved status 142
agrarian societies 154
ascribed status 142
dramaturgical analysis 165
ethnomethodology 164
formal organization 148
Gemeinschaft 159
Gesellschaft 159
horticultural societies 153
hunting and gathering societies 152
impression management (presentation of self) 165
industrial societies 155
master status 143
mechanical solidarity 158
nonverbal communication 167
organic solidarity 158
pastoral societies 153

personal space 169
postindustrial societies 156
primary group 148
role 145
role conflict 145
role exit 146
role expectation 145
role performance 145
role strain 146
secondary group 148
self fulfilling prophecy 163
social construction of reality 163
social group 147
social institution 149
social interaction 139
social structure 139
status 141
status symbol 144

Chapter 5

KEY PEOPLE
(identified at page number shown)

Daniel Bell 156
Emile Durkheim 157
Helen Rose Fuchs Ebaugh 146
Harold Garfinkel 164
Erving Goffman 165
Edward Hall 169

Arlie Hochschild 166
Gerhard Lenski and Jean Lenski 150
David Snow and Leon Anderson 142
Ferdinand Tonnies 157
Tracy Watson 145
Jacqueline Wiseman 163

CHAPTER OUTLINE

I.   SOCIAL STRUCTURE: THE MACROLEVEL PERSPECTIVE

   A.   **Social interaction** is the process by which people act toward or respond to other people.

   B.   **Social structure** is the complex framework of social institutions (such as the economy) and the social practices (such as rules and social roles) that make-up a society and that organize and establish limits on people's behavior

      1.   This structure is essential for the survival of society and for the well-being of individuals

      2.   This structure provides for a social web for familial support and social relationships that connects each person to the larger society.

   C.   Social structure creates boundaries that define which persons or groups will be the "insiders" and which will be the "outsiders."

      1.   *Social marginality* is the state of being part insider and part outsider in the social structure. Social marginality results in stigmatization.

      2.   A *stigma* is any physical or social attribute or sign that so devalues a person's social identity that it disqualifies that person from full social acceptance.

II. COMPONENTS OF SOCIAL STRUCTURE

   A.   A **status** is a socially defined position in a group or society characterized by certain expectations, rights, and duties.

      1.   A **status set** is comprised of all the statuses that a person occupies at a given time.

      2.   Ascribed and achieved statuses:

         a.   An **ascribed status** is a social position conferred at birth or received involuntarily later in life. Examples include race/ethnicity, age, and gender.

         b.   An **achieved status** is a social position a person assumes voluntarily as a result of personal choice, merit, or direct effort. Examples of achieved statuses include occupation, education and income. Ascribed statuses have a significant influence on the achieved statuses we occupy.

      3.   A **master status** is the most important status a person occupies; it dominates all of the individual's other statuses and is the overriding ingredient in determining a person's general social position (e.g., being poor or rich is a master status).

66

    4.   **Status symbols** are material signs that inform others of a person's general social position. Examples include a wedding ring or a Rolls-Royce automobile.

  B.   A **role** is a set of behavioral expectations associated with a given status.

    1.   **Role expectation** -- a group's or society's definition of the way a specific role ought to be played -- may sharply contrast with **role performance** -- how a person actually plays the role.

    2.   **Role conflict** occurs when incompatible role demands are placed on a person by two or more statuses held at the same time (e.g., a woman whose roles include full time employee, mother, wife, caregiver for an elderly parent, and community volunteer).

    3.   **Role strain** occurs when incompatible demands are built into a single status that a person occupies (e.g., a doctor in a public clinic who is responsible for keeping expenditures down and providing high quality patient care simultaneously). Sexual orientation, age, and occupation frequently are associated with role strain.

    4.   **Role exit** occurs when people disengage from social roles that have been central to their self identity (e.g., ex convicts, ex nuns, retirees, and divorced women and men).

  C.   A **social group** consists of two or more people who interact frequently and share a common identity and a feeling of interdependence.

    1.   A **primary group** is a small, less specialized group in which members engage in face to face, emotion based interactions over an extended period of time (e.g., one's family, close friends, and school or work related peer groups).

    2.   A **secondary group** is a larger, more specialized group in which the members engage in more impersonal, goal oriented relationships for a limited period of time (e.g., schools, churches, the military, and corporations).

    3.   A **social network** is a series of social relationships that link an individual to others.

    4.   A **formal organization** is a highly structured group formed for the purpose of completing certain tasks or achieving specific goals (e.g., colleges, corporations, and the government).

  D.   A **social institution** is a set of organized beliefs and rules that establish how a society will attempt to meet its basic social needs. Examples of social institutions include the family, religion, education, the economy, the government, mass media, sports, science and medicine, and the military.

III.   SOCIETIES, TECHNOLOGY, AND SOCIOCULTURAL CHANGE

  A.   **Hunting** and **Gathering Societies**, preindustrial societies, use simple technology for hunting animals and gathering vegetation; their technology is limited to tools and weapons used for basic subsistence.

  B.   **Horticultural Societies** and **Pastoral Societies**, preindustrial societies, have existed throughout the world at some time.

    1.   **Pastoral Societies** are based on technology that supports the domestication of large animals to provide food, and emerged in mountainous regions and areas with low amounts of annual rainfall. They typically remain nomadic as they seek new grazing lands and water sources for their animals.

    2.   **Horticultural Societies** are based on technology that supports the cultivation of plants to provide food. These societies emerged in more fertile areas that were better suited for growing plants through the use of hand tools.

  C.   **Agrarian Societies** use the technology of large-scale farming including animal-drawn or energy-powered plows and equipment, to produce their food supply; most of the world's population lives in agrarian societies that are in various stages of industrialization.

  D.   **Industrial Societies** are based on technology that mechanizes production; this mode of production transforms predominantly rural and agrarian societies into urban and industrial societies.

  E.   **Postindustrial Societies** are societies in which technology supports a service-and-information-based economy; knowledge is viewed as the basic source of innovations and policy formulation; education becomes a most important social institution and scientific research becomes institutionalized.

IV.   STABILITY AND CHANGE IN SOCIETIES

  A.   Sociologists Emile Durkheim and Ferdinand Tonnies developed typologies to explain how stability and change occur in the social structure of societies.

  B.   Durkheim's Typology:

    1.   **Mechanical solidarity** refers to the social cohesion in preindustrial societies where there is minimal division of labor and people feel united by shared values and common social bonds.

    2.   **Organic solidarity** refers to the social cohesion found in industrial societies in which people perform very specialized tasks and feel united by their mutual dependence.

  C.   Tonnies' Typology:

    1.   According to Ferdinand Tonnies, the ***Gemeinschaft*** is a traditional society in which social relationships are based on personal bonds of friendship and kinship and on intergenerational stability. Relationships are based on ascribed statuses.

    2.   The ***gesellschaft*** is a large, urban society, in which social bonds are based on impersonal and specialized relationships, with little long term commitment to the group or consensus on values. Relationships are based on achieved statuses.

  D.   Social Structure and Homelessness - in examining the relationship between social structure and homelessness, several explanations are provided for *Gesellschaft* societies.

    1.   The homeless have made bad decisions which eventually led to homelessness; they are responsible for the consequences of their actions.

    2.   Homelessness is rooted in poverty; it is a result of steady, across the board lowering of the standard of living of the working class and the lower class — a social class phenomena.

V.   SOCIAL INTERACTION: THE MICROLEVEL PERSPECTIVE

  A.   Social interaction within a given society has certain shared meanings across situations; however, everyone does not interpret social interaction rituals in the same way.

  B.   The **social construction of reality** is the process by which our perception of reality is shaped largely by the subjective meaning that we give to an experience. Our definition of the situation can result in a **self-fulfilling prophecy** -- a false belief or prediction that produces behavior that makes the original false belief come true.

C. **Ethnomethodology** is the study of the commonsense knowledge that people use to understand the situations in which they find themselves.

   1. This approach challenges existing patterns of conventional behavior in order to uncover people's background expectancies, that is, their shared interpretation of objects and events, as well as the actions they take as a result.

   2. To uncover people's background expectancies, ethnomethodologists frequently conduct breaching experiments in which they break "rules" or act as though they do not understand some basic rule of social life so that they can observe other people's responses.

D. **Dramaturgical analysis** is the study of social interaction that compares everyday life to a theatrical presentation.

   1. This perspective was initiated by Erving Goffman, who suggested that day to day interactions have much in common with being on stage or in a dramatic production.

   2. Most of us engage in **impression management**, or **presentation of self** -- people's efforts to present themselves to others in ways that are most favorable to their own interests or image.

   3. Social interaction, like a theater, has a front stage -- the area where a player performs a specific role before an audience -- and a back stage -- the area where a player is not required to perform a specific role because it is out of view of a given audience.

E. The Sociology of Emotions

   1. Arlie Hochschild suggests that we acquire a set of feeling rules, which shape the appropriate emotions for a given role or specific situation.

   2. Emotional labor occurs when employees are required by their employers to feel and display only certain carefully selected emotions.

   3. Gender, class, and race are related to the expression of emotions necessary to manage one's feelings.

F. **Nonverbal communication** is the transfer of information between persons without the use of speech (e.g. facial expressions, head movements, body positions, and other gestures). Personal space is the immediate area surrounding a person that the person claims as private. Age, gender, kind of relationship, and social class are important factors in allocation of personal space. Power differentials between people are reflected in personal space and privacy.

VI. FUTURE CHANGES IN SOCIETY, SOCIAL STRUCTURE, AN INTERACTION

A. The social structure in the U.S. has been changing rapidly in the past decades (e.g., more possible statuses for persons to occupy and roles to play than at any other time in history).

B. Ironically, at a time when we have more technological capability, more leisure activities and types of entertainment, and vast quantities of material goods available for consumption, many people experience high levels of stress, fear for their lives because of crime, and face problems such as homelessness.

C. While some individuals and groups continue to show initiative in trying to solve some of our pressing problems, the future of this country rests on our collective ability to deal with major social problems at both the macrolevel (structural) and the microlevel of society.

PRACTICE TESTS

MULTIPLE CHOICE QUESTIONS

Select the response that best answers the question or completes the statement:

1. The stable pattern of social relationships that exist within a particular group or society are referred to as:

    a. social structure.

    b. social interaction.

    c. social dynamics.

    d. social constructions of reality.

2. According to the text, a recent arrives immigrant often experiences:

    a. social depletion.

    b. social marginality.

    c. social disintegration.

    d. social misappropriation.

3. A _____ is a socially defined position in a group or society.

    a. location

    b. set

    c. status

    d. role

4. Maxine is an attorney, a mother, a resident of California, and a Jewish American. All of these socially defined positions constitute her:

    a. role pattern.

    b. role set.

    c. ascribed statuses.

    d. status set.

5. A master status:

    a. historically has been held only by men.

    b. is comprised of all of the statuses that a person occupies at a given time.

    c. is the most important status a person occupies.

    d. is a social position a person always assumes voluntarily.

6. According to the text, a wedding ring and a Rolls Royce automobile are both examples of:

   a. conspicuous consumption.

   b. status symbols.

   c. status markers.

   d. master status indicators.

7. _____ is (are) the dynamic aspect of a status.

   a. Role

   b. Norms

   c. Groups

   d. People

8. In her study of women athletes in college sports programs, sociologist Tracey Watson found role _____ in the traditionally incongruent identities of being a woman and being an athlete.

   a. strain

   b. distancing

   c. conflict

   d. confusion

9. According to the text, lesbians and gay men often experience role _____ because of the pressures associated with having an identity heavily stigmatized by the dominant cultural group.

   a. strain

   b. distancing

   c. conflict

   d. confusion

10. When a homeless person is able to become a domiciled person, sociologists refer to the process as:

    a. role disengagement.

    b. role exit.

    c. role engulfment.

    d. role relinquishment.

11. All of the following are examples of a primary group, **except**:

    a. family.

    b. close friends.

    c. peer groups.

    d. students in a lecture hall.

12. Which of the following statements **best** describes the characteristics of a secondary group?

    a. a small, less specialized group in which members engage in impersonal, goal oriented relationships over an extended period of time.

    b. a small, less specialized group in which members engage in face to face, emotion based interactions over an extended period of time.

    c. a larger, more specialized group in which members engage in face to face, emotion based interactions over an extended period of time.

    d. a larger, more specialized group in which members engage in impersonal, goal oriented relationships over an extended period of time.

13. According to the text, the Salvation Army and other caregiver groups that provide services for the homeless and others in need are examples of:

    a. primary groups.

    b. formal organizations.

    c. informal organizations.

    d. social networks.

14. Sociologists use the term _____ to refer to a set of organized beliefs and rules that establish how a society will attempt to meet its basic social needs.

    a. social structure

    b. social expectations

    c. social networking

    d. social institutions

15. Which one of the following types of societies is more egalitarian?

    a. hunting and gathering

    b. horticultural and pastoral

    c. agrarian

    d. industrial

16. Most of the world's population lives in _____ societies.

    a. horticultural and pastoral

    b. postindustrial

    c. agrarian

    d. industrial

17. Emile Durkheim referred to the social cohesion found in industrial societies as:

    a. organic solidarity.

    b. mechanical solidarity.

    c. *Gemeinschaft.*

    d. *Gesellschaft.*

18. A young person who has been told repeatedly that she or he is not a good student and, as a result, stops studying and receives failing grades is an example of a(n):

    a. selective perception.

    b. objective deduction.

    c. subjective reality.

    d. self fulfilling prophecy.

19. Ethnomethodologist Harold Garfinkel assigned different activities to his students to see how breaking the unspoken rules of behavior created confusion. His research involved a series of:

    a. shared expectancies.

    b. breaching experiments.

    c. dramaturgical analyses.

    d. impression managements.

20. According to sociologist Arlie Hochschild, people acquire a set of _____, which shape the appropriate emotions for a given role or specific situation.

    a. role expectations

    b. emotional experiences

    c. feeling rules

    d. nonverbal cues

TRUE FALSE QUESTIONS

1. Most homeless persons are on the streets by choice or because they were deinstitutionalized by mental hospitals.
    True or False

2. Sociologists use the term status to refer only to high level positions in society.
    True or False

3. Historically, the most common master statuses for women have related to positions in the family, such as daughter, wife, and mother.
    True or False

4. Role performance does not always match role expectation.
    True or False

5. Role conflict occurs when incompatible role demands are placed on a person by two or more statuses held at the same time.
    True or False

6. Role distancing occurs when social identities are inconsistent with one's own identity.
    True or False

7. Role exit usually does not require a creation of a new identity.
    True or False

8. Close friends would be an example of a primary group.
    True or False

9. Social solidarity exists when a group remains cohesive when facing obstacles.
   True or False

10. Social networks work the same way for men and women and for people from different racial ethnic groups.
    True or False

11. Agrarian societies are based on technology that supports the cultivation of plants to provide food.
    True or False

12. Societies do not make a clear transition from industrialism to post-industrialism.
    True or False

13. Relationships in *Gemeinschaft* societies are based on achieved rather than ascribed status.
    True or False

14. Race/ethnicity, gender, and social class play a part in the way that social interaction is interpreted.
    True or False

15. Age, gender, and social class are strong influences in the allocation of personal space.
    True or False

FILL IN THE BLANK QUESTIONS

1. The process by which people act toward or respond to other people in defined as _____ .

2. A status gained as a result of personal ability is defined as a/an _____ status.

3. _____ societies based on technology that supports the cultivation of plants to provide food.

4. Societies based on technology that supports the domestication of large animals to provide food are known as _____ societies.

5. The process by which our perception of reality is largely shaped by the subjective meaning that we give to the experience is known as the _____ .

6. The _____ means that people analyze a social context in which they find themselves, determine what is in their best interest, and adjust their attitudes and actions accordingly.

7. The study of social interaction that compares everyday life to a theatrical presentation is known as _____ .

8. _____ refers to people's efforts to present themselves to others in ways that are most favorable to their own interests or image.

9. The transfer of information between persons without the use of words is called _____ .

10. The immediate area surrounding a person that the person claims as private is defined as _____ .

SHORT ANSWER/ESSAY QUESTIONS

1. What are the major components of social structure? Give examples of each.

2. What are the five major components of societies? List some of the major characteristics of each type. In which pre-industrial society is the social inequality the highest? The lowest? Why? Which type of society brought about some of the greatest innovations in all of human history?

3. How is homelessness related to the social structure of a society? In what type of society do you think there might be more homelessness? Why?

4. What do we mean by the social construction of reality? Give some examples.

5. What are some of the projected future changes in the social structure in the United States? How should our society react to these changes?

STUDENT CLASS PROJECTS AND ACTIVITIES

1. Utilizing the concept of social networks as discussed in the text, trace your own social networks. Construct diagrams linking yourself to your family and other relatives, and to your friends and to other acquaintances. After constructing the diagrams, answer the following questions/statements: (1) Describe the members in your network (who are they; and what is their gender, approximate age, and current employment, if applicable?). (2) How and why are they linked to you (3) Summarize the impact of each person in your network; are the ties weak or strong? Why? (4) What persons in your network are most important now? Why? (5) What persons in your network will be especially important to you in future years? (6) Is there any potential for anyone in your network to harm your in any fashion? What can/should you do about this? (7) Is there any potential for anyone in your network to provide you with special advantages for a potential career? Explain in detail your responses to the above questions. Write your paper in the manner described by your instructor and submit your paper on the due date.

2. As mentioned in the text, changes in social structure have a dramatic impact on individuals, groups, and societies. Many nations in the world today are experiencing radical changes as they attempt to modernize; while many contemporary societies are experiencing great change as they become more complex with the introduction of new technology. You are to select any country that is experiencing such change utilizing at least one of the typologies mentioned in the text (that o f Durkheim or Tonnies). Countries that could illustrate the former are the People's Republic of China; any of the 15 Republics of the U. S. S. R.; any of the countries of the former Yugoslavia; many of the countries of South America, such as Brazil; many of the countries of Africa, such as Zaire; many of the countries of South East Asia or the Pacific Rim, such as Thailand, South Korea, Malaysia, Laos; Iran; or India. Countries that could illustrate the former are: Japan, the United States, Canada, France, Germany, or Britain. You should examine the changes from both a

microlevel and a macrolevel perspective. Trace the changes in (1) the statuses, (2) the roles, (3) groups, (4) social institutions, and (5) in the society for both the individual and the country as a whole. You should also explain the effects these changes will have on the future options and opportunities of people living in that particular country. Submit your paper to your instructor, following any specific guidelines for your finished paper.

3.   The text uses homelessness as a concrete example to help students understand the difficult concept of social structure. Providing effective solutions to this problem is even more difficult. Many politicians suggest that one reason for the increase in homelessness is a direct result of the shortage of available low-income housing. You are to research and write an issue paper on this topic: "Should more low-income housing be created to help the homeless?" In your paper, you should provide the following: (1) a background of this problem; (2) factual information germane to homelessness; (3) the positions of opposing viewpoints; (4) arguments for and against the issue; (5) your own position and resolution of homelessness. Suggested note: you may attempt a synthesis of opposing positions, leave the issue essentially unresolved, or provide a new position, or a completely different, innovative program.

INTERNET ACTIVITIES

1.   *Emotions: Observing the Fusion Between Body, Mind and Society.* This is a fantastic web site that will help you understand the connections between sociology, psychology and physiology as they address the topic of emotions. The site contains links to research articles, survey data, and an online bibliography. www.trinity.edu/mkearl/spsy-emo.html

2.   This site contains an article entitled *Homelessness in a Small Southern City* in the Electronic Journal of Sociology. This would be a good opportunity to expose yourself to actual research data in order to help balance all the other kinds of information about this social problem that you encounter in the media. www.sociology.org/content/vol005.002/home99.html

3.   A selection from Erving Goffman's *Presentation of Self in Everyday Life*. This passage is about Impression Management. You should read Goffman in his own words. http://www2.pfeiffer.edu/~lridener/courses/IMPMGT.HTML

4.   From this page, you can explore non-verbal communication. This page was created to introduce the University of California video series on NONVERBAL COMMUNICATION that was produced by Dane Archer, a Professor at the University of California at Santa Cruz. http://nonverbal.ucsc.edu

5.   To learn about how we can help the homeless, go to *54 Ways You Can Help the Homeless by Rabbi Charles A. Kroloff*. This site deals with topics like characteristics of the homeless, what to do when confronted by the homeless, and how to end homelessness. www.tinman.org/sue/articles/54WaysYouCanHelpTheHomeless.html

INFOTRAC EXERCISES

1. Search for articles using the subject guide **Social Structure**. You will get 76 periodical references. Choose the article entitled: *PATHWAYS TO ADULTHOOD IN CHANGING SOCIETIES: Variability and Mechanisms in Life Course Perspective*. This would make a great resource for a small group discussion. The article would help you to connect the curriculum content to the lives of your students. The author, Michael J. Shanahan, suggests new lines of inquiry that focus on the interplay between agency and social structures in the shaping of lives.

2. Look for research projects related to the study of **emotions.** Bring in copies of articles of interest. This becomes an effective way to discuss empirical research using such "fuzzy" categories like emotions. You can emphasize research methods, science, and the sociology of emotions.

3. These three articles were accessed using InfoTrac. Each is a good starting point for a discussion on **social structure and interaction**. Each in its own way can inspire the sociological imagination. Find other research articles that help you understand the powerful influence of society on you individual life.

    a. *Restoring American cultural institutions.* Jerry L. Martin. Society. Jan-Feb 1999 v36 i2 p35(6).

    b. *Responses to humiliation.* (The Decent Society) Arthur Ripstein. Social Research. Spring 1997 v64 n1 p90 (22).

    c. *On moral issues Americans prefer persuasion.* (The Communication Network survey) Society, Nov-Dec 1997 v35 n1 p2 (1).

Solutions

MULTIPLE CHOICE QUESTIONS

1. A p. 139

2. B p. 141

3. C p. 141

4. D p.142

5. C p. 143

6. B p. 144

7. A p. 145

8. C p. 145

9. A p. 146

10. B p. 147

11. D p. 148

12. D p. 148

13. B p. 149

14. D p. 149

15. A p. 152

16. C p. 155

17. A p. 158

18. D p. 163

19. B p. 164

20. C p. 166

TRUE FALSE QUESTIONS

1. F p. 142

2. F p. 141

3. T p. 143

4. T p. 145

5. T p. 145

6. T p. 146

7. F p. 146

8. T p. 148

9. T p. 148

10. F p. 148

11. F p. 154

12. T p. 156

13. F p. 159

14. T p. 161

15. T p. 169

FILL IN THE BLANK QUESTIONS

1. social interaction

2. achieved

3. Horticultural

4. pastoral

5. social construction of reality

6. definition of the situation

7. dramaturgical analysis

8. Impression management

9. nonverbal communication

10. personal space

Chapter 6

GROUPS AND ORGANIZATIONS

BRIEF CHAPTER OUTLINE

Social Groups

- Groups, Aggregates, and Categories
- Types of Groups

Group Characteristics and Dynamics

- Group Size
- Group Leadership
- Group Conformity
- Groupthink
- Social Exchange/Rational Choice Theories

Formal Organizations in Global Perspective

- Types of Formal Organizations
- Bureaucracies
- Shortcomings of Bureaucracies
- Bureaucracy and Oligarchy

Alternative Forms of Organization

- Organizational Structure in Japan

Organizations in the Future

CHAPTER SUMMARY

Groups are a key element of our social structure and much of our social interaction takes place within them. A **social group** is a collection of two or more people who interact frequently, share a sense of belonging, and have a feeling of interdependence. Social groups may be either **primary groups** -- small, personal groups in which members engage in emotion based interactions over an extended period -- or **secondary groups** -- larger, more specialized groups in which members have less personal and more formal, goal oriented relationships. All groups set boundaries to indicate who does and who does not belong: an **ingroup** is a group to which we belong and with which we identify; an **outgroup** is a group we do not belong to or perhaps feel hostile toward. The size of a group is one of its most important features. The smallest groups are **dyads** -- groups composed of two members -- and **triads** -- groups of three. In order to maintain ties with a group, many members are willing to conform to norms established and reinforced by group members. Three types of **formal organizations** -- highly structured secondary groups formed to achieve specific goals in an efficient manner -- are normative, coercive, and utilitarian organizations. A **bureaucracy** is a formal organization characterized by hierarchical authority, division of labor, explicit procedures, and impersonality in personnel concerns. The **iron law of oligarchy** refers to the tendency of organizations to become a bureaucracy ruled by the few. A recent movement to humanize bureaucracy has focused on developing human resources. The best organizational structure for the future is one that operates humanely and that includes opportunities for all, regardless of race, gender, or class.

LEARNING OBJECTIVES

After reading Chapter 6 you should be able to:

1. Distinguish between aggregates, categories, and groups from a sociological perspective.

2. Distinguish between primary and secondary groups and explain how people's relationships differ in each.

3. State definitions for ingroup, outgroup, and reference group and describe the significance of these concepts in everyday life.

4. Contrast functionalist and conflict perspectives on the purposes of groups.

5. Describe dyads and triads and explain how interaction patterns change as the size of a group increases.

6. Distinguish between the two functions of leadership and the three major styles of group leadership.

7. Describe the experiments of Solomon Asch and Stanley Milgram and explain their contributions to our understanding about group conformity and obedience to authority.

8. Explain what is meant by groupthink and discuss reasons why it can be dangerous for organizations.

9. Describe the social exchange/rational choice theories.

10. Compare normative, coercive, and utilitarian organizations and describe the nature of membership in each.

11. Summarize Max Weber's perspective on rationality and outline his ideal characteristics of bureaucracy.

12. Describe the informal structure in bureaucracies and list its positive and negative aspects.

13. Discuss the major shortcomings of bureaucracies and their effects on workers, clients or customers, and levels of productivity.

14. Describe the iron law of oligarchy and explain why bureaucratic hierarchies and oligarchies go hand in hand.

15. Evaluate U.S. and Japanese models of organization.

KEY TERMS
(defined at page number shown and in glossary)

aggregate 176
authoritarian leaders 184
bureaucracy 192-193
bureaucratic personality 199
category 176
conformity 185
democratic leaders 184
dyad 182
expressive leadership 184
goal displacement 199
groupthink 188
ideal type 193

informal structure 195
ingroup 178
instrumental leadership 184
iron law of oligarchy 202
laissez-faire leaders 184
network 179
outgroup 178
rationality 193
reference group 179
small group 182
triad 182

KEY PEOPLE
(identified at page number shown)

Solomon Asch 185
Charles H. Cooley 177
Amitai Etzioni 190
Joe Feagin 200
Irving Janis 188
Rosabeth Moss Kanter 200

Robert Michels 202
Stanley Milgram 187
Georg Simmel 182
William Graham Sumner 178
Max Weber 193

CHAPTER OUTLINE

I.   SOCIAL GROUPS

    A.   Groups, Aggregates, and Categories

        1.   A **social group** is a collection of two or more people who interact frequently with one another, share a sense of belonging, and have a feeling of interdependence.

        2.   An **aggregate** is a collection of people who happen to be in the same place at the same time but share little else in common.

        3.   A **category** is a number of people who may never have met one another but share a similar characteristic.

    B.   Types of Groups

        1.   Primary and Secondary Group

            a.   According to Charles H. Cooley, a **primary group** is a small group whose members engage in face-to-face, emotion-based interactions over an extended period of time.

      b.   A **secondary group** is a larger, more specialized group in which the members engage in more impersonal, goal-oriented relationships for a limited period of time.

  2.   Ingroups and Outgroups

      a.   According to William Graham Sumner, an **ingroup** is a group to which a person belongs and with which the person feels a sense of identity.

      b.   An **outgroup** is a group to which a person does not belong and toward which the person may feel a sense of competitiveness or hostility.

  3.   Reference Groups

      a.   A **reference group** is a group that strongly influences a person's behavior and social attitudes, regardless of whether that individual is an actual member.

      b.   Reference groups help us explain why our behavior and attitudes sometimes differ from those of our membership groups; we may accept the values and norms of a group with which we identify rather than one to which we belong.

  4.   Networks

      a.   A **network** is a web of social relationships that link one person with other people and, through them, with other people they know.

      b.   Networks extend far beyond to not only persons that are known, but also the people that know of you.

II.   GROUP CHARACTERISTICS AND DYNAMICS

  A.   Group Size

    1.   A **small group** is a collectively small enough for all members to be acquainted with one another and to interact simultaneously.

    2.   According to Georg Simmel, small groups have distinctive interaction patterns which do not exist in larger groups.

      a.   In a **dyad** -- a group composed of two members -- the active participation of both members is crucial for the group's survival and members have a more intense bond and a sense of unity not found in most larger groups.

      b.   When a third person is added to a dyad, a **triad** -- a group composed of three members -- is formed, and the nature of the relationship and interaction patterns change.

    3.   As group size increases, members tend to specialize in different tasks, and communication patterns change.

  B.   Group Leadership

    1.   Leaders are responsible for directing plans and activities so that the group completes its task or fulfills its goals.

    2.   Leadership functions:

      a.   **Instrumental leadership** is goal or task oriented; if the underlying purpose of a group is to complete a task or reach a particular goal, this type of leadership is most appropriate.

        b.   **Expressive leadership** provides emotional support for members; this type of leadership is most appropriate when harmony, solidarity, and high morale are needed.

    3.   Leadership styles:

        a.   **Authoritarian leaders** make all major group decisions and assign tasks to members.

        b.   **Democratic leaders** encourage group discussion and decision making through consensus building.

        c.   **Laissez-faire leaders** are only minimally involved in decision making and encourage group members to make their own decisions.

C.   Group Conformity

    1.   **Conformity** is the process of maintaining or changing behavior to comply with the norms established by a society, subculture, or other group.

    2.   In a series of experiments, Solomon Asch found that the pressure toward group conformity was so great that participants were willing to contradict their own best judgment if the rest of the group disagreed with them.

    3.   Stanley Milgram (a former student of Asch's) conducted a series of controversial experiments and concluded that people's obedience to authority may be more common than most of us would like to believe.

    4.   Irving Janis coined the term **groupthink** to describe the process by which members of a cohesive group arrive at a decision that many individual members privately believe is unwise.

D.   Groupthink

    1.   Irving Janis coined the term **groupthink** to describe the process by which members of a cohesive group arrive at a decision that many individual members privately believe is unwise.

    2.   The tragic launch of the space shuttle *Challenger* example of this process.

E.   Social Exchange/Rational Choice Theories

    1.   Social Exchange/Rational Choice theories focus on the process by which actors settle on one optimal outcome out of a range of possible choices.

    2.   Social Exchange theories are based on the assumption of self-interest as the basic motivating factor.

    3.   Key elements of rational choice theories include *actors* and *resources*.

III.   FORMAL ORGANIZATIONS IN GLOBAL PERSPECTIVE

A.   A *formal organization* is a highly structured secondary group formed for the purpose of achieving specific goals in the most efficient manner (e.g., corporations, schools, and government agencies).

B.   Types of Formal Organizations

    1.   Amitai Etzioni classified formal organizations into three categories based on the nature of membership.

2. We voluntarily join *normative* organizations when we want to pursue some common interest or to gain personal satisfaction or prestige from being a member. Examples include political parties, religious organizations, and college social clubs.

3. People do not voluntarily become members of *coercive* organizations — associations people are forced to join. Examples include total institutions, such as boot camps and prisons.

4. We voluntarily join *utilitarian* organizations when they can provide us with a material reward we seek. Examples include colleges and universities, and the workplace.

C. Bureaucracies

1. **Bureaucracy** is an organizational model characterized by a hierarchy of authority, a clear division of labor, explicit rules and procedures, and impersonality in personnel matters.

2. According to Max Weber, bureaucracy is the most "rational" and efficient means of attaining organizational goals because it contributes to coordination and control. **Rationality** is the process by which traditional methods of social organization, characterized by informality and spontaneity, gradually are replaced by efficiently administered formal rules and procedures.

3. An **ideal type** is an abstract model which describes the recurring characteristics of some phenomenon; the ideal characteristics of bureaucracy include:

   a. Division of Labor -- each member has a specific status with certain assigned tasks to fulfill.

   b. Hierarchy of Authority -- a chain of command that is based on each lower office being under the control and supervision of a higher one.

   c. Rules and Regulations -- standardized rules and regulations establish authority within an organization and usually are provided to members in a written format.

   d. Qualifications - Based Employment-- hiring of staff members and professional employees is based on specific qualifications; individual performance is evaluated against specific standards; and promotions are based on merit as spelled out in personnel policies.

   e. Impersonality -- interaction is based on status and standardized criteria rather than personal feelings or subjective factors.

4. An organization's **informal structure** is composed of those aspects of participants' day to day activities and interactions that ignore, bypass, or do not correspond with the official rules and procedures of the bureaucracy.

   a. The Hawthorne studies made social scientists aware of the presence of informal networks and their effect on workers' productivity; they concluded that the level of productivity was determined by the workers' informal networks, not by the levels set by management.

   b. There are positive and negative aspects of thoughts about informal structure in organizations; one emphasizes control (or eradication) of informal groups; the other suggests that they should be nurtured.

D.   Shortcomings of Bureaucracy

    1.   Inefficiency and Rigidity

        a.   **Goal displacement** occurs when the rules become an end in themselves (rather than a means to an end), and organizational survival becomes more important than achievement of goals

        b.   The term **bureaucratic personality** is used to describe those workers who are more concerned with following correct procedures than they are with getting the job done correctly.

    2.   Resistance to Change

        a.   Once bureaucratic organizations are created, they tend to resist change.

        b.   "Parkinson's Law" and the "Peter Principle" provide theories about problems of bureaucracies.

    3.   Perpetuation of Race, Class, and Gender Inequalities

        a.   Some bureaucracies perpetuate inequality of race, class, and gender.

        b.   This form of organizational structure created a specific type of work or learning environment that historically was typically created for middle and upper-middle-class white men.

E.   Bureaucracy and Oligarchy

    1.   Max Weber believed that bureaucracy was a necessary evil because it achieved coordination and control and thus efficiency in administration; however, he believed such organizations stifled human initiative and creativity.

    2.   Bureaucracy generates an enormous degree of unregulated and often unperceived social power in the hands of a very few leaders.

    3.   According Robert Michels, this results in the **iron law of oligarchy** -- a bureaucracy ruled by a few people.

IV.   ALTERNATIVE FORMS OF ORGANIZATION

A.   "Humanizing" bureaucracy includes: (1) less rigid, hierarchical structures and greater sharing of power and responsibility; (2) encouragement of participants to share their ideas and try new approaches; and (3) efforts to reduce the number of people in dead end jobs and to help people meet outside family responsibilities while still receiving equal treatment inside the organization.

B.   The Japanese model of organization has been widely praised for its innovative structure, which (until recently) has included:

    1.   Lifetime Employment-- Workers were guaranteed permanent employment after an initial probationary period.

    2.   Quality Circles -- small workgroups that meet regularly with managers to discuss the group's performance and working conditions.

    3.   Limitations-an economic recession in Japan has forced factory closings and reassignments; some analysts suggest that production goals set by managers (not workers) must still be met.

V.   NEW ORGANIZATIONS IN THE FUTURE

A. There is a lack of consensus among organizational theorists about the "best" model of organization; however, some have suggested a horizontal model in which both hierarchy and functional or departmental boundaries largely would be eliminated.

B. In the horizontal structure, a limited number of senior executives would still exist in support roles (such as finance and human resources); everyone else would work in multidisciplinary teams that would perform core processes (e.g., product development or sales).

C. It is difficult to determine what the best organizational structure for the future might be; however, everyone can benefit from humane organizational environments that provide opportunities for all people regardless of race, gender, or class.

PRACTICE TESTS

MULTIPLE CHOICE QUESTIONS

Select the response that best answers the question or completes the statement:

1. According to the introductions the culture of the FBI:
    a. promoted anarchy.
    b. enhanced cooperation among employees.
    c. prevented it from an early detection of 9/11.
    d. worked with all arms of the government.

2. A(n) _____ is a collection of people who happen to be in the same place at the same time while a(n) _____ is a number of people who may never have met one another but share a similar characteristic.
    a. aggregate category
    b. category - aggregate
    c. social group - aggregate
    d. category - social group

3. John had thought about trying out for the football team, but because he is not very athletic, he decides to hang out with the "stoners" at his school. He harbors some feelings of hostility for the football team. For John, the football team represents a(n):
    a. reference group.
    b. secondary group.
    c. ingroup.
    d. outgroup.

4. A _____ is an alliance created in an attempt to reach a shared objective or goal.
    a. triad
    b. coalition
    c. dyad
    d. reference group

5. _____leadership is goal or task oriented; _____leadership provides emotional support for members.
   a. authoritarian - democratic
   b. authoritarian - laissez faire
   c. expressive - instrumental
   d. instrumental - expressive

6. A group leader at a business related seminar is only minimally involved with the decisions made by the group and encourages members to make their own choices. This illustrates a(n) _____ leader.
   a. expressive
   b. democratic
   c. laissez faire
   d. authoritarian

7. In one of Solomon Asch's experiments, a subject was asked to compare the length of lines printed on a series of cards without knowing that all other research "subjects" actually were assistants to the researcher. The results of Asch's experiments revealed that:
   a. 85 percent of the subjects routinely chose the correct response regardless of the assistants' opinions.
   b. 33 percent of the subjects routinely chose to conform to the opinion of the assistants by giving an incorrect answer.
   c. 10 percent of the subjects routinely chose to conform to the opinion of the assistants by giving an incorrect answer.
   d. the opinion of the assistants had no influence on the subjects' opinions.

8. In reference to the experiments by Stanley Milgram, the text points out that:
   a. obedience to authority may be less common than most people would like to believe.
   b. many of the subjects questioned the ethics of the experiment.
   c. research such as this raises important questions concerning research ethics.
   d. most of the subjects were afraid to conform because the use of electrical current was involved.

9. According to the text, the tragic loss of the space shuttle *Challenger* is an example of:
   a. groupthink.
   b. obedience to authority.
   c. compliance.
   d. the iron law of oligarchy.

10. All of the following are types of formal organizations, <u>except</u> _____ organizations.
   a. normative
   b. anomic
   c. coercive
   d. utilitarian

11. Membership in _____ organizations is involuntary.

    a. normative

    b. anomic

    c. coercive

    d. utilitarian

12. According to Max Weber, rationality refers to:

    a. the process by which bureaucracy is gradually replaced by alternative types of organization such as quality circles.

    b. the process by which traditional methods of social organization are gradually replaced by bureaucracy.

    c. the level of sanity (or insanity) of people in an organization.

    d. the logic used by organizational leaders in decision making.

13. All of the following are ideal type characteristics of bureaucratic organizations, as specified by Max Weber, **except**:

    a. coercive leadership.

    b. impersonality.

    c. hierarchy of authority.

    d. division of labor.

14. In higher education, student handbooks, catalogs, and course syllabi are examples of:

    a. informal structures in bureaucracy.

    b. impersonality.

    c. hierarchy of authority.

    d. rules and regulations.

15. In the Hawthorne studies, workers in the "bank wiring room":

    a. worked harder when management offered them financial incentives.

    b. adhered to the formal rules of the organization because they believed they would lose their jobs otherwise.

    c. tended to work slowly in the morning but work rapidly in the afternoon when managers were most likely to see them.

    d. determined the level of productivity within informal networks, not by the levels set by management.

16. The _____ approach to management views informal networks as a type of adaptive behavior workers engage in because they experience a lack of congruence between their own needs and the demands of the organization.

    a. authoritarian

    b. human relations

    c. public relations

    d. quality circles

17. All of the following are shortcomings of bureaucracy, **except**:
    a. impersonality
    b. inefficiency and rigidity
    c. resistance to change
    d. perpetuation of race, class, and gender inequalities

18. The statement that best expresses the Peter Principle is:
    a. People rise to the level of their incompetence.
    b. Work expands to fill the time available for its completion.
    c. When things can go wrong, they will.
    d. If it ain't broke, don't fix it.

19. According to sociologist Joe R. Feagin's recent research on racial and ethnic inequalities in organizations, many middle class African Americans today:
    a. are included in informal communications networks at work.
    b. have mentors who take an interest in furthering their careers.
    c. have found that entry into dominant white bureaucratic organizations has brought about integration for them.
    d. have experienced an internal conflict between the ideal of equal opportunity and the prevailing norms of many organizations.

20. According to Robert Michels, all organizations encounter:
    a. the Peter Principle.
    b. the iron law of oligarchy.
    c. Murphy's Law.
    d. groupthink.

TRUE FALSE QUESTIONS

1. People in aggregates share a common purpose.
   True or False

2. Although formal organizations are secondary groups, they also contain many primary groups within them.
   True or False

3. According to functionalists, people form groups to meet instrumental and expressive needs.
   True or False

4. If one member withdraws from a dyad, the group ceases to exist.
   True or False

5. Laissez faire leaders encourage group discussion and decision making through consensus building.
   True or False

6. Stanley Milgram's research focused on people's obedience to authority.
    True or False

7. The research of Solomon Asch demonstrated that few people actually will bow to social pressure in small-group settings.
    True or False

8. Recent research on sexual harassment by psychologist John Pryor suggests that there is a relationship between group conformity and harassment.
    True or False

9. The explosion of the space shuttle *Columbia* has been cited as an example of group think.
    True or False

10. In the utilitarianism doctrine of rational choice theory, the purpose of all action should be to bring about the greatest happiness to the greatest number of people.
    True or False

11. Over the past century, the number of formal organizations increased dramactically in the United States.
    True or False

12. An ideal type is an abstract model that describes the recurring characteristics of some phenomenon.
    True or False

13. The formal structure of an organization has been referred to as "bureaucracy's other face."
    True or False

14. In the Hawthorne studies, those workers who worked too hard were referred to as "chiselers."
    True or False

15. Women and people of color who are employed in positions traditionally held by white men often experience categorical exclusion from the informal structures..
    True or False

FILL IN THE BLANK QUESTIONS

1. According to _____ , small groups have distinctive interaction patterns that do not exist in larger groups.

2. Sociologist _____ coined the terms ingroup and outgroup.

3. The term primary group was coined by _____ .

4. A series of controversial experiments dealing with people's obedience to authority were conducted by _____ .

5. The term groupthink was coined by _____ .

6. Sociologist _____ analyzed how the power structure of bureaucratic hierarchies negatively affect white women and people of color.

7. The term iron law of oligarchy was coined by _____ .

8. Many U.S. corporations use _____ to achieve better product quality and to lower productive costs.

9. Officials in a bureaucracy practice _____ when they emphasize rules and procedures more than the achievement of the goals.

10. The term _____ describes workers more concerned with following correct procedures than they are with getting the job done correctly.

SHORT ANSWER/ESSAY QUESTIONS

1. According to the social exchange/rational choice theory, what might some men gain from sexually harassing workers? What are some possible losses or penalties? What do women gain or lose by reporting incidents of sexual harassment?

2. Define and provide an example of each of the following three theories: (1) Parkinson's law; (2) Peter Principle; and (3) Michel's Iron Law of Oligarchy.

3. What is bureaucracy? What are some of the strengths and weaknesses of bureaucracies?

4. What is groupthink? How might one affect or be affected by groupthink?

5. What were the insights gained from Stanley Milgram's research? Do these insights outweigh the personal costs to the subjects of the research?

STUDENT CLASS PROJECTS AND EXERCISES

1. Prior to taking office, the U.S. President-elect announces to the public his/her choice of all the cabinet and chief advisory appointments. These appointments profoundly shape many of the policies and directions the U.S. Federal Government, which is one of the largest bureaucracies in the country. As a required written project, select ten of these positions. Describe the position, in terms of the purpose of the office; the requirements, if any, for the position; and the length of the term of that position. Name and briefly describe the credentials of the person who occupies that office. Some examples of cabinet posts are: U.S. Attorney General, Agriculture Secretary, Secretary of the Interior, Transportation Secretary, Secretary of State, Secretary of Defense, Education Secretary, Energy Secretary, Secretary of Veterans Affairs, Commerce Secretary, Labor Secretary, Secretary of the Treasury, etc. Some examples of non-cabinet appointments are: Office of Management and Budget, White House Chief of Staff, White House Council of Economic Advisers, Environmental Protection Agency Administrator, etc. Submit your paper at the designated time according to the format and instructions provided by your instructor.

2. One example of a formal organization is your college or university. Gather information about the characteristics of the organization. Is it constructed according to the specific characteristics of a bureaucracy as described by Max Weber? Explain your response. You may gather information from the college catalog, available organizational charts, and/or via interviews with personnel who work in the organization. Draw and organizational chart to demonstrate the characteristics.

3. Visit a factory with an assembly line, preferably a large factory. Obtain or construct an organizational chart of the factory. Try to speak with several employees who occupy different positions in the factory. Carefully record all responses. The questions are: (1) What is their specific job description? (2) Why do they work there? (3) What is their specific responsibility? (4) Are they satisfied with their position? Why? Why not? (5) What about the formal and informal aspect of the work environment? What is the degree of friendship with other workers or management? (6) Do they have any control over their responsibilities? Explain. (7) Are there any improvements they would make? If so, what specifically? Submit your papers at the appropriate date, following directions provided by your professor.

INTERNET ACTIVITIES

1. Go to *Verstehen, the Max Weber* web site and read about
    Bureaucracy, Rationality, Oligarchy and Ideal Types.
    www.faculty.rsu.edu/~felwell/Theorists/Weber/Whome.htm

2. Here are a number of *McDonaldization* sites. There are even more "out there" on the World Wide
    Web. As you begin to study this theory take a look at the WWW and ask for more information.
    Hold a "show and tell" with other class members and relate ideas from these sites to what you have
    learned about groups and organizations and Weber's theories.
    a.   www.mcdonaldization.com/main.shtml
    b.   www.stedwards.edu/bss/farrall/mcdonize.htm
    c.   www.geocities.com/mcdonaldization/
    d.   www.umsl.edu/~rkeel/010/mcdonsoc.html

3. Federal organizations are taking some heat for intelligence failures related to the September 11th
    terrorist attacks. Take a look at some of these online essays, editorials, and commentaries to
    get a feel for the current discourse.
    a.   www.infed.org/bornandbred/lead-bk.htm
    b.   http://oilempire.us/warnings.html
    c.   http://pub17.ezboard.com/fhumanrightsfrm18.showMessage?topicID=5.topic

4. To learn more about leadership and styles of leading, access the *Leadership Booklist*
    for a thorough listing and description of important works on leadership. Print
    and save for future use in other classes and your own professional development.
    www.infed.org/bornandbred/lead-bk.htm

INFOTRAC EXERCISES

1. Look for articles on **Social Isolation** that compare the consequences of web interaction rather
    than face-to-face interaction in a group. Note that much of the research to date finds negative
    consequences-loneliness and other psychological consequences). After looking at this research,
    why do you think people miss interacting with a group face to face?

2. Look for research on **conformity**. What types of situations seem to increase or decrease
    conformity? What types of group membership is more likely to increase conformity (e.g., gangs,
    cults, etc.)?

3. Search for the keyword **leadership style** in the title, abstract or citation of articles. Have your
    students work in small groups to hold a seminar on leadership. Use information from any of these
    articles and from this chapter to construct a brochure on "How to Be a Successful Leader."

4. There are 425 periodical references listed under the category of **bureaucracy**. Try and discover
    the meaning of this common word. Bring in to class examples of these articles. From these articles
    see if you can construct a definition of the concept along with its essential dimensions.

Solutions

MULTIPLE CHOICE QUESTIONS

1. C pp. 175

2. A p. 176

3. D p. 178

4. B p. 182

5. D p. 184

6. C p. 184

7. B p. 185

8. C p. 187

9. A p. 188

10. B pp. 191-192

11. C p. 192

12. B p. 193

13. A pp. 193

14. D p. 193

15. D p. 195

16. B p. 197

17. A p. 198-200

18. A p. 200

19. D p. 200

20. B p. 200

TRUE FALSE QUESTIONS

1. T p. 176

2. T p. 178

3. T p. 181

4. T p. 182

5. F p. 184

6. T p. 186

7. F p. 185

8. T p. 188

9. T p. 189

10. T p. 189

11. T p. 191

12. T p. 193

13. F p. 195

14. F p. 195

15. T p. 197

FILL IN THE BLANK QUESTIONS

1. Georg Simmel

2. William Graham Sumner

3. Charlse H. Cooley

4. Stanley Milgrim

5. Irving Janis

6. Rosabeth Kanter

7. Robert Michels

8. quality circles

9. goal displacement

10. bureaucratic personality

Chapter 7

DEVIANCE AND CRIME

BRIEF CHAPTER OUTLINE

What Is Deviance?
- Who Defines Deviance?
- What is Social Control?

Functionalist Perspectives on Deviance
- What Causes Deviance, and Why Is It Functional for Society?
- Strain Theory: Goals and Means to Achieve Them
- Opportunity Theory: Access to Illegitimate Opportunities

Symbolic Interactionist Perspectives on Deviance
- Differential Association Theory and Differential Reinforcement Theory
- Rational Choice Theory
- Control Theory: Social Bonding
- Labeling Theory

Conflict Perspectives on Deviance
- Deviance and Power Relations
- Deviance and Capitalism
- Feminist Approaches
- Approaches Focusing on Race, Class, and Gender

Postmodernist Perspectives on Deviance

Crime Classifications and Statistics
- How the Law Classifies Crime
- How Sociologists Classify Crime
- Crime Statistics
- Terrorism and Crime
- Street Crimes and Criminals
- Crime Victim

The Criminal Justice System
- The Police
- The Courts

- Punishment and Corrections
- Death Penalty

Deviance and Crime in the United States in the Future

The Global Criminal Economy

CHAPTER SUMMARY

By definition, **deviance** is any behavior, belief, or condition that violates significant social norms in the society or group in which it occurs. Crime is a form of deviant behavior that violates criminal law and is punishable by fines, jail terms, and other sanctions. A subcategory, **juvenile delinquency**, refers to a violation of a law or the commission of a status offence by young people. All societies create norms in order to define, reinforce, and to help teach acceptable behavior. They also have various mechanisms of **social control**, systematic practices developed by social groups to encourage conformity and to discourage deviance. What causes deviance, and why is it functional for society? Functionalists suggest that deviance is inevitable in all societies and serves several functions: it clarifies rules, unites groups, and promotes social change. Functionalists use **strain theory** and opportunity theory, such as **access to illegitimate opportunity structures** and to argue that socialization into the core value of material success without the corresponding legitimate means to achieve that goal accounts for much of the crime committed by people from lower income backgrounds, especially when a person's ties to society are weakened or broken. **Symbolic Interactionists** use **differential association theory, differential reinforcement theory, rational choice theory of deviance, social bonding theory** and **labeling theory** to explain how a person's behavior is influenced and reinforced by others. Conflict theorists suggest that people with economic and political power define as criminal any behavior that threatens their own interests and are able to use the law to protect their own interests. Postmodernists' perspectives on deviance examine the intertwining nature of knowledge, power, and technology on social control and discipline. While the law classifies crime into felonies and misdemeanors based on the seriousness of the crime, sociologists categorize crimes according to how they are committed and how society views them. Four general categories of crime include: **conventional, occupational, corporate crime, organized crime**, and **political crime**. Studies show that many more crimes are committed than are reported in official crime statistics. In explaining terrorism and crime, the rational choice approach suggests that terrorists are rational actors who constantly calculate the gains and losses of participation in violent—and often suicidal—acts against others. Gender, age, class, and race are key factors in official crime statistics. The criminal justice system includes the police, the courts, punishment, and corrections. These agencies often have considerable discretion in dealing with deviance. The death penalty, or capital punishment, has been used in the United States as an appropriate and justifiable response to very serious crimes and continues to be controversial. As we move into the future, we need new approaches for dealing with crime and delinquency. Equal justice under the law needs to be guaranteed, regardless of race, class, gender, or age. Global crime -- the networking of powerful criminal organizations and their associates in shared activities around the world – has expanded rapidly in the era of global communications and rapid transportation networks. Reducing global crime will require a global response, including the cooperation of law enforcement agencies around the world.

LEARNING OBJECTIVES

After reading Chapter 7, you should be able to:

1. Explain the nature of deviance and describe its most common forms.

2. Discuss the functions of deviance from a functionalist perspective and outline the principal features of strain, opportunity, and control theories.

3. Describe the key components of differential association theory and differential reinforcement theory from the symbolic interactionist perspective.

4. Identify rational choice, social bonding, and labeling theories and explain why they are examples of interactionist perspectives.

5. Discuss conflict perspectives on deviance and note the strengths and weaknesses of critical and feminist approaches to deviance and crime.

6. Examine the simultaneous effects of race, class, and gender on deviant behavior.

7. Define and explain the postmodernist perspectives on deviance.

8. Distinguish between legal and sociological classification of crime.

9. Describe the types of behavior included in conventional crimes.

10. Differentiate between occupational and corporate crime and explain "criminals."

11. Describe organized crime and political crime and explain how each may weaken social control in a society.

12. Explain why official crime statistics may not be an accurate reflection of the actual number and kinds of crimes committed in the United States.

13. Explain how the rational choice approach explains terrorism and crime.

14. Describe the criminal justice system and explain how police, courts, punishment and corrections have considerable discretion in dealing with offenders.

15. State the four major goals of punishment and explain how disparate treatment of the poor, all people of color, and white women is evident in the U.S. prison system.

16. Discuss the issues of the death penalty, and subsequent Supreme Court decisions related to capital punishment.

KEY TERMS

(defined at page number shown and in glossary)

conventional (street) crime 227
corporate crime 230
crime 212
criminology 213
deviance 210
differential association theory 218
illegitimate opportunity structures 217
juvenile delinquency 213
labeling theory 220
occupational (white-collar) crime 229

organized crime 231
political crime 231
primary deviance 221
punishment 238
rational choice theory of deviance 219
secondary deviance 221
social bond theory 219
social control 213
strain theory 215
tertiary deviance 221

KEY PEOPLE

(identified at page number shown)

Regina Arnold 224
Howard Becker 220
William Chambliss 221
Richard Cloward and Lloyd Ohlin 217
Katherine Daly and Meda Chesney-Lind 223
Emile Durkheim 214
Michel Foucault 224-225
Travis Hirshci 219

Edwin Lemert 221
Coramae Richey Mann 235
Robert Merton 215
Richard Quinney 223
Walter Reckless 219
Edwin Sutherland 218
Lewsi Yablonsky 217

CHAPTER OUTLINE

I. WHAT IS DEVIANCE?
   A. By definition, **deviance** is any behavior, belief or condition that violates significant social norms in the society or group in which it occurs.
      1. Deviance is relative and it varies in its degree of seriousness: some forms of deviant behavior are officially defined as a crime.
      2. **Crime** is a form of deviant behavior that violates criminal law and is punishable by fines, jail terms, and other negative sanctions.
      3. **Juvenile delinquency** refers to a violation of law or the commission of a status offence by young people.
   B. What is social control?
      1. All societies have norms that govern acceptable behavior and mechanisms of **social control**, systematic practices developed by social groups to encourage conformity and discourage deviance.
      2. **Criminology** is the systematic study of crime and the criminal justice system, including police, courts, and prisons.

II. FUNCTIONALIST PERSPECTIVES ON DEVIANCE

    A. What causes deviance, and why is it functional for society?

        1. Emile Durkheim regarded deviance as a natural and inevitable part of all societies.

        2. Deviance is universal because it serves three important functions:

            a. Deviance clarifies rules.

            b. Deviance unites a group.

            c. Deviance promotes social change.

        3. Functionalists acknowledge that deviance also may be dysfunctional for society; if too many people violate the norms, everyday existence may become unpredictable, chaotic, and even violent.

    B. Strain Theory: Goals and Means to Achieve Them

        1. According to **strain theory**, people feel strain when they are exposed to cultural goals that they are unable to obtain because they do not have access to culturally approved means of achieving those goals. Robert Merton identified five ways in which people adapt to cultural goals and approved ways of achieving them:

            a. Conformity;

            b. Innovation;

            c. Ritualism;

            d. Retreatism; and

            e. Rebellion.

    C. Opportunity Theory: Access to Illegitimate Opportunities

        1. According to Richard Cloward and Lloyd Ohlin, for deviance to occur people must have access to **illegitimate opportunity structures** -- circumstances that provide an opportunity for people to acquire through illegitimate activities what they cannot achieve through legitimate channels.

III. SYMBOLIC INTERACTIONIST PERSPECTIVES ON DEVIANCE

    A. Differential Association Theory and Differential Reinforcement Theory

        1. **Differential association theory** states that individuals have a greater tendency to deviate from societal norms when they frequently associate with persons who are more favorable toward deviance than conformity.

    B. Rational Choice Theory

        1. The **rational choice theory of deviance** states that deviant behavior occurs when a person weighs the costs and benefits nonconventional or criminal behavior and determines that the benefits will outweigh the risks involved in such actions.

    C. Control Theory: **Social Bonding**

        1. **Social bond** theory holds that the probability of deviant behavior increases when a person's ties to society are weakened or broken.

    D. Labeling Theory

        1. **Labeling theory** states that deviants are those people who have been successfully labeled as such by others.

        2. **Primary deviance** is the initial act of rule breaking.

3. **Secondary deviance** occurs when a person who has been labeled a deviant accepts that new identity and continues the deviant behavior.

4. **Tertiary deviance** occurs when a person labeled a deviant seeks to normalize the behavior by relabeling it as non-deviant.

IV. CONFLICT PERSPECTIVES ON DEVIANCE

   A. Deviance and Power Relations

   1. According to conflict theorists, people in positions of power maintain their advantage by using the law to protect their own interests.

   B. Deviance and Capitalism

   1. According to the critical approach, the way laws are made and enforced benefits the capitalist class by ensuring that individuals at the bottom of the social class structure do not infringe on the property or threaten the safety of those at the top.

   C. Feminist Approaches

   1. While there is no single feminist perspective on deviance and crime, three schools of thought have emerged:

      a. Liberal feminism is based on the assumption that women's deviance and crime is a rational response to gender discrimination experienced in work, marriage, and interpersonal relationships.

      b. Radical feminism is based on the assumption that women's deviance and crime is related to patriarchy (male domination over females) that keeps women more tied to family, sexuality, and home, even if women also have full time paid employment.

      c. Socialist feminism is based on the assumption that women's deviance and crime is the result of women's exploitation by capitalism and patriarchy (e.g., their overrepresentation in relatively low wage jobs and their lack of economic resources).

   2. Feminist scholars of color have pointed out that these schools of feminist thought do not include race and ethnicity in their analyses.

   3. Approaches Focusing on Race, Class, and Gender

      a. According Arnold's research, criminal behavior of women in her study was linked to class, gender, and racial oppression, which the women experienced daily in their families and at work and school.

      b. According to feminist sociologist and criminologist research on women as both victims and perpetrators is long overdue.

      c. The research of Martin and Junk found that women in the criminal justice system experience significant barriers in justice occupations.

V. POSTMODERNIST PERSPECTIVES ON DEVIANCE

   A. Postmodernists perspective on deviance examines the intertwining nature of knowledge, power, and technology on social control and discipline.

   B. Technologies make widespread surveillance and disciplinary power possible in many settings.

   1. These settings include state-police network, factories, schools, and hospitals.

2.   Discipline would not sweep uniformly through society due to opposing forces that would use their power to oppose such surveillance.

VI.   CRIME CLASSIFICATIONS AND STATISTICS

    A.   How the Law Classifies Crime

        1.   Crimes are divided into felonies and misdemeanors based on the seriousness of the crime.

        2.   the Uniform Crime Report (UCR), compiled by the F.B.I., is the major source of information on crimes reported in the United States.

    B.   How Sociologists Classify Crime

        1.   Sociologists categorize crimes based on how they are committed and how society views the offenses.

            a.   **Conventional** or **street crime** is all violent crime, certain property crimes, and certain morals crimes.

            b.   **Occupational** or **white-collar crime** is illegal activities committed by people in the course of their employment or financial affairs; **corporate crime** is an illegal act committed by corporate employees on behalf of the corporation and with its support

            c.   **Organized crime** is a business operation that supplies illegal goods and services for profit.

            d.   **Political crime** refers to illegal or unethical acts involving the usurpation of power by government officials, or illegal/unethical acts perpetrated against the government by outsiders seeking to make a political statement, undermine the government, or overthrow it.

    C.   Crime Statistics

        1.   Official crime statistics, such as those found in the *Uniform Crime Report*, provide important information on crime; however, the data reflect only those crimes that have been reported to the police.

        2.   The National Crime Victimization Survey and anonymous self reports of criminal behavior have made researchers aware that the incidence of some crimes, such as theft, is substantially higher than reported in the UCR.

        3.   Crime statistics do not reflect many crimes committed by persons of upper socioeconomic status in the course of business because they are handled by administrative or quasi judicial bodies.

    D.   Terrorism and Crime

        1.   The United States and other nations, as of 2001, are confronted with world terrorism and crime.

        2.   The nebulous nature of the "enemy" and other limitations has resulted in a "war on terrorism."

    E.   Street Crimes and Criminals

        1.   Gender and Crime

a.   The three most common arrest categories for both men and women are driving under the influence of alcohol or drugs (DUI), larceny, and minor or criminal mischief types of offenses.

b.   Liquor law violations (such as underage drinking), simple assault, and disorderly conduct are middle range offenses for both men and women, and the rate of arrests for murder, arson, and embezzlement are relatively low for both men and women.

c.   There is a proportionately greater involvement of men in major property crimes and violent crime.

2.   Age and Crime

a.   Arrest rates for index crimes are highest for people between the ages of 13 and 25, with the peak being between ages 16 and 17.

b.   Rates of arrest remain higher for males than females at every age and for nearly all offenses.

3.   Social Class and Crime

a.   Individuals from all social classes commit crimes; they simply commit different kinds of crime.

b.   Persons from lower socioeconomic backgrounds are more likely to be arrested for violent and property crimes; only a very small proportion of individuals who commit white collar or elite crimes will ever be arrested or convicted.

4.   Race and Crime

a.   In 2002, whites (including Latinos/as) accounted for about 66 percent of all arrests for index crimes; arrest rates for whites were higher in non violent property crimes such as fraud and larceny theft, but were lower than the rates for African Americans in violent crimes such as robbery and murder.

b.   In 2002, African Americans made up about 12 percent of the U.S. population but accounted for almost 30 percent of all arrests.

c.   In 2002, Latinos/as made up about 12 percent of the U.S. population and accounted for about 13 percent of all arrests; over two-thirds of their offences were for nonindex crimes such as alcohol and drugs-related offences and disorderly conduct.

d.   In 2002, about 1 percent of all arrests were Asian-Americans or Pacific Islanders.

e.   About 1 percent of all arrests were Native Americans, designated in the UCR as "American Indian" or "Alaskan Native."

f.   Arrest records tend to produce over generalizations about who commits crime because arrest statistics are not an accurate reflection of the crimes actually committed in our society.

g.   Arrests should not be equated with guilt: being arrested does not mean that a person is guilty of the crime.

5.   Crime Victims

a. Men are more likely to be victimized by crime although women tend to be more fearful of crime, particularly those directed toward them, such as forcible rape.

b. The elderly also tend to be more fearful of crime, but are the least likely to be victimized. Young men of color between the ages of 12 and 24 have the highest criminal victimization rates.

c. The burden of robbery victimization falls more heavily on males than females, African Americans more than whites, and young people more than middle aged and older persons.

VII. THE CRIMINAL JUSTICE SYSTEM

A. The criminal justice system includes the police, the courts, and correctional facilities. This system is a collection of bureaucracies that has considerable discretion the use of personal judgment regarding whether to take action on a situation and, if so, what kind of action to take.

B. The **police** are responsible for crime control and maintenance of order.

1. *Racial profiling* remains a highly charged issue.

2. The current emphasis of community-oriented policing has enhanced the image of police departments.

C. The courts determine the guilt or innocence of those accused of committing a crime.

D. **Punishment** is any action designed to deprive a person of things of value (including liberty) because of something the person is thought to have committed. **Corrections** is often used in place of punishment.

1. Historically, punishment has had four major goals: *retribution*, *general deterrence*, *incapacitation*, and *rehabilitation*.

2. Newer approaches, such as *restoration*, promote peacemaking, rather than punishment for offenders.

3. *Corrections* is a major activity today; more than one out of 20 males; one out of 100 females are under some form of correctional control.

4. Some argue that a *determinate sentence* with *mandatory sentencing guidelines* would help reduce disparities in corrections based on race, ethnicity, and class.

E. The Death Penalty

1. For many years, capital punishment, or the **Death Penalty**, has been used in the United States.

2. Scholars have documented race and class biases in the imposition of the death penalty in this country.

3. Questions that remain today regarding capital punishment include the execution of:

a. Possible innocent individuals

b. Juvenile offenders

c. Those not having effective legal counsel

d. Those believed to be insane

VIII. DEVIANCE AND CRIME IN THE UNITED STATES IN THE FUTURE

    A.   Although many people in the United States agree that crime is one of the most important problems facing this country, they are divided over what to do about it.

    B.   The best approach for reducing delinquency and crime ultimately is prevention: to work with young people before they become juvenile offenders so as to help them establish family relationships, build self esteem, choose a career, and get an education which will help them pursue that career, as well as to promote social justice regardless of race, class, gender, or age.

IX.   THE GLOBAL CRIMINAL ECONOMY

    A.   Global Crime--the networking of powerful criminal organizations and their associates in shared activities around the world-have expanded rapidly in the era of global communications and rapid transportation networks.

    B.   Global networking and forming strategic alliances allow participants to escape police control and live beyond the laws of any one nation.

    C.   Reducing global crime will require a global response, including the cooperation of law enforcement agencies around the world.

PRACTICE TESTS

MULTIPLE CHOICE QUESTIONS

Select the response that best answers the question or completes the statement.

1.   The text defines deviance as any:

    a.   aberrant behavior.

    b.   behavior, belief, or condition that violates social norms.

    c.   serious violation of consistent moral codes.

    d.   perverted act.

2.   _____ refer(s) to systematic practices developed by social groups to encourage conformity and to discourage deviance.

    a.   Law

    b.   Folkways

    c.   Mores

    d.   Social control

3.   According to functionalists such as Emile Durkheim, deviance serves all of the following functions, **except**:

    a.   deviance helps us to identify social dynamite and social junk in a society.

    b.   deviance clarifies rules.

    c.   deviance promotes social change.

    d.   deviance unites a group.

4. According to _____ theory, people are sometimes exposed to cultural goals that they are unable to obtain because they do not have access to culturally approved means of achieving those goals.

   a. containment

   b. status inaccessibility

   c. strain

   d. conflict

5. All of the following are included in Robert Merton's modes of adaptation to cultural goals and approved ways of achieving them, **except**:

   a. retribution.

   b. ritualism.

   c. retreatism.

   d. rebellion.

6. According to _____ theory, a teenager living in a poverty ridden area of a central city is unlikely to become wealthy through a Harvard education, but some of his desires may be met through behaviors such as theft, drug dealing, and robbery.

   a. deviance management

   b. control

   c. illegitimate opportunity structures

critical

1. Which theory would suggest that people must be taught that the risks of engaging in criminal behavior far outweigh any benefits gained from their actions?

   a. postmodern.

   b. critical.

   c. social bonding.

   d. rational choice.

2. _____ theories suggest that the probability of delinquency increases when a person's social bonds are weak and when peers promote antisocial values and violent behavior.

   a. Deviance management

   b. Control

   c. Illegitimate opportunity structures

   d. Critical

3. According to Edwin Lemert's typology, _____ deviance is exemplified by a person under the legal drinking age who orders an alcoholic beverage at a local bar but is not "caught" and labeled a deviant.

   a. primary

   b. secondary

   c. tertiary

   d. adolescent

4. The _____ approach argues that criminal law protects the interests of the affluent and powerful.
   a. functionalist
   b. liberal feminist
   c. interactionist
   d. conflict

5. _____ feminism explains women's deviance and crime as a rational response to gender discrimination experienced in work, marriage, and interpersonal relationships.
   a. Radical
   b. Communist
   c. Liberal
   d. Marxistt

6. Marxist/Socialist feminists argue that women's deviance and crime occurs because:
   a. women are exploited by other women.
   b. women are exploited by capitalism and patriarchy.
   c. women experience gender discrimination in work, marriage, and interpersonal relationships.
   d. women are consumers and tend to purchase more than they can afford.

7. All of the following theorists are correctly matched with their theory, **except**:
   a. Howard Becker -- labeling theory
   b. Robert Merton -- strain theory
   c. Travis Hirschi -- differential association
   d. Meda Chesney Lind -- feminist approach

8. Violent crime, certain property crimes, and certain morals crimes are referred to as _____ crime.
   a. misdemeanor
   b. organized
   c. political
   d. conventional

9. All of the following are index crimes, **except**:
   a. traffic violations.
   b. larceny in excess of $50.
   c. armed robbery.
   d. murder.

10. Much _____ crime is a violation of positions of trust at the expense of the general public..
    a. occupational or corporate
    b. street
    c. organized
    d. conventional

11. Drug trafficking, prostitution, loan sharking, and money laundering are examples of _____ crime.
    a. occupational/white collar
    b. street
    c. organized
    d. conventional

12. All of the following are examples of political crime, **except**:
    a. unethical or illegal use of government authority for the purpose of material gain.
    b. money laundering.
    c. engaging in graft through bribery, kickbacks, or "insider" deals.
    d. dubious use of public funds and public property.

13. According to the text, rates of arrest:
    a. are about the same for males and females at every age group and for most offenses.
    b. are slightly higher for females than males in the younger age levels and for violent crimes.
    c. are about the same for males and females for prostitution due to more stringent enforcement of criminal laws pertaining to male customers.
    d. remain higher for males than females at every age and for nearly all offenses.

14. All of the following are functions of punishment, **except**:
    a. deterrence.
    b. retribution.
    c. social protection.
    d. elimination of social dynamite and social junk.

TRUE FALSE QUESTIONS

1. People may be regarded as deviant if they express a radical or unusual belief system.
True or False

2. According to sociologists, deviance is relative.
True or False

3. Deviance is found in all societies.
True or False

4. A person who accepts culturally approved goals, but rejects the approved means of achieving them is a representation of Mertons's ritualism.
True or False

5. According to differential association theory, people learn the necessary techniques and motivation for deviant behavior from people with whom they associate.
True or False

6. Moral entrepreneurs use their views of right and wrong to establish rules for their daily lives.
True or False

7. According the research of Chambliss, the group known as the "Saints" became negatively stigmatized and eventually dropped out of school.
True or False

8. Members of stigmatized groups who are costly to society but relatively harmless are categorized as social dynamite.
True or False

9. Karl Marx wrote extensively about deviance and crime.
True or False

10. Recently, functionalist theorists have examined the relationship between class, race, and crime.
True or False

11. A felony is a serious crime with punishment from imprisonment to death.
True or False

12. The UCR is published annually by the CIA.
True or False

13. Moral crimes are often referred to as victimless crimes.
True or False

14. According to the rational choice approach, terrorists are rational actors who constantly calculate the gains and losses of participation in violence and sometimes suicidal acts against others.
True or False

15. A recent study by the justice department found that Native Americans are more likely to be victims of violent crimes than are members of any other racial ethic group.
True or False

FILL IN THE BLANK QUESTIONS

1. _____ is the systematic study of crime and the criminal justice system.

2. According to _____ criminal behavior is learned within intimate personal groups.

3. According to the research of Chambliss the _____ were negatively labeled whereas the _____ were positively labeled, even though they were both involved in criminal behavior.

4. The _____ views the cause of women's crime as originating in patriarchy.

5. _____ crime comprises illegal activities committed by people in the course of their employment of financial affairs.

6. _____ crimes are illegal acts committed by corporate employees on behalf of the corporation.

7. According to the research of _____ and _____ , three basic gang types: criminal , conflict, and retreatist, emerge on the basis of what types of structures of illegitimate opportunities are available.

8. According to sociologist, _____ people with economic and political power define as criminal any behavior that threatens their own interest.

9. _____ theory holds that the probability of deviant behaviors increases when a person's ties to society are weakened or broken.

10. _____ theory refers to the systematic practices that social groups develop in order to encourage conformity to norms, rules, and laws and to discourage deviance.

SHORT ANSWER/ESSAY QUESTIONS

1. What is meant by deviant behavior? What are some factors that help determine whether an act will be viewed as deviant?

2. What are the key assumptions of the symbolic interactionist perspective in deviance?

3. What are the primary assumptions of conflict and feminist perspectives on deviance? What are some of the gaps in research that these two perspectives have attempted to fill?

4. What is it meant by the global criminal economy? What are some examples? How can global crime be reduced?

5. How are age, race, class, and gender related to crime statistics?

STUDENT CLASS PROJECTS AND ACTIVITIES

1. The organized crime syndicate, the Mafia, has a long and interesting history. You are to research the origin, the purpose, and the growth of the Mafia in Italy and Sicily, noting some similarities and differences of each. In addition to tracing the history of both of these organizations, explain the growth of the Mafia in the United States. Explain some of the original neighborhood programs that the Mafia sponsored. Explain why you think it is difficult to eradicate this crime syndicate.

2. Research the topic of crime rates in a cross-cultural perspective, with specific emphasis on comparing the rates of the U.S. with those of other industrialized countries. Summarize your findings, provide some explanations for your findings, and provide a bibliography of your references. Submit your papers at the appropriate time, following the instructions you have been given in the writing of your paper.

3. As indicated in your textbook, global crime--the networking of powerful criminal organizations and their associates in shared activities around the world--is a relatively new phenomenon, although theses organizations have existed for many years in their country of origin. You are to: 1) select five global criminal organizations; 2) explain the origin, purpose, and growth of the organization; 3) describe some of their illegal activity; 4) examine and explain some key factors in the success of expansion of their criminal activity; 5) provide some possible solutions for reducing global crime; and 6) critique your solutions. What would it take for your solutions to work?

4. Research the identification and expansion of world terrorism. What nations of the world today support and/or sponsor world terrorism? Why? In your research, identify various diverse "cells" of terrorist. Who are their leaders? What theoretical approaches best explain the existence of terrorists? What are some possible solutions for eradicating world terrorism and crime? Provide bibliographic references in your writing up this project. Follow any additional instructions provided by your professor and submit your paper at the appropriate time.

INTERNET ACTIVITIES

1. *"Defining Deviancy Down": How Senator Moynihan's Misleading Phrase About Criminal Justice Is Rapidly Being Incorporated Into Popular Culture.* www.albany.edu/scj/jcjpc/vol2is5/deviancy.html

2. Videos available from Court TV on recent trials or specific topics in the criminal justice system typically are well researched, objectively presented, and of great interest to students. The Court TV website offers streaming video feeds that you could use if your class is connected to the Internet. Study specific court cases then follow the progress of each case from this web site - even see video clips on your computer. www.courttv.com/video/

3. The Internet has become a highly useful source for obtaining statistical data and current information about crime in the United States. Search these sites and bring back to class important crime facts.

    a. www.icpsr.umich.edu/NACJD/

    b. www.ojp.usdoj.gov/bjs/pubalp2.htm

    c. www.ojp.usdoj.gov/bjs/welcome.html

    d. www.ojp.usdoj.gov/bjs/cvict.htm

    e. www.ojp.usdoj.gov/bjs/drugs.htm

    f. www.ncjrs.org/

INFOTRAC EXERCISES

1. Take a look at the <u>Juvenile Crime Bill of 1999</u> (draft). What kind of picture does it tend to paint about juvenile justice in America?

2. Search through the articles on <u>youth gangs</u>. Make up a your own questionnaire based on factual information you find during your search.

3. Search for information on <u>peer groups</u>. You will need to type in *Age Groups* in the search box. Go to the periodical listings. Compose a list of research findings from these articles.

4. There are numerous subdivisions under <u>deviant behavior</u>. Work in small groups and select a category of interest and present findings to the class. Groups can make a poster with facts that they find within these categories.

5. Using the periodical references on <u>deviant behavior</u>, come to class with three articles in which you can identify one of the theories of deviance from this chapter. (You are not allowed to use articles with the theory in the title!)

6. Look up the word <u>Terrorism</u> and compare the various pieces of legislation that have been enacted to address this expanding problem.

Solutions

MULTIPLE CHOICE QUESTIONS

1. B p. 210

2. D p. 213

3. A p. 214

4. C p. 215

5. A pp. 215-216

6. C p. 217

MULTIPLE CHOICE QUESTIONS

7. D p. 219

8. B p. 220

9. A p. 221

10. D p. 222

11. C p. 223

12. B p. 224

13. C p. 219

14. D p. 227

15. A p. 227

16. A p. 230

17. C p. 231

18. B p. 231-232

19. D p. 233

20. D p. 238-239

TRUE FALSE QUESTIONS

1. T pp. 211-212

2. T p. 211

3. T p. 214

4. F p. 216

5. T p. 218

6. F p. 220

7. F p. 221

8. F p. 222

9. F p. 222

10. F p. 224

11. T p. 225

12. F p. 227

13. T p. 229

14. F p. 232

15. T p. 236

FILL IN THE BLANK QUESTIONS

1. Criminology

2. differential association theory

3. roughnecks, saints

4. radical feminist approach

5. Occupational (white collar)

6. Corporate

7. Cloward, Ohlin

8. Richard Quinney

9. Social bond

10. Social control

Chapter 8

GLOBAL STRATIFICATION

BRIEF CHAPTER OUTLINE

What Is Social Stratification?

Global Systems of Stratification

- Slavery

- The Caste System

- The Class System

Wealth and Poverty in Global Perspective

Problems in Studying Global Inequality

- The "Three Worlds" approach

- The Levels of Development Approach

Classification of Economies by Income

- Low-income economies

- Middle-income economies

- High-income economies

Measuring Global Wealth and Poverty

- Absolute, Relative, and Subjective Poverty

- The Gini Coefficient and Global Quality of Life Issues

Global Poverty and Human Development Issues

- Life expectancy

- Health

- Education and Literacy

- Persistent Gaps in Human Development

Theories of Global Inequality

- Development and Modernization Theory

- Dependency Theory

- World Systems Theory

- The New International Division of Labor Theory

Chapter 8

Global Inequality in the Future

CHAPTER SUMMARY

Social stratification is the hierarchical arrangement of large social groups based on their control over basic resources. A key characteristic of systems of stratification is the extent to which the structure is flexible. **Slavery**, a form of stratification in which people are owned by others, is a closed system. *Bonded labor* or *debt bondage* creates a form of slavery in the global economy. In a **caste system**, people's status is determined at birth based on their parents' position in society. The **class system**, which exists in the United States, is a type of stratification based on ownership of resources and on the type of work people do. The social and economic gaps between the **developed nations** and the developing nations of the world are much more pronounced than they are in the United States. One approach to defining global stratification is through the **"Three Worlds" approach. First world** nations are the rich, industrialized countries having primarily capitalistic economies and democratic political systems. **Second World** nations are those countries having a moderate level of economic development and a moderate standard of living. **Third World** countries are the poorest countries with little or no industrialization, having lowest standards of living, shortest life expectancy, and highest mortality. Closely linked to the "three worlds" concept are the levels of development approach using terms such as developed nations, developing nations, less developed nations, and underdevelopment. The World Bank classifies nations into three economic categories: low-income economies, middle-income economies, and high-income economies. Using the **gross domestic product** is now a means of measuring wealth and power on a global basis. The World Bank uses the **Gini Coefficient** as its measure of income inequality. Using the Human Development Index, the United Nations Development Program has established three new criteria for measuring the level of development in a country: life expectancy, education, and living standards. Because of **social exclusion**, a *fourth world* is developing; one where people are being systematically barred from access to positions that would enable their having an autonomous livelihood. Overall, the gap between the poorest nations and the middle-income nations has continued to widen. Social scientist use three primary theoretical perspectives to explain the persistence of global inequality: (1) development and modernization theory; (2) dependency theory; and (3) world systems theory. According to the *new international division of labor theory*, commodity production is being split into fragments that can be assigned to any global area which can produce the most profitable combination of capital and labor. The future prospects of global inequality range from more to less optimistic predictions. As we enter the future, we can enjoy global prosperity only by ensuing that other people around the world have the opportunity to survive and thrive in their own surroundings.

LEARNING OBJECTIVES

After reading Chapter 8, you should be able to:

1. Define social stratification and describe the major sources of stratification found in societies.

2. Define life chances and explain its effects upon

3. Explain social mobility and distinguish between intergenerational and intragenerational mobility

4. Describe the key characteristics of the three major systems of stratification.

5. Define global stratification and explain how it contributes to economics inequality.

6. Identify and explain the two dimensions of global stratification according to Gunner Myrdal.

7. Define and describe the "three worlds" approach used to classify nations of the world.

8. Explain the levels of development approach used for describing global stratification.

9. Identify and explain the Fourth World approach for describing global inequality.

10. Classify and describe nations of the world by the three economic categories.

11. Explain how poverty is defined on a global basis.

12. Identify and explain the use of the Gini coefficient.

13. Discuss global poverty and its effects upon human development.

14. Explain how and why slavery continues to exist in the global economy.

15. Compare and contrast the three major theories of global inequality.

16. Explain the new international division of labor theory.

17. Describe the future prospects of global inequality.

KEY TERMS

(defined at page number shown and in glossary)

caste system 254
class system 256
core nations 275
dependency theory 274
intergenerational mobility 250
intragenerational mobility 251
life chances 250

modernization theory 270
peripheral nations 275
semiperipheral nations 275
slavery 250
social exclusion 259
social mobility 250
social stratification 250

KEY PEOPLE

(identified at page number shown)

Manual Castells 259
Gary Gereffi 274
Ping-Chun Hsiung 274
Serge Latouche 260
Harriet Martineau 252

Gunner Myrdal 257
George C. Marshall 259
Walt Rostow 270
Harry S. Truman 260
Immanuel Wallerstein 275

CHAPTER OUTLINE

I.   WHAT IS SOCIAL STRATIFICATION?

    A.   **Social stratification** is the hierarchical arrangement of large social groups based on their control over basic resources.

    B.   Max Weber's term **life chances** describes the extent to which persons within a particular layer of stratification have access to important scarce resources.

II.   GLOBAL SYSTEMS OF STRATIFICATION

    A.   Systems of stratification may be open or closed based on the availability of **social mobility** -- the movement of individuals or groups from one level in a stratification system to another.

        1.   **Intergenerational mobility** is the social movement experienced by family members from one generation to the next.

        2.   **Intragenerational mobility** is the social movement of individuals within their own lifetime

    B.   **Slavery**, a closed system, is an extreme form of stratification in which some people are owned by others.

        1.   *Bonded labor* or *debt bondage*, refers to a situation when people give themselves into slavery as security against a loan or when they inherit a debt from a relative.

        2.   Bales argues that there are slaves in almost every country, including the United States.

        3.   Most slaves work in non-technical labor, cloth and carpet making, domestic service and prostitution.

    C.   A **caste system** is a system of social inequality in which people's status is permanently determined at birth based on their parents' ascribed characteristics.

    D.   The **class system** is a type of stratification based on the ownership and control of resources and on the type of work people do.

III. WEALTH AND POVERTY IN GLOBAL PERSPECTIVE

    A.   *Global stratification* refers to the unequal distribution of wealth, power, and prestige on a global basis.

    B.   Global stratification results in people having vastly different life styles and life chance both within and among the nations of the world.

IV.   PROBLEMS IN STUDYING GLOBAL INEQUALITY

    A.   One of the problems is determining what terminology should be used to refer to the distribution of resources in various nations.

    B.   After World War II, the "three worlds" approach was utilized to distinguish among nations based upon their economic development and their standard of living.

        1.   First World nations consist of the rich, industrialized nations that primarily have capitalistic economic systems and democratic political systems.

        2.   Second World nations consist of the countries with at least moderate level of economic development and a moderate standard of living.

3. Third World nations consist of the poorest countries with little or no industrialization and the lowest standards of living, shortest life expectancies, and high mortality rate.

4. Recently, the term *Fourth World* is used to describe the "multiple black holes of **social exclusion**" of people in wide-range areas of the world, including those from sub-Saharan Africa to U.S. inner-city ghettos.

C. The levels of development approach include concepts such as developed nations, developing nations, less developed nations, and underdevelopment.

1. Leaders of the developed nations argue that economic development and growth is the primary way to solve poverty problems of the underdeveloped nations.

2. This viewpoint requires that people in the lesser developed nations accept the beliefs and values of people in the developed nations.

3. If nations could increase the GNP, then social and economic inequality among their citizens could be reduced.

4. However, improving a country's GNP did not tend to reduce the poverty of the poorest people in that country and inequality increased even with greater economic development; some analysts blamed high rates of population growth in the underdeveloped nations.

V. CLASSIFICATION OF ECONOMIES BY INCOME

A. The World Bank classifies nations into three economic categories.

B. Low-income economies are nations that have a GNP per capita of $735 or less in 2002. About half of the world's population lives in the sixty-three low-income economies.

C. Middle-income economies are nations that have a GNP per capita of betwen $736 and $9,075 in 2002. About one-third of the world's population resides in the 92 nations with middle-income economies.

D. High-income economies are nations that have a GNI per capita of more than $9,075 in 2002 and are found in 52 nations.

VI. MEASURING GLOBAL WEALTH AND POVERTY

A. Absolute, relative, and subjective poverty are measurements of poverty defined on a global basis.

B. The **Gini Coefficient** and Global Quality of Life Issues

1. The World Bank uses as its measure of income inequality the Gini coefficient, which ranges from zero (when everyone has the same income) to 100 (when one person receives all the income).

2. Using this measure, the World Bank concluded that inequality increased in specific nations in 2003.

VII. GLOBAL POVERTY AND HUMAN DEVELOPMENT ISSUES

A. Since the 1970s, the United Nations has focused on human development as a crucial factor fighting poverty.

B. Average life expectancy has increased by about a third in the past three decades and is now more than 70 years in 87 countries; however, the

C.   Health is defined by the World Health Organization as a stage of complete physical, mental, and social well-being and not merely the absence of disease or infirmity. Many people in low-income nations suffer from infectious and other diseases. New diseases have recently emerged in countries all over the world, while some middle-income countries are experiencing rapid growth in degenerative diseases such as cancer and coronary heart diseases.

D.   What is literacy and why is it important for human development? UNESCO defines a literate person as "someone who can, with understanding, both read and write a short, simple statement on their everyday life." The adult literacy rate in the low-income countries is about half of that of the high-income countries.

E.   Persistent gaps in human development paint an overall dismal picture for the world's poorest people.

    1.   The gap between the poorest nations and the middle-income nations has continued to widen.

    2.   Although more women have paid employment than in the past, more and more women are still finding themselves in poverty because of increases in single person and single-parent households headed by women and low-wage work employment.

VIII. THEORIES OF GLOBAL INEQUALITY

A.   The most widely known development theory is **modernization theory**.

    1.   This perspective links global inequality to different levels of economic development and suggests that low-income economies can move to middle-and high-income economies by achieving self-sustained economic growth.

    2.   Along with intensive economic growth, the less developed nations can improve their standard of living with accompanying changes in people's beliefs, values, and attitudes toward work.

B.   **Dependency theory** states that global poverty can partially be attributed to the exploitation of the low-income countries by the high-income countries.

    1.   Dependency theory has been more often applied to the newly industrializing countries (NICs) of Latin America.

    2.   Scholars examining the NICs of East Asia found that dependency theory had little or no relevance to economic growth and development in that part of the world.

C.   **World Systems theory** suggests that under capitalism, a global system is held together by economic ties.

    1.   The capitalist world-economy is a global system divided into a hierarchy of three major types of nations-core, semiperipheral, and peripheral.

    2.   **Core nations** are dominant capitalist centers characterized by high levels of industrialization and urbanization.

    3.   **Semiperipheral nations** are more developed than peripheral nations, but less developed than core nations.

    4.   **Peripheral nations** are dependent on core nations for capital, have little or no industrialization (other than brought in by core nations), and have uneven patterns of urbanization.

D. According to the new international division of labor theory, commodity production is being split into fragments that can be assigned to whichever part of the world can provide the most profitable combination of capital and labor.

   1. The global nature of these activities is referred to as global commodity chains, a complex pattern of international labor and production.

   2. Producer-driven commodity chains describe industries in which transnational corporations play a central part in controlling the production process.

   3. Buyer-driven commodity chains refers to industries wherein large retailers, brand-named merchandisers, and trading companies set up decentralized production network in various middle-and low-income counties.

IX. GLOBAL INEQUALITY IN THE FUTURE

A. Social scientists describe an optimistic or a pessimistic scenario for the future depending upon the theoretical framework they apply in studying global inequality.

   1. Some analysts highlight the human rights issues embedded in global inequality; others focus primarily on an economic framework.

   2. In the future, continued population growth, urbanization, and environmental degradation threaten even the meager living conditions of those residing in high-income countries, the quality of life diminishes as natural resources are depleted.

   3. A more optimistic scenario suggests that with modern technology and worldwide economic growth, it might be possible to reduce absolute poverty and to increase people's opportunities, ensuring that people all over the world have the opportunity to survive and thrive in their own surroundings.

PRACTICE TESTS

MULTIPLE CHOICE QUESTIONS

Select the response that best answers the question or complete the statement:

1. Sociologists use the term _____ to refer to the hierarchical arrangements of large social groups based on their control over basic resources.

   a. social stratification
   b. social layering
   c. social distinction
   d. social accumulation

2. The extent to which individuals have access to important societal resources is known as:

   a. relative poverty.
   b. absolute poverty.
   c. social mobility.
   d. life chances.

3. A young woman's father is a carpenter; she graduates from college with a degree in accounting, becomes a CPA, and has a starting salary that represents more money than her father ever made in one year. This illustrates _____ mobility.

    a. intragenerational

    b. intergenerational

    c. horizontal

    d. subjective

4. All of the following are **true** statements about slavery, **except**:

    a. Slavery is a closed system in which "slaves" are treated as property.

    b. Slaves were forcibly imported to the United States as a source of cheap labor.

    c. Slavery has ended throughout the world.

    d. Some people have been enslaved because of unpaid debts, criminal behavior, or war and conquest.

5. A _____ system is a system of social inequality in which people's status is permanently determined at birth based on their parents' ascribed characteristics.

    a. class

    b. slavery

    c. capitalist

    d. caste

6. A young woman who comes from an impoverished background works at two full-time jobs in order to save enough money to attend college. Ultimately, she earns a degree, attends law school, graduates with highest honors, and is hired by a firm at a starting salary of $75,000. This person has experienced _____ mobility.

    a. horizontal

    b. vertical

    c. direct

    d. indirect

7. The unequal distribution of wealth, power, and prestige on a global basis is referred to as

    a. global stratification.

    b. global layering.

    c. global distinction.

    d. global accumulation.

8. First world nations are best represented by the countries of:

    a. Japan, the United States, China.

    b. New Zealand, the United States, Great Britain.

    c. Canada, China, Korea.

    d. Russia, Australia, Japan.

9. The term _____ refers to all the goods and services produced in a country in a given year.

    a. WHO

    b. GDP

    c. NIC

    d. GNI

10. Low-income economies are primarily found in _____ nations.

    a. Asian and South American

    b. Eastern European and African

    c. African and South American

    d. Asian and African

11. The situation wherein women around the world tend to be more impoverished than men is referred to as:

    a. global feminization stratification.

    b. global feminization.

    c. global feminization of poverty.

    d. global feminization of labor.

12. Lower-middle income economies include the nations of:

    a. Russia, Romania, Bolivia.

    b. South Korea, the Ukraine, Mexico.

    c. Mexico, Guatemala, Russia.

    d. Mozambique, Bosnia, Turkey.

13. High-income economies are found in _____ nations.

    a. 51

    b. 15

    c. 38

    d. 25

14. The movement of jobs and economic resources from one nation to another is defined as:

    a. deindustrialization.

    b. capital flight.

    c. transnational flight.

15. The closing of plants and factories because of their obsolescence or employment of cheaper workers in other nations is known as:

    a. capital flight.

    b. capital destabilization.

    c. deindustrialization.

    d. reindustrialization.

16. The World Bank uses the term _____ to indicate all of the goods and services produced within a country's economy during a given year:
    a. GDP
    b. GNP
    c. GPA
    d. GPO

17. _____ poverty is a condition in which people do not have the means to secure the most basic necessities of life.
    a. subjective poverty
    b. relative poverty
    c. absolute poverty
    d. standard poverty

18. The World Bank uses the term _____ as its measure of income inequality.
    a. GNP
    b. Gini coefficient
    c. relative poverty
    d. Mrydal coefficient

19. According to the _____ theory, the capitalist world-economy is a global system divided into a hierarchy of three major types of nations.
    a. world systems
    b. dependency
    c. development and modernization
    d. new international division of labor

20. According to the _____ theory, commodity production is split into fragments that can be assigned to the part of the world that can provide the most profitable combination of capital and labor.
    a. world systems
    b. new international division of labor
    c. dependency
    d. development and modernization

TRUE OR FALSE QUESTIONS

1. According to Max Weber, lifestyle describes the extent to which persons within a particular layer of stratification have access to important scarce resources.
   True or False

2. Gunner Mrydal believed that the poorest people living in extremely poor nations experience much greater economic hardship than do the poor who live in more affluent countries of the world.
   True or False

T   3.   The Fourth World is a term originally designated for indigenous people who are descended from a country's aboriginal population.
          True or False

T   4.   Castells uses the term "Fourth World" to refer to the new developing countries in the continent of Africa.
          True or False

F   5.   In utilizing the "three worlds" approach for studying global inequality, China is an example of a Third World Nation.
          True or False

T   6.   Ideas regarding underdevelopment were popularized by U.S. President Harry S. Truman.
          True or False

T   7.   According to the development approach in studying global inequality, an increase in the standard of living of a century meant that a nation was moving toward economic development.
          True or False

F   8.   High rates of population growth taking place in the underdeveloped nations have led to an increase in greater economic development of those countries.
          True or False

T   9.   About half of the world's population lives in the 64 low-income economies, according to the World Bank classification.
          True or False

F   10. According to the classification of economies by income, many countries referred to as "middle income" have very few of their population living in poverty.
          True or False

F   11. Subjective poverty is defined as a condition in which people do not have the means to secure the most basic necessities.
          True or False

T   12. Since the 1970s, the United Nations has more actively focused on human development as a crucial factor for fighting poverty.
          True or False

F   13. The numbers of people dying worldwide from hunger-related diseases is the equivalent of 200 jumbo jet crashes per day with no survivors.
          True or False

T   14. About 17 million people die each year from diarrhea, malaria, tuberculosis, and other infectious and parasitic illnesses.
          True or False

T   15. According to UNESCO, women in low-income countries comprise about two-thirds of those who are illiterate.
          True or False

FILL IN THE BLANK QUESTIONS

1. Slavery in the United States was a topic of concern for _____ , on eof the first women social scientists.

2. According to Manuel Castells, _____ is the process by which certain individuals and groups are systematically barred from access to positions that would enable them to have an autonomous livelihood.

3. According to Swedish economist, _____ , social inequality and economic inequality are the main causes of the poverty of a nation.

4. The concepts of underdevelopment and underdevelopment nations emerged out of the _____ plan following World War II.

5. The _____ is defined as all the goods and services produced within a country's economy during a given year.

6. The movement of one individual or group from one level in a stratification system to another is defined as _____ .

7. Sociologist _____ is closely associated with World Systems Theory.

8. According to World Systems Theory, _____ nations are dominant capitalist centers characterized by high levels of industrialization and urbanization.

9. According to World Systems Theory, _____ nations are more developed than peripheral nations, but less developed than core nations.

10. _____ stratification refers to the unequal distribution of wealth, power, and prestige on a global basis.

SHORT ANSWER/ESSAY QUESTIONS

1. What do you think are the future prospects for greater equality across and within nations" Cite at least one theoretical framework from this chapter that provides an optimistic scenario and one that provides a pessimistic scenario for the future. Which do you agree with more? Why?

2. What is the global stratification and what effects does it have upon economic inequality?

3. Where and why does slavery exist in today's global economy? What are some of the various forms of slavery in the world today? What happens to people who are enslaved?

4. What is literacy and why is it important for human development? Why is it especially important for women?

5. Why is the majority of the world's population growing richer while the poorest one-fifth of the world's population remain poor? How are global poverty and human development related? What steps could be taken to reduce global poverty?

STUDENT CLASS PROJECTS AND ACTIVITIES

1. Select one present independent country (or republic) that used to be a republic that comprised the Union of Soviet Republics (before September, 1991): (1) Armenia; (2) Azerbaijan; (3) Belorussia; (4) ; (5) Georgia; (6) Kasakhstan; (7) Kirghizia; (8) Latvia; (9) Lithuania; (10) Moldavia; (11) Russian S.F.S.R.; (12) Tadshikistan; (13) Turkmenistan; (14) Ukraine; and (15) Uzbekistan. Or select one independent country that used to be part of a whole (such as Bosnia or Croatia or the former country of Yugoslavia). You are to prepare a research report of a minimum of five typewritten pages about their respective republic, or country. Your reports must include: (1) the population: (2) ethnic breakdown of various population groups; (3) date that the country first became a part of the whole and the date that the country became independent from the whole; (4) brief historical background of the country; (5) size (in square miles); (6) major goods, service, and raw products produced; (7) various religious practices; (8) language that is spoken; (9) typical lifestyle of the people; (10) the social and economic status of the people either within their own group or in comparison to an outside group, (11) political sentiments of the people, i.e., is there a strong sense of nationalism; (12) any other information that enhances the understanding of this country or republic. Submit your paper at the appropriate time, following the instructions of your instructor.

2. Drawing upon World Systems Theory most closely associated with the work of Immanuel Wallerstein, select three countries that are members of ASEAN (Association of South East Asian Nations) who best represent the three major types of nations in the hierarchical position of nations in the global economy. Prepare a research report on the economic conditions of each of the three you selected, including information such as (1) the status of the major infrastructures of each country, such as their transportation systems, their power plants, their telecommunications systems; (2) the status of their financial capital and (3) the status of their human capital. i.e., the human skills needed to handle. Provide substantial explanations of why and how you selected the countries representing each specific category. Include an analysis of the resources and obstacles characterizing each specific country. Are there any global cities (or command posts) in any of the countries that you selected? Provide any other information that supports you selections.

3. In the later part of the twentieth century, countries in various parts of the globe began to form economic, political and/or social alliances. Research past and present such alliances, noting the purpose of the alliance, the status of that alliance today, countries that are part of the alliance, and possible or probable future alliances. Some possibilities of the past, present, and future are (1) Atlantic Rim; (2) Asian Pacific (Pacific Rim); (3) the Group of Seven; (4) the Group of 77; (5) NAFTA; (6) Hemispheric Free Trade Area (HFTA); (7) Asia Pacific Economic Cooperation (APEC); (8) the EU (European Union); (9) North Atlantic Free Trade Area; (10) Mediterranean Rim; (11) NATO; and (12) OPEC.

4. Research the lives of the world's ten richest people, according to the latest Forbes magazine poll. (1) Provide a minimum one-paragraph biographical sketch on each of the "top ten." (2) Explain how each of them obtained their wealth. (3) What countries do they represent? (4) Who did they replace from the previous year's poll? (5) What are some similarities and differences among the top ten. Submit your paper at the appropriate time, following the instruction of your professor.

INTERNET ACTIVITIES

1. Visit the United Nations Economic and Social Development Web Site. This site has links to information about crime, trade, drugs, population, etc. from a global perspective. www.un.org/esa/

2. Another organization to visit is the World Bank Group. To read about poverty, click on *Poverty Reduction Strategy Papers*. What are some of the proposed ways to reduce or end poverty? www.worldbank.org

3. UNESCO stands for the United Nations Educational, Scientific, and Cultural Organization. What is the mission of UNESCO? To read a quick summary of important facts, click on *Did You Know*? This list of quick facts addresses literacy, primary education and childhood development, who finances education. How will reducing global illiteracy help the United States, and other countries? www.unesco.org

4. A site devoted to international issues of women's health is the *International Women's Health Coalition*. Read about their population policies and efforts to increase AIDS awareness for women around the world. www.iwhc.org/

5. From these sites you can take a surfing trip to gain facts about stratification, poverty and conflict. To generate a deeper level of interest bring facts and resources to class. A typed up "fact sheet" can be turned in for credit. www.globalissues.org/TradeRelated/Poverty.asp

6. Visit this site to read an essay entitled "Global Poverty in the Late 20th Century" by Michel Chossudovsky, Professor of Economics at the University of Ottawa. Write three critical thinking questions based on their reading of the essay. www.heise.de/tp/english/special/eco/6099/1.html

INFOTRAC EXERCISES

1. Look up **Human Rights Violations** and search for articles that address the human rights violations in Serbia, Russia, China, Saudi Arabia, and Sierra Leone to name a few.

2. Type in under subject **gini coefficient** and see how this measure of income inequality is used in actual research articles.

3. There are a number of articles under the subject **Women and Poverty**. Find articles related to global poverty. What cultural values are related in some of these articles?

4. There are a number of subdivisions under the subject search for **Developing Countries**. Under the subdivision Environmental Aspects students can learn about the interrelationship between the social structure and the physical environment.

Solutions

MULTIPLE CHOICE QUESTIONS

1. A p. 250

2. D p. 250

3. B p. 250

4. C p. 251-252

5. D p. 254

6. B p. 256

7. A p. 256

8. B p. 258-259

9. D p. 260

10. D p. 261

11. C p. 262

12. A p. 263

13. D p. 264

14. A p. 264

15. C p. 264

16. A p. 264

17. C p. 265

18. B p. 266

19. A p. 275

20. B p. 276

TRUE OR FALSE QUESTIONS

1. F p. 250

2. T p. 257

3. T p. 259

4. T p. 259

5. F p. 259

6. T p. 260

7. T p. 260

8. F p. 260

9. T p. 261

10. F p. 262

11. F p. 265

12. T p. 267

13. F p. 268

14. T p. 268

15. T p. 269

FILL IN THE BLANK QUESTIONS

1. Harriet Martineau

2. social exclusion

3. Gunnar Myrdal

4. marshall

5. gross domestic product

6. social mobility

7. Immanuel Wallerstein

8. core

9. semiperiphial

10. Global

Chapter 9

SOCIAL CLASS IN THE UNITED STATES

BRIEF CHAPTER OUTLINE

Income and Wealth Differences in the United States
- Comparing Income and Wealth
- Distribution of Income and Wealth

Classical Perspectives on Social Class
- Karl Marx: Relationship to the Means of Production
- Max Weber: Wealth, Prestige, and Power

Contemporary Sociological Models of the U.S. Class Structure
- The Weberian Model of the U.S. Class Structure
- The Marxian Model of the U.S. Class Structure
- The New Class Society?

Consequences of Inequality
- Physical and Mental Health and Nutrition
- Housing
- Education
- Crime and Lack of Safety

Poverty in the United States
- Who Are the Poor?
- Economic and Structural Sources of Poverty
- Solving the Poverty Problem

Sociological Explanations of Social Inequality in the United States
- Functionalist Perspectives
- Conflict Perspectives
- Symbolic Interactionist Perspectives

U.S. Stratification in the Future

CHAPTER SUMMARY

Throughout human history, people have argued about the distribution of scarce resources in society. **Income** —the economic gain derived from wages, salaries, income transfers, or ownership of property—and **wealth**—the value of all of a person's or family's economic aspects—is unevenly distributed in the United States. In the past two decades, both income equality and wealth inequality has widened. Karl Marx and Max Weber acknowledged social class as a key determinant of social inequality and social change. According to Marx, capitalistic societies are comprised of two classes -- the capitalists, who own the means of production, and the workers, who sell their labor to the owners. By contrast, Weber developed a multidimensional concept that focuses on the interplay of **wealth, prestige**, and **power**. Sociologists have developed several models of the class structure: one is the broadly based Weberian approach; the second on a Marxian approach, and the third is based on a study of society today: the new class society. Among the most prosperous nations in today's world, the United States has the highest degree of inequality of income distribution. The stratification of society into different social groups results in wide discrepancies in income, wealth, and access to available goods and services (including health, good nutrition, and education). Sociologists distinguish between **absolute poverty**, which exists when people do not have the means to secure the basic necessities of life, and **relative poverty**, which exists when people may be able to afford basic necessities but are still unable to maintain an average standard of living. There are both economic and structural sources of poverty. Low wages are a key problem, as are unemployment and underemployment. Recent suggestions for solving the poverty problem range from (1) changing past welfare programs that established state-level workfare programs and mandatory time limits on welfare benefits; and (2) providing better training and education in order that the poor might be able to "work their way out of poverty." Functionalist's perspectives on the U.S. class structure view classes as broad groupings of people who share similar levels of privilege based on their roles in the occupational structure. According the Davis-Moore thesis, positions that are most important within a society, requiring the most talent and training, must be highly rewarded. Conflict perspectives are based on the assumption that social stratification is created and maintained by one group in order to enhance and protect its own economic interests. Symbolic interactionists focus on the micro-level analysis; such as examining the social and psychological factors that influence the contributions of the wealthy to charitable and arts organizations. As a gap between rich and poor, employed and unemployed widens, social inequality will increase in the future if nothing is done. Given that the well-being of all people is linked, some analysts are urging a joint effort to regain the American Dream by attacking poverty so that everyone has a job, a living wage, and an equal life chance.

LEARNING OBJECTIVES

After reading Chapter 9, you should be able to:

1. Identify and compare the terms income and wealth

2. Describe some of the benefits of wealth.

3. Compare and contrast the distribution of income and wealth in the United States.

4. Describe Karl Marx's perspective on class position and class relationships.

5. Outline Max Weber's multidimensional approach to social stratification and explain how people are ranked on all three dimensions.

6. Outline the functionalist model of the U.S. class structure and briefly describe the key characteristics of each class.

7. Outline the conflict model of the U.S. class structure and briefly describe the key characteristics of each class.

8. Outline the major characteristics of the new class society.

9. Discuss the distribution of income and wealth in the United States and describe how this distribution affects life chances.

10. Distinguish between absolute and relative poverty and describe the characteristics and lifestyle of those who live in poverty in the United States.

11. Describe the feminization of poverty and explain why two out of three impoverished adults in the United States are women.

12. Discuss some economic and structural sources of poverty.

13. Provide some of the attempts of the United States to solve the poverty problem.

14. Distinguish between functionalist and conflict explanations of social inequality.

15. Explain the symbolic interactionist perspectives of social inequality in the United States.

KEY TERMS

(defined at page number shown and in glossary)

absolute poverty 308
alienation 291
capitalist class (or bourgeoisie) 291
class conflict 292
classism 304
feminization of poverty 309
job deskilling 311
income 286

meritocracy 312
pink collar occupations 298
power 294
prestige 394
relative poverty 308
socioeconomic status (SES) 295
wealth 286
working class (or proletariat) 291

KEY PEOPLE

(identified at page number shown)

Peter Blau and Otis Duncan 295
John Butler 303
Patricia Hill Collins 295
Kingsley Davis and Wilbert Moore 311
Barbara Ehrenrich 298
Karl Marx 291

Diana Pearce 309
Robert Perrucci and Earl Wyson 303
Dennis Gilbert and Joseph A. Kahl 296
Max Weber 293
Eric Olin Wright 300

CHAPTER OUTLINE

I.   INCOME and WEALTH DIFFERNECES IN THE UNITED STATES

    A.   Comparing Income and Wealth

        1.   **Income** is the economic gain derived from wages, salaries, income transfers (governmental aid), or ownership of property.

        2.   **Wealth** includes not only income but also property such as buildings, land, farms, houses, factories, cars, and other assets.

    B.   Distribution of Income and Wealth

        1.   In the past two decades, income inequality has widened; the poor have been more likely to stay poor, and the affluent have been more likely to stay affluent.

        2.   Wealth inequality has increased; the disparities are even more pronounced when compared across racial and ethic categories.

II.   CLASSICAL PERSPECTIVES ON SOCIAL CLASS

    A.   Karl Marx: Relationships to the Means of Production

        1.   According to Marx, class position in capitalistic societies is determined by people's work situation, or relationship to the means of production.

            a.   The **bourgeoisie** or **capitalist class** consists of those who privately own the means of production; the **proletariat**, or **working class**, must sell their labor power to the owners in order to earn enough money to survive.

            b.   Class relationships involve inequality and exploitation; workers are exploited as capitalists expropriate a surplus value from their labor; continual exploitation results in workers' **alienation**, a feeling of powerlessness and estrangement from other people and from oneself.

        2.   The **capitalist class** maintains its position by control of the society's superstructure -- comprised of the government, schools, and other social institutions, which produce and disseminate ideas perpetuating the existing system; this exploitation of workers ultimately results in **class conflict**—the struggle between the capitalist class and working class.

    B.   Max Weber: Wealth, Prestige, and Power

        1.   Weber's multidimensional approach to stratification examines the interplay among wealth, prestige, and power as being necessary in determining a person's class position.

            a.   Weber placed people who have a similar level of *wealth* -- the value of all of a person or family's economic assets, including income, personal property, and *income* producing property -- and income in the same class.

            b.   **Prestige** is the respect or regard with which a person or status position is regarded by others, and those who share similar levels of social prestige belong to the same status group regardless of their level of wealth.

            c.   **Power** -- the ability of people or groups to carry out their own goals despite opposition from others -- gives some people the ability to shape society in accordance with their own interests and to direct the actions of others.

2. Wealth, prestige, and power are separate continuums on which people can be ranked from high to low; individuals may be high on one dimension while being low on another.

3. **Socioeconomic status (SES)** -- a combined measure that attempts to classify individuals, families, or households in terms of indicators such as income, occupation, and education -- is used to determine class location.

III. CONTEMPORARY SOCIOLOGICAL MODELS OF THE U.S. CLASS STRUCTURE

    A. The Weberian Model of the Class Structure

        1. The Upper (or Capitalist) Class is the wealthiest and most powerful class, comprised of people who own substantial income producing assets.

        2. The Upper-Middle Class is based on a combination of three factors: university degrees, authority and independence on the job, and high income. Examples of occupations for this class are highly educated professionals such as physicians, stockbrokers, or corporate managers.

        3. The Middle Class is characterized by a minimum of a high school diploma or a community college degree.

        4. The Working Class is comprised of semiskilled machine operatives, clerks and salespeople in routine, mechanized jobs, and workers in **pink collar occupations** -- relatively low paying, nonmanual semiskilled positions primarily held by women.

        5. The Working Poor live from just above to just below the poverty line; they hold unskilled jobs, seasonal migrant employment in agriculture, lower paid factory jobs, and service jobs (e.g., such as counter help at restaurants).

        6. The Underclass includes people who are poor, seldom employed, and caught in long term deprivation that results from low levels of education and income and high rates of unemployment.

    B. The Marxian Model of the U.S. Class Structure

        1. These criteria can be used to determine the class placement for all workers in a capitalist society.

            a. Erik Olin Wright outlined four criteria for placement in the class structure: (a) ownership of the means of production; (b) purchase of the labor of others (employing others); (c) control of the labor of others (supervising others on the job); and (d) sale of one's own labor (being employed by someone else).

        2. The Capitalist Class is composed of those who have inherited fortunes, own major corporations, or are top corporate executives who own extensive amounts of stock or control company investments.

        3. The Managerial Class includes upper level managers -- supervisors and professionals who typically do not participate in company wide decisions -- and lower level managers who may be given some control over employment practices, such as the hiring and firing of some workers.

        4. The Small-Business Class consists of small business owners, craftspeople, and some doctors and lawyers who may hire a small number of employees but largely do their own work.

5.   The Working Class is made up of blue collar workers, including skilled workers (e.g., electricians, plumbers, and carpenters), unskilled blue collar workers (e.g., laundry and restaurant workers), and white collar workers who do not own the means of production, do not control the work of others, and are relatively powerless in the workplace.

C.   The New Class Society?

1.   According to sociologists Perrucci and Wysong, the beginning of 21st century is characterized by a new class society in which transnational corporations, high technology, and disposable workers encounter new and increasingly polarizes class lines.

2.   The two largest classes—the *privileged class* and the *new working class* posses fundamentally different and opposed interests; consequently, when one class improves, the other loses.

IV.   CONSEQUENCES OF INEQUALITY

A.   Physical and Mental Health and Nutrition

1.   As people's economic status increases so does their health status; the poor have shorter life expectancies and are at greater risk for chronic illnesses and infectious diseases. About 41 million people in the United States are without health insurance coverage.

B.   Housing

1.   Homelessness is a major problem in the U.S.

2.   Lack of affordable housing and substandard housing are also central problems brought about by economic inequality.

C.   Education

1.   Education and life chance are directly linked; while functionalists view education as an "elevator" for social mobility, conflict theorists stress that schools are agencies for reproducing the capitalist class system and perpetuating inequality in society.

2.   Poverty affects the ability of many young people to finish high school, much less enter college.

D.   Crime and Lack of Safety

1.   Both crime and lack of safety on the streets and at home are consequences of inequality

2.   Poverty and violence are linked; street violence is often not random at all—but a response to profound social inequalities in the inner city.

V.   POVERTY IN THE UNITED STATES

A.   Although some people living in poverty are unemployed, many hardworking people with full time jobs also live in poverty.

B.   The official poverty line is based on what is considered to be the minimum amount of money required for living at a subsistence level.

C.   Sociologists distinguish between **absolute poverty** -- when people do not have the means to secure the most basic necessities of life -- and **relative poverty** -- when people may be able to afford basic necessities but still are unable to maintain an average standard of living.

D. Who Are the Poor?

1. Age: Children are more likely to be poor than older persons; older women are twice as likely to be poor as older men; older African Americans and Latinos/as are much more likely to live below the poverty line than are non Latino/a whites.

2. Gender: About two thirds of all adults living in poverty are women; this problem is described as the **feminization of poverty** -- the trend in which women are disproportionately represented among individuals living in poverty.

3. Race and Ethnicity: white Americans (non Latinos/as) account for approximately two thirds of those below the official poverty line; however, a disproportionate percentage of the poverty population is made up of African Americans, Latinos/as, and Native Americans.

E. Economic and Structural Sources of Poverty

1. An economic source of poverty is the low wages paid for many jobs: half of all families living in poverty are headed by someone who is employed, and one third of those family heads work full time.

2. Poverty also is exacerbated by structural problems such as (a) deindustrialization -- millions of U.S. workers have lost jobs as corporations have disinvested here and opened facilities in other countries where "cheap labor" exists -- and (b) **job deskilling** -- a reduction in the proficiency needed to perform a specific job that leads to a corresponding reduction in the wages paid for that job.

F. Solving the Poverty Problem

1. The United States has attempted to solve the poverty problem with social welfare programs; however, the primary beneficiaries have not always been the poor.

2. A lack of consensus exists regarding both the definition of the problem and the possible solutions for it.

VI. SOCIOLOGICAL EXPLANATIONS OF SOCIAL INEQUALITY IN THE UNITED STATES

A. Functionalist Perspectives

1. According to the Davis-Moore thesis:

   a. All societies have important tasks that must be accomplished and certain positions that must be filled.

   b. Some positions are more important for the survival of society than others.

   c. The most important positions must be filled by the most qualified people.

   d. The positions that are the most important for society and require scarce talent, extensive training, or both, must be the most highly rewarded.

   e. The most highly rewarded positions should be those that are functionally unique (no other position can perform the same function), and those positions upon which others rely for expertise, direction, or financing.

2. This thesis assumes that social stratification results in **meritocracy** -- a hierarchy in which all positions are rewarded based on people's ability and credentials.

B. Conflict Perspectives

1. From a conflict perspective, inequality does not serve as a source of motivation for people; powerful individuals and groups use ideology to maintain their favored positions at the expense of others.

2. Core values, laws, and informal social norms support inequality in the United States (e.g., legalized segregation and discrimination produce higher levels of economic inequality).credentials.

C. Symbolic Interactionist Perspectives

1. Symbolic interactionists focus on microlevel concerns such as the effects of wealth and poverty on people's lives.

2. Some studies focus on the social and psychological factors that influence the rich to contribute to charitable and arts organizations.

3. Other researchers have examined the social and psychological aspects of life in the middle class; few have examined rare insights into the social interactions between people from vastly different social classes.

VII. U.S. SOCIAL STRATIFICATION IN THE FUTURE

A. According to some social scientists, wealth will become more concentrated at the top of the U.S. class structure; as the rich have grown richer, more people have found themselves among the ranks of the poor.

B. The gap between the earnings of workers and the income of managers and top executives in the U.S.A. has widened.

C. Structural sources of upward mobility are shrinking while the rate of downward mobility has increased; the persistence of economic inequality is related to profound global economic changes.

D. Some call for a united effort to regain the American Dream by attacking poverty.

PRACTICE TESTS

MULTIPLE CHOICE QUESTIONS

Select the response that best answers the question or completes the statement:

1. All of the following are components of wealth, **except**:

   a. income

   b. a position on the local school board

   c. bank accounts

   d. insurance policies

2. In examining the unequal distribution of income and wealth in the United States, the text notes that:

   a. the wealthiest 20 percent of households receive almost 50 percent of the total income "pie."

   b. the poorest 20 percent of households receive about 30 percent of the total income "pie."

   c. income inequalities between the rich and the poor narrowed greatly in 1999.

   d. Differences in median income of married couples and female-headed households narrowed during the 1990's.

3. According to the texts regarding poverty and wealth in the United States:

    a. men account for two out of three impoverished adults.

    b. people no longer believe in the American Dream.

    c. many of the poor are "working poor".

    d. income is more unevenly distributed than wealth.

4. According to Karl Marx's theory of class relations:

    a. the bourgeoisie consists of those who own the means of production.

    b. The proletariat consists of those who own the means of production.

    c. class relationships involve inequality and exploitation.

    d. wealth, prestige, and power are all important in determining a person's class position

5. According to Karl Marx _____ is a feeling of powerlessness and estrangement from other people and from oneself.

    a. alienation

    b. meritocracy

    c. class conflict

    d. classism

6. When workers overthrow the capitalists, according to Marx, they would eventually create a/an _____ society.

    a. class

    b. caste

    c. egalitarian

    d. stratified

7. According to _____, class position is determined by people's relationship to the means of production.

    a. Karl Marx

    b. Max Weber

    c. Emile Durkheim

    d. Dennis Gilbert and Joseph A. Kahl

8. All of the following statements regarding Marx's analysis of class are correct, **except**:

    a. Class relationships involve inequality and exploitation.

    b. The exploitation of workers by the capitalist class ultimately will lead to the destruction of capitalism.

    c. The capitalist class maintains its position by control of the society's superstructure.

    d. Wealth, prestige, and power are separate continuums on which people can be ranked from high to low.

136

9. According to Max Weber, _____ is the respect or regard with which a person or status position is regarded by others.

    a. admiration

    b. power

    c. prestige

    d. rank

10. Entrepreneurs, as identified by Weber are those who:

    a. do not have to work.

    b. work for wages.

    c. are a privileged commercial class.

    d. live off their investments.

11. Prestige ratings for selected occupations in the United States have shown that the occupation of _____ consistently receives the highest ranking.

    a. attorney

    b. physician

    c. accountant

    d. dentist

12. According to the Weberian model of the U.S. class structure, members of the _____ class have earned most of their money in their own lifetime as entrepreneurs, presidents of corporations, top level professionals, and so forth.

    a. upper upper

    b. lower upper

    c. upper middle

    d. middle

13. The text points out that a combination of three factors qualifies people for the upper middle class. Which of the following is not one of these factors?

    a. university degrees.

    b. authority and independence on the job.

    c. inherited wealth.

    d. high income.

14. Over the past fifty years, Asian Americans, Latinos/as, and African Americans have placed great emphasis on _____ as a means of attaining the American Dream.

    a. education

    b. affirmative action

    c. unemployment compensation

    d. vocational training

15. Women employed in pink collar occupations are mainly classified in the:
    a. working class.
    b. working poor.
    c. middle class.
    d. upper middle class.

16. In the Weberian Model of the U.S. Class Structure, medical technicians, nurses, lower-level managers, and semi-professionals make up the _____ class.
    a. upper
    b. middle
    c. working
    d. lower

17. All of the following are included in Erik O. Wright's typology of the class structure, **except** the _____ class.
    a. capitalist
    b. managerial
    c. middle
    d. working

18. According to Perucci's and Wysong's typology of the class structure, wealthy owners and high income employers make up the
    a. comfort class.
    b. credentialed class.
    c. excluded class.
    d. superclass.

19. The trend in which women disproportionately are represented among individuals living in poverty is referred to as:
    a. absolute poverty.
    b. relative poverty.
    c. situational poverty.
    d. the feminization of poverty.

20. According to the functionalist explanation of social inequality:
    a. all societies have important tasks that must be accomplished and certain positions that must be filled.
    b. the most important positions must be filled by the most qualified people.
    c. the most highly rewarded positions should be those that are functionally unique and on which other positions rely.
    d. all of the above.

TRUE FALSE QUESTION

1. People no longer believe in the "American Dream."
   True or False

2. TANF does not require recipients with young children to work.
   True or False

3. Both Marx and Weber viewed class as an important determinant of social inequality.
   True or False

4. Most people in the U.S. identify themselves as the middle class.
   True or False

5. Of all the class categories, according to the Weberian Model, the one most shaped by formal education is the upper class.
   True or False

6. An estimated thirty percent of the U.S. population is the working class.
   True or False

7. The working poor account for about 10 percent of the U.S. population.
   True or False

8. About 3 to 5 percent of the U.S. population is the underclass.
   True or False

9. More people today are self-employed or own a small business than at any time in U.S. past.
   True or False

10. People of color have owned small businesses in the United States throughout U.S. history.
    True or False

11. The working class consists of about 50 percent of all employees of the U.S.
    True or False

12. About 41 million people in the United States are without health insurance coverage.
    True or False

13. Relative poverty exists when people do not have the means to secure the most basic necessities of life.
    True or False

14. About two third of all adults living in poverty are men.
    True or False

15. The Davis Moore thesis assumes that social stratification results in meritocracy.
    True or False

FILL IN THE BLANK QUESTIONS

1. _____ is the value of all of a person's or family's economic assets.

2. _____ is the ability of people or groups to achieve their goals despite opposition from others.

3. _____ is a combined measure that attempts to classify individuals, families, or households in terms of indicators such as income, occupation, and education to determine class.

4. Karl Marx identified _____ as the struggle between the capitalist class and the working class.

5. Occupations that are relatively low-paying, non-manual, semi-skilled positions primarily held by women are called _____ occupations.

6. _____ refers to the belief that persons in the upper or privileged class are superior to those in the lower or working class.

7. The poverty that exists when people do not have the means to secure the most basic necessities of life is known as _____ poverty.

8. _____ poverty exists when people may be able to afford basic necessities but are still unable to maintain an average standard of living.

9. The trend in which women are disproportionately represented among individuals living in poverty is known as _____ .

10. A hierarchy in which all positions are rewarded based upon people's ability and credentials is termed _____ .

SHORT ANSWER/ESSAY QUESTIONS

1. What is the "American Dream?" What assumption is it based upon? What are some of the facts about the "American Dream?"

2. What are some of the characteristics of the "new class society"? What are the two largest classes in the new class and why do they possess fundamentally different and opposed interests?

3. What are some of the consequences of inequality in the United States?

4. Who are the poor in the United States? Why does poverty persist in the United States? What are some economic and structural sources of poverty?

5. What do you think are your own social mobility chances? Will you be better or worse off than your parents? Your grandparents?

STUDENT CLASS PROJECTS AND ACTIVITIES

1. Using theories, concepts, facts, and discussions found in this chapter, as well as from other sources, write a proposal for a long-term plan that would reduce income inequality in our nation. Write your proposal as if you were going to present it to Congress. Document your facts and figures and present compelling evidence and information supporting your proposal. You must give sufficient goals and objectives of your proposal and provide proof that your plan is a feasible one. Type up your proposal and submit your paper at the appropriate time and in the style provided by your instructor.

2. Examine social stratification in either your own hometown, or the town/city in which your now reside. Conduct a driving route that will take you into a variety of neighborhoods that represent the six social classes as discussed on pages 280-283 of the text. You can probably secure census track data that will be particularly helpful for this project. Drive through the various neighborhoods recording the characteristics of the neighborhoods, the type of housing, probable lifestyles, the streets and the condition of the streets, the landscaping, any vehicles, and other signs that would indicate social class. Look for symbols of wealth or poverty, such as fences, recreational facilities, statues, flagpoles, water fountains, trees, and noise level, or the absence of such. Record anything unique or special about each neighborhood. Look for children in the neighborhoods and describe the children and their activities. Look for signs of conspicuous consumption and/or conspicuous waste. Submit a five-page paper describing each neighborhood using the above information as specific guidelines for the descriptions. In the writing of your project, focus on what you learned and how you felt about conducting this project. Follow any other specific guidelines provided by your instructor (if there are any) and submit your paper in the appropriate format at the appropriate time.

INTERNET ACTIVITIES

1. To read about welfare reform, go to the Urban Institute, a non-partisan economic and social policy research organization. Once there, look for the ***Focus on***... box, and click on Welfare Reform to find current research on this topic. www.urban.org

2. The Bureau of Labor Statistics provides a wide range of economic data-you can look at the *Economy at a Glance* section, which provides a regional and state-by-state breakdown of economic data, or you can look at *Industry at a Glance* (which provides the same kind of information on specific industries). Click on your state or the region in which you live to get current data. www.bls.gov/eag/

3. *Harvard University's Inequality and Social Policy Web Site Think Tank Links*. Send students to this web site to explore some of the ideas that people are talking and "thinking" about in regards to inequality and social policy. www.ksg.harvard.edu/inequality/Focus/links.htm

4. Use these websites to collect facts about poverty in the United States. Guide your students to use critical thinking skills to construct reasoned judgments about "who are the poor?"

    a. The U.S. Census Bureau *Income Statistics* www.census.gov/ftp/pub/hhes/www/income.html

    b. The U.S. Census Bureau *Poverty Statistics* www.census.gov/ftp/pub/hhes/www/poverty.html

    c. The 2001 Health and Human Services *2001 Poverty Guidelines* http://aspe.hhs.gov/poverty/01poverty.htm

INFOTRAC EXERCISES

1. Look up **Social Class**. Search for articles that address the plight of poor children. Bring a summary and articles to class. Collectively construct a picture of the problems facing children in poverty.

2. Do a keyword search for the **American Dream**. What are the different ways that this term is used? What articles use the term to address social class issues? How often is this term used in a positive way? How has it become a negative symbol in our culture? Why do you think we use the word *dream* when we talk about our social condition?

3. Look up **Karl Marx**. There are a number of references to his work The Communist Manifesto. You may want to actually read portions of this historic document.

4. There are a number of concepts in this chapter that could be researched in more depth using InfoTrac: **Caste System**, **Class System**, **Slavery** and **Poverty**.

5. Discover the relationship between **social networks** and **occupational prestige**. Find the article, *Social Networks and Prestige Attainment: New Empirical Findings* (The American Journal of Economics and Sociology, Oct 1999).

Solutions

MULTIPLE CHOICE QUESTIONS

1. B p. 286

2. A p. 287

3. C p. 287

4. C p. 291

5. A p. 291

6. C p. 292

7. A p. 291

8. D pp. 291-292

9. C p. 294

10. C p. 294

11. B p. 295

12. B p. 297

13. C p. 297

14. A p. 297

15. A p. 298

16. B p. 297

17. C p. 300

18. D p. 303

19. D p. 309

20. D p. 311

TRUE FALSE QUESTION

1. F p. 288

2. F p. 287-288

3. T p. 291

4. T p. 296

5. F p. 297

6. T p. 298

7. F p. 298

8. T p. 299

9. T p. 302

10. T p. 303

11. T p. 303

12. T p. 304

13. F p. 308

14. F p. 309

15. T p. 312

FILL IN THE BLANK QUESTIONS

1. Income

2. Power

3. Socioeconomic status

4. class conflict

5. pink collar

6. Classism

7. absolute

8. Relative

9. feminization of poverty

10. meritocracy

Chapter 10

RACE AND ETHNICITY

BRIEF CHAPTER OUTLINE

Race and Ethnicity

- Social Significance of Race and Ethnicity
- Racial Classification and the Meaning of Race
- Dominant and Subordinant Groups

Prejudice

- Stereotypes
- Racism
- Theories of Prejudice
- Measuring Prejudice

Discrimination

Sociological Perspectives on Race and Ethnic Relations

- Symbolic Interactionist Perspectives
- Functionalist Perspectives
- Conflict Perspectives
- An Alternative Perspective: Critical Race Theory

Racial and Ethnic Groups in the United States

- Native Americans
- White Anglo Saxon Protestants (British Americans)
- African Americans
- White Ethnic Americans
- Asian Americans
- Latinos/as (Hispanic Americans)
- Middle Eastern Americans

Global Racial and Ethnic Inequality in the Future

- Worldwide Racial and Ethnic Struggles
- Growing Racial and Ethnic Diversity in the United States

CHAPTER SUMMARY

Issues of race and ethnicity permeate all levels of interaction in the United States. A **race** is a category of people who have been singled out as inferior or superior, often on the basis of physical characteristics such as skin color, hair texture, and eye shape. By contrast, an **ethnic group** is a collection of people distinguished, by others or by themselves, primarily on the basis of cultural or nationality characteristics. Race and ethnicity are ingrained in our consciousness and often form the basis of hierarchical ranking and determine who gets what resources. A **dominantgroup** is one that is advantaged and has superior resources and rights in a society while a **subordinategroup** is one whose members, because of physical or cultural characteristics, are disadvantaged and subjected to unequal treatment by the dominant group and who regard themselves as objects of collective discrimination. **Prejudice** is a negative attitude based on faulty generalizations about the members of selected racial and ethnic groups and is rooted in **stereotypes** and *ethnocentrism*. **Racism** is a set of attitudes, beliefs, and practices that is used to justify the superior treatment of one racial or ethnic group and the inferior treatment of another racial or ethnic group. **Discrimination** -- actions or practices of dominant group members that have a harmful impact on members of a subordinate group -- may be either **individual** or **institutional discrimination** -- involving day to day practices of organizations and institutions that have a harmful impact on members of subordinate groups. According to the interactionist contact hypothesis, increased contact between people from divergent groups should lead to favorable attitudes and behavior when a specific set of criteria are met. Two functionalist perspectives -- **assimilation** and **ethnic pluralism** -- focus on how members of subordinate groups become a part of the mainstream. Conflict theories analyze economic stratification and access to power in race and ethnic relations: caste and class perspectives, **internal colonialism**, **split labor market theory**, gendered racism, and racial formation theory. Critical race theory derives its foundation from the U.S. civil rights tradition and the writings of several civil rights leaders. The unique experiences of Native Americans, White Anglo Saxon Protestants/British Americans, African Americans, White Ethnics, Asian Americans, Latinos/as (Hispanic Americans), and Middle Easterners are discussed, and the increasing racial ethnic diversity of the United States is examined. Globally, many racial and ethnic groups seek self-determination creating ethnic wars in some areas. In the future, it is hoped that the superpower nations with the aid of the United Nations will suppress ethnic violence. In the United States, racial and ethnic diversity is increasing; several possibilities of this increase remain.

LEARNING OBJECTIVES

After reading Chapter 10, you should be able to:

1. Define race and ethnic group and explain their social significance.

2. Explain the sociological usage of dominant group and subordinant group and note why these terms may be misleading.

3. Discuss prejudice and explain the major theories of prejudice.

4. Discuss discrimination and distinguish between individual and institutional discrimination.

5. Describe interactionist perspectives on racial and ethnic relations.

6. Distinguish between assimilation and ethnic pluralism and explain why both are functionalist perspectives on racial and ethnic relations.

7. Explain the key assumptions of conflict perspectives on racial and ethnic relations and note the group(s) to which each applies.

8. Know the major premises of critical race theory.

9. Trace the intergroup relationships of racial and ethnic groups in the United States.

10. Explain how the experiences of Native Americans have been different from those of other racial and ethnic groups in the United States.

11. Describe how the African American experience in the United States has been unique when compared with other groups.

12. Compare and contrast the experiences of Chinese Americans, Japanese Americans, Korean Americans, Filipino Americans, and Indochinese Americans in the United States.

13. Describe the experiences of Mexican Americans, Puerto Ricans, and Cuban Americans in the United States.

14. Discuss racial and ethnic struggles from a global perspective.

KEY TERMS

(defined at page number shown and in glossary)

assimilation 332	prejudice 324
authoritarian personality 327	race 320
discrimination 327	racism 325
dominant group 324	scapegoat 327
ethnic group 320	segregation 331
ethnic pluralism 331	social distance 327
genocide 328	split labor market 332
individual discrimination 328	stereotypes 324
institutional discrimination 328	subordinate group 324
internal colonialism 332	

KEY PEOPLE

(identified at page number shown)

Robert Blauner 332	Robert Merton 328
Emory Bogardus 327	Michael Omi and Howard Winant 321
W.E.B. DuBois 331	William Julius Wilson 332
Joe R. Feagin 328	

CHAPTER OUTLINE

I. RACE AND ETHNICITY

    A.   A **race** is a category of people who have been singled out as inferior or superior, often on the basis of physical characteristics such as skin color, hair texture, and eye shape.

    B.   An **ethnic group** is a collection of people distinguished, by others or by themselves, primarily on the basis of cultural or nationality characteristics.

    C.   Social significance of race and ethnicity: Race and ethnicity are bases of hierarchical ranking in society; the dominant group holds power over other (subordinate) ethnic groups.

    D.   Racial classifications in the U.S. census mirror how the meaning of race has continued to change over the past century in the U.S.

    E.   A **dominantgroup** is one that is advantaged and has superior resources and rights in a society; a **subordinategroup** is one whose members, because of physical or cultural characteristics, are disadvantaged and subjected to unequal treatment by the dominant group and who regard themselves as objects of collective discrimination.

II. PREJUDICE

    A.   **Prejudice** is a negative attitude based on faulty generalizations about members of selected racial and ethnic groups. Prejudice is often based on stereotypes.

    B.   **Stereotypes** are overgeneralizations about the appearance, behavior, or other characteristics of all members of a category. Ethnocentrism is maintained and perpetuated by stereotypes.

    C.   **Racism** is a set of attitudes, beliefs, and practices that is used to justify the superior treatment of one racial or ethnic group and the inferior treatment of another.

    D.   The frustration-aggression hypothesis states that people who are frustrated in their efforts achieve a highly desired goal will respond with a pattern of aggression toward a **scapegoat** -- a person or group that is incapable of offering resistance to the hostility or aggression of others.

    E.   Theories of prejudice include the frustration aggression hypothesis, social learning theory, and the theory of the **authoritarian personality**, which is characterized by excessive conformity, submissiveness to authority, intolerance, insecurity, a high level of superstition, and rigid, stereotypic thinking.

    F.   To measure prejudice, some sociologist use **social distance,** which is the extent to which people are willing to interact and establish relationships with members of racial and ethnic groups other than their own.

III. DISCRIMINATION

    A.   **Discrimination** is defined as actions or practices of dominant group members that have a harmful impact on members of a subordinate group.

    B.   Robert Merton identified four combinations of attitudes and responses:

        1.   Unprejudiced nondiscriminators -- persons who are not personally prejudiced and do not discriminate against others;

2. Unprejudiced discriminators -- persons who may have no personal prejudice but still engage in discriminatory behavior because of peer group prejudice or economic, political, or social interests;

3. Prejudiced nondiscriminators -- persons who hold personal prejudices but do not discriminate due to peer pressure, legal demands, or a desire for profits;

4. Prejudiced discriminators -- persons who hold personal prejudices and actively discriminate against others.

C. Discriminatory actions vary in severity from the use of derogatory labels to violence against individuals and groups.

1. **Genocide** is the deliberate, systematic killing of an entire people or nation.

2. More recently, the term "ethnic cleansing" has been used to define a policy of "cleansing" geographic areas (such as in Yugoslavia) by forcing persons of other races or religions to flee -- or die.

D. Discrimination also varies in how it is carried out.

1. **Individual discrimination** consists of one on one acts by members of the dominant group that harm members of the subordinate group or their property.

2. **Institutional discrimination** is the day to day practices of organizations and institutions that have a harmful impact on members of subordinate groups.

IV. SOCIOLOGICAL PERSPECTIVES ON RACE AND ETHNIC RELATIONS

A. Symbolic Interactionist Perspectives

1. The *contact hypothesis* suggests that contact between people from divergent groups should lead to favorable attitudes and behavior when a specific set of criteria is met.

2. However, scholars have found that increasing contact may have little or no effect on existing prejudices.

B. Functionalist Perspectives

1. **Assimilation** is a process by which members of subordinate racial and ethnic groups become absorbed into the dominant culture.

2. **Ethnic pluralism** is the coexistence of a variety of distinct racial and ethnic groups within one society.

3. **Segregation** is the spatial and social separation of categories of people by races, ethnicity, class, gender, and/or religion.

C. Conflict Perspectives

1. The **caste perspective** views racial and ethnic inequality as a permanent feature of U.S. society.

2. **Class perspectives** emphasize the role of the capitalist class in racial exploitation.

3. **Internal colonialism** occurs when members of a racial or ethnic group are conquered, or colonized, and forcibly placed under the economic and political control of the dominant group.

4. **Split labor market** refers to the division of the economy into two areas of employment, a primary sector composed of higher paid (usually dominant group) workers in more secure jobs, and a secondary sector comprised of lower paid (often

subordinate group) workers in jobs with little security and frequently hazardous working conditions.

5. *Gendered racism* refers to the interactive effect of racism and sexism in the exploitation of women of color.

6. The *theory of racial formation* states that actions of the government substantially define racial and ethnic relations in the United States.

D. An Alternative Perspective: Critical Race Theory

1. One premise is that racism is so ingrained in the U.S. society that is appears to be ordinary and natural to many people.

2. *Interest convergence* is a crucial factor in bringing about social change.

3. Formal equality under the law does not necessarily equate to actual equality in society.

4. Ironies and contradictions exist in civil rights law, which are actually self-serving.

V. RACIAL AND ETHNIC GROUPS IN THE UNITED STATES

A. Native Americans

1. Historically, Native Americans experienced the following kinds of treatment in the United States:

    a. Genocide

    b. Forced Migration

    c. Forced Assimilation

2. Today, about two million Native Americans live in the United States (primarily in the southwest), and about one third live on reservations.

3. Native Americans are the most disadvantaged racial or ethnic group in the United States in terms of income, employment, housing, nutrition, and health (especially among individuals living on reservations).

B. White Anglo Saxon Protestants (British Americans)

1. Although many English settlers initially were indentured servants or sent here as prisoners, they quickly emerged as the dominant group, creating a core culture to which all other groups were expected to adapt.

2. Like other racial and ethnic groups, British Americans are not all alike; social class and gender affect their life chances and opportunities.

C. African Americans

1. Slavery was rationalized by stereotyping African Americans as inferior and childlike; however, some slaves and whites engaged in active resistance that eventually led to the abolition of slavery.

2. Slavery was rationalized by stereotyping African Americans as inferior and childlike; however, some slaves and whites engaged in active resistance that eventually led to the abolition of slavery.

3. *Lynching* -- a killing carried out by a group of vigilantes seeking revenge for an actual or imagined crime by the victim -- was used by whites to intimidate African Americans into staying "in their place."

4. During World Wars I and II, African Americans were a vital source of labor in war production industries; however, racial discrimination continued both on and off the job.

    a. After African Americans began to demand sweeping societal changes in the 1950s, racial segregation slowly was outlawed by the courts and the federal government.

    b. Civil rights legislation attempted to do away with discrimination in education, housing, employment, and health care.

5. Today, African Americans make up about 13 percent of the U.S. population; many have made significant gains in education, employment, and income in the past three decades; however, other African Americans have not fare so well; for example, the African American unemployment rate remains twice as high as that of whites, and young people in central city areas face a bleak future.

D. The term *white ethnics Americans* is used to identify immigrants who came from European countries other than England. Ireland, Poland, Italy, Greece, Germany, Yugoslavia, Russia and other former Soviet republics are examples.

E. The term *Asian Americans* refers to many diverse groups with roots in Asia.

  1. Chinese Americans

    a. The initial wave of Chinese immigration occurred between 1850 and 1880 when Chinese men came to the United States seeking gold in California and jobs constructing the transcontinental railroads.

    b. Chinese Americans were subjected to extreme prejudice and stereotyping; the Chinese Exclusion Act of 1882 was passed because white workers feared for their jobs.

    c. In the 1960s, the second and largest wave of Chinese immigration came from Hong Kong and Taiwan.

    d. Today, one third of all Chinese Americans were born in the United States; as a group, they have enjoyed considerable upward mobility, but many Chinese Americans live in poverty in Chinatowns.

  2. Japanese Americans

    a. The earliest Japanese immigrants primarily were men who worked on sugar plantations in the Hawaiian Islands in the 1860s; the immigration of Japanese men was curbed in 1908; however, Japanese women were permitted to enter the U.S. for several more years because of the shortage of women.

    b. Internment: During World War II, when the United States was at war with Japan, nearly 120,000 Japanese Americans were placed in internment camps because they were seen as a security threat; many Japanese Americans lost all that they owned during the internment.

    c. In spite of the extreme hardship faced as a result of the loss of their businesses and homes during World War II, many Japanese Americans have been very successful.

  3. Korean Americans

a.   The first wave of Korean immigrants were male workers who arrived in Hawaii between 1903 and 1910; the second wave came to the mainland following the Korean War in 1964 (e.g., the wives of servicemen, and Korean children who had lost their parents in the war); and the third wave arrived after the Immigration Act of 1965 permitted well educated professionals to migrate to the U.S.

b.   Korean Americans have helped each other open small businesses by pooling money through the *kye* -- an association that grants members money on a rotating basis to gain access to more capital.

4.   Filipino Americans

a.   Most of the first Filipino immigrants were men who were employed in agriculture; following the Immigration Act of 1965, Filipino physicians, nurses, technical workers, and other professionals moved in large numbers to the U.S. mainland.

b.   Unlike other Asian Americans, most Filipinos have not had the start up capital necessary to open their own businesses, and workers generally have been employed in the low wage sector of the dual labor market.

5.   Indochinese Americans

a.   Most Indochinese Americans (including people from Vietnam, Cambodia, Thailand, and Laos) have come to the U.S. in the past two decades.

b.   Vietnamese refugees who had the resources to flee at the beginning of the Vietnam War were the first to arrive. Next came Cambodians and lowland Laotians, referred to as "boat people" by the media.

c.   Today, most Indochinese Americans are foreign born; about half live in western states, especially California. Even though most Indochinese immigrants spoke no English when they arrived in this country, some of their children have done very well in school and have been stereotyped as "brains".

F.   Latinos/as (Hispanic Americans)

1.   Mexican Americans or Chicanos/as have experienced disproportionate poverty as a result of internal colonialism.

a.   More recently, Mexican Americans have been seen as cheap labor at the same time that they have been stereotyped as lazy.

b.   When anti-immigration sentiments are running high, Mexican Americans often are the objects of discrimination.

c.   Today, the families of many Mexican Americans have lived in the United States for four or five generations and have made significant contributions in many areas.

2.   When Puerto Rico became a possession of the United States in 1917, Puerto Ricans acquired U.S. citizenship and the right to move freely to and from the mainland; while living conditions have improved substantially for some, others have continued to live in poverty in Spanish Harlem and other barrios.

3.   Cuban Americans have fared somewhat better than other Latinos; early waves of Cuban immigrants were affluent business and professional people; the second

wave of Cuban Americans in the Mariel boatlift of the 1970s fared worse; and more recent arrivals have developed their own ethnic and economic enclaves in cities such as Miami.

G.   Middle Eastern Americans

    1.   Since 1970, many immigrants have arrived in the United States from Middle Eastern countries such as Egypt, Syria, Lebanon, Saudi Arabia, Kuwait, Yemen, Iran, and Iraq.

    2.   While some are from working class families, those coming from Lebanon, Syria, Iran, and Kuwait primarily came from middle and upper-income family backgrounds.

    3.   In the United States, Islamic schools and centers often bring together people from a diversity of middle-eastern countries such as Egypt and Pakistan.

    4.   Like other minority groups, middle Eastern Americans are often treated as categories rather than as individual human beings.

VI.   GLOBAL RACIAL AND ETHNIC INEQUALITY IN THE FUTURE

A.   Worldwide Racial and Ethnic Struggles

    1.   The cost of self-determination -- the right to choose one's own way of life -- often is the loss of life and property in ethnic warfare (e.g., Yugoslavia, Spain, Britain, Romania, Russia, Moldova, Georgia, the Middle East, Africa, Asia, and Latin America).

    2.   Some analysts predict that the "superpower" nations, including the United States, Great Britain, Japan, and Germany, will suppress ethnic violence with the assistance of the United Nations, which will serve a peacekeeping function by monitoring and enforcing agreements between rival factions.

B.   Growing Racial and Ethnic Diversity in the United States

    1.   Racial and ethnic diversity is increasing in the United States: in the year 2000, white Americans made up 70 percent of the population, in contrast to 80 percent in 1980; by 2056, the roots of the average U.S. resident will be Africa, Asia, Hispanic countries, the Pacific Islands, and the Middle East -- not white Europe.

    2.   Interethnic tensions may ensue between whites and people of color; people may continue to employ sincere fictions -- personal beliefs that are a reflection of larger societal mythologies, such as "I am not a racist" -- even when these are inaccurate perceptions.

    3.   Some analysts believe that there is reason for cautious optimism; throughout U.S. history subordinate racial and ethnic groups have struggled to gain the freedom and rights which were previously withheld from them, and movements comprised of both whites and people of color will continue to oppose racism in everyday life, to aim at healing divisions among racial groups, and to teach children about racial tolerance.

PRACTICE TESTS

MULTIPLE CHOICE QUESTIONS

Select the response that best answers the question or completes the statement:

1. All of the following are characteristics of ethnic groups, **except**:
   a. unique cultural traits.
   b. a feeling of ethnocentrism.
   c. territoriality.
   d. the same skin color.

2. According to the text, the terms "majority group" and "minority group" are:
   a. accurate because "majority groups" always are larger in number than "minority groups."
   b. misleading because people who share ascribed racial or ethnic characteristics automatically constitute a group.
   c. less accurate terms than "dominant group" and "subordinate group," which more accurately reflect the importance of power in the relationships.
   d. no longer used because they are "politically incorrect."

3. _____ is a negative attitude based on faulty generalizations about members of selected racial and ethnic groups.
   a. Prejudice
   b. Discrimination
   c. Stereotyping
   d. Genocide

4. According to the text, the use of Native American names, images, and mascots by sports teams is an example of:
   a. prejudice.
   b. discrimination.
   c. stereotyping.
   d. genocide.

5. Racism tends to intensify in times of:
   a. low emplloyment
   b. economic uncertainty.
   c. low rates of immigration.
   d. economic equality

6. All of the following are examples of overt racism, **except**:
   a. a police detective who repeatedly refers to African Americans in derogatory terms while discussing police department procedures with the author of a screenplay.
   b. stereotyping.
   c. segregation of students by race/ethnicity in public schools.
   d. hate crimes perpetrated against victims because of their race/ethnicity, sexual orientation, or religion.

153

7. Sociologist Emory Bogardus developed a scale to measure:

    a. racial ethnic prejudice in society.

    b. stereotyping.

    c. social distance.

    d. income differentials by race/ethnicity.

8. According to sociologist Robert Merton's typology, an umpire who is prejudiced against African Americans and deliberately makes official calls against them when they are at bat, is an example of a(n):

    a. unprejudiced nondiscriminator.

    b. unprejudiced discriminator.

    c. prejudiced nondiscriminator.

    d. prejudiced discriminator.

9. Institutional discrimination consists of:

    a. one on one acts by members of the dominant group that harm members of the subordinate group or their property.

    b. day to day practices of organizations and institutions that have a harmful impact on members of subordinate groups.

    c. the division of the economy into two areas of employment, a primary sector or upper tier, and a secondary sector or lower tier.

    d. the deliberate, systematic killing of an entire people or nation.

10. A prejudiced judge giving harsher sentences to all African-American defendants and is not supported by the judicial system in that action is an example of _____ discrimination.

    a. indirect institutionalized

    b. direct institutionalized

    c. small group

    d. isolate

11. According to the contact hypothesis, contact between people from divergent groups should lead to favorable attitudes and behaviors when certain factors are present. Members of each group must have all of the following, **except**:

    a. equal status.

    b. pursuit of the same goals.

    c. being competitive with one another to achieve their goals.

    d. positive feedback from interactions with each other.

12. _____ is a process by which members of subordinate racial and ethnic groups become absorbed into the dominant culture.

    a. Assimilation

    b. Ethnic pluralism

    c. Accommodation

    d. Internal colonialism

13. _____ is the coexistence of a variety of distinct racial and ethnic groups within one society.

  a. Assimilation

  b. Ethnic pluralism

  c. Accommodation

  d. Internal colonialism

14. Based on early theories of race relations by W. E. B. Du Bois, sociologist Oliver C. Cox suggested that African Americans were enslaved because:

  a. of prejudice based on skin color.

  b. they were the cheapest and best workers that owners could find for heavy labor in the mines and on plantations.

  c. they allowed themselves to be dominated by wealthy people.

  d. they agreed to work for passage to the United States, believing that they would be released after a period of indentured servitude.

15. Sociologist _____ has suggested that class is more important than race in explaining "black white relations" in the United States.

  a. William Julius Wilson

  b. Joe R. Feagin

  c. Oliver C. Cox

  d. Robert Merton

16. According to _____ , sports reflect the interests of the wealthy and powerful; athletes are exploited in order for coaches, managers, and owners to gain high levels of profit and prestige.

  a. interactionists

  b. sportsologists

  c. functionalists

  d. conflict theorists

17. The division of the economy into a primary sector, composed of higher paid workers in more secure jobs, and a secondary sector, composed of lower-paid workers in jobs with little security and hazardous working conditions is referred to as:

  a. the split labor market.

  b. racial formation.

  c. gendered racism.

  d. stacking.

18. According to _____ theory, interest convergence is a critical factor in changing race and ethnic inequality.

  a. functionalists

  b. symbolic interactionists

  c. critical race

19. The experiences of Native Americans in the United States have been characterized by:
    a. slavery and segregation.
    b. restrictive immigration laws.
    c. genocide, forced migration, and forced assimilation.
    d. internment.

20. The label _____ was first used by the U.S. government to designate people of Latin American and Spanish descent living in the United States.
    a. Mexican-American
    b. Hispanic
    c. Chicano
    d. Latino/Latina

TRUE FALSE QUESTIONS

1. Sociologists suggest that race is a socially constructed reality, not a biological one.
   True or False

2. Racial classifications in the U.S. census have remained unchanged for the past century.
   True or False

3. The terms "majority group" and "minority group" are misleading because, numerically speaking, "minority" means a group that is fewer in number than a "majority" group.
   True or False

4. Analysts have found that whites that accept racial stereotypes have no greater desire for social distance from people of color than do whites that reject negative stereotypes.
   True or False

5. The extermination of 6 million European Jews by Nazi Germany is an example of genocide.
   True or False

6. Discrimination is an individual activity; it is never based on norms of an organization or community.
   True or False

7. Equalitarian pluralism is an ideal typology that has never actually been identified in any society.
   True or False

8. De facto segregation refers to racial separation and inequality enforced by custom.
   True or False

9. The internal colonialism model helps explain the continued exploitation of immigrant groups such as the Chinese, Filipinos, and Vietnamese.
   True or False

10. The term "gendered racism" refers to the interactive effect of racism and sexism in the exploitation of women of color.
    True or False

11. White Anglo Saxon Protestants (WASPS) have been the most privileged group in the United States.
    True or False

12. The term "white ethnics" was coined to identify immigrants who came from European countries other than England, such as Ireland, Poland, Germany, and Italy.
    True or False

13. White ethnics have not experienced discrimination in the United States.
    True or False

14. Asian Americans are the fastest growing ethnic minority group in the United States.
    True or False

15. It is predicted that by 2056, the roots of the average U.S. resident will be in Africa, Asia, Hispanic countries, the Pacific Islands, and the Middle East.
    True or False

FILL IN THE BLANK QUESTIONS

1. In the nineteenth-century biologists divided the world's population in to three racial categories: _____ , _____ , and _____ .

2. The term _____ refers to individuals who share some common cultural or national characteristics.

3. Sociologists emphasize that race is a _____ , not a biological one.

4. _____ can either be a positive bias in favoring a group or can be a negative bias against a group.

5. _____ is an attitude that is used to justify the superior or inferior treatment of another racial or ethnic group.

6. Highly prejudiced individuals tend to have an _____ which is charactertized by excessive conformity, intolerance, and rigid stereotypes.

7. _____ involves actions or practices of dominant group members that have a harmful impact on members of a subordinate group.

8. The day-to-day practices of organizations and institutions that have a harmful impact on members of subordinate groups is termed _____

9. Segregation may be enforced by custom, _____ , or by law which is an example of _____ segregation.

10. The process by which members of subordinate racial and ethnic groups become absorbed into the dominant culture is known as _____ .

SHORT ANSWER/ESSAY QUESTIONS

1. How do racial groups, ethnic groups, minority and majority groups differ? What are some groups that may be one, but not any of the other?

2. What are some social factors that have prevented African-Americans from achieving full equality in the United States?

3. What is the fastest growing ethnic minority group in the United States today? Why?

4. Why is education a crucial issue for Latinos/as? Which Latino/a group has fared the best? Why?

5. Why are race and ethnicity so socially significant? In your response, provide both historic and contemporary explanations.

STUDENT CLASS PROJECTS AND ACTIVITIES

1. Investigate pluralism on your campus by conducting a brief campus study. Record your information in a written paper. Ask the following questions and include any others you may want to ask: (1) What is the number and percentage of the different ethnic or racial groups enrolled on the campus? (2) What is the number and percentage of "foreign" students? (3) What percentage of various ethnic groups holds important campus offices? Identify the office and the race or ethnicity of the office holder; (4) What percentage of racial or ethnic groups are in the campus sororities and fraternities and other organizations? (5) What percentage of racial or ethnic groups comprises both the male and female athletes who receive college or university scholarships? (6) Based on the research, evaluate your campus. How pluralistic is it? This information may be available from the admissions or registrar's office, student activities or athletic office. Write up your results following any additional instructions from your professor and submit your paper on the correct due date.

2. Conduct an informal survey of 20 people who appear to be an ethnic or racial minority in our country. Ask these specific questions and record the responses: (1) Ask the respondent's name, general address, and specific race or ethnicity; (2) Do you ever experience racism or bigotry or discrimination in some form in our society; (3) If so, what was it? (4) Can you remember the first time you were hurt in some way? (5) Can you remember a more recent time? (6) How did you respond? (7) How would you like to have responded? Provide any other questions that you would like to ask and then provide a summary, conclusion and evaluation of this project. Submit your papers at the appropriate time following any other specific instructions given by your instructor.

3. Examine your own ethnicity or racial heritage, if known. If your ethnicity or race is mixed, then select the one that you believe to be the most dominant heritage in your life. If your ethnicity or race is unclear, or not known, then examine your own socialization into an ethnic or racial group. Note that many people, because of adoption or other factors, may not know their original ethnic heritage, but may be able to identify their own racial heritage. Prepare a minimum five-page report

on your experience as a member of your particular group. Gather as much background information as possible in exploring your own ethnic or racial heritage. If known, trace the ethnic history of your own family, such as the approximate date of your ancestors' migration to the United States, the obstacles they faced, their cultural practices and experiences from childhood, usual activities, and family experiences. Include activities with extended kin members, type of education received, if any, and church and neighborhood experiences. Record any other event or experience that influenced your identity and membership in the group. Include any other information you desire, but do provide a conclusion and evaluation of this project. Submit your paper at the appropriate time following any other instructions provided by your professor.

INTERNET ACTIVITIES

1. Take a tour through cyberspace searching for general information about race and ethnicity. Search through these sites to collect relevant facts about racial and ethnic groups. These are good introductory sites for writing papers and collecting data.

    a. http://eserver.org/race

    b. www.trinity.edu/mkearl/race.html

    c. http://resi.tamu.edu/index.html

2. This site contains an essay by Tom Lovell on the work of Shelby Steele. Specific reference is made to Steele's term "race holding." www.raleightavern.org/steele.html

3. These are sites that are more specific to various racial and ethnic groups in the U.S. Students wishing to go more in depth with a study of specific racial and ethnic groups should start here.

    a. www.aawc.com/aawc0.html(African-American)

    b. www.lif.org/(Latino)

    c. http://goldsea.com/Air/Issues/issues.html(Asian-American)

    d. www.hanksville.org/NAresources/(Native American)

INFOTRAC EXERCISES

1. Scan the newspaper for articles dealing with **racism**. What are some common themes that emerge? (Qualitative research)

2. **Ethnic cleansing** remains a powerful tool for one group to eliminate another. There are two categories listed in InfoTrac, genocide and forced migration. Look for articles that describe where ethnic cleansing is taking place, and with what consequences.

3. Select one of the **ethnic minority groups** addressed in this chapter. What are some of the issues related to each group? How do research articles and newspaper articles about this group differ in their treatment of these groups?

4. Search for these theoretical concepts in articles contained in the archives of InfoTrac: **Scapegoat, Contact Hypothesis, Psychological Assimilation, Internal Colonialism, Split Labor Market, and Critical Race Theory.**

Solutions

MULTIPLE CHOICE QUESTIONS

1. D p. 320

2. C p. 324

3. A p. 324

4. C p. 324

5. B p. 325

6. B p. 325

7. C p. 327

8. D p. 328

9. B p. 328

10. D p. 328

11. C p. 329

12. A p. 330

13. B p. 331

14. B p. 332

15. A p. 332

16. D p. 332

17. A p. 333

18. C p. 334

19. C p. 334

20. B p. 346

TRUE FALSE QUESTIONS

1. T p. 320

2. F p. 323

3. T p. 324

4. F p. 327

5. T p. 328

6. F p. 328

7. F p. 331

8. T p. 331

9. T p. 332

10. T p. 333

11. T p. 337

12. T p. 343

13. F p. 331

14. T p. 344

15. T p. 350

FILL IN THE BLANK QUESTIONS

1. Negroid, Caucasoid, Mongaloid

2. ethnicity

3. sociall constructed reality

4. Prejudice

5. Racism

6. authoritarian personality

7. Discrimination

8. institutional discrimination

9. de facto, de jure

10. assimilation

Chapter 11

SEX AND GENDER

BRIEF CHAPTER OUTLINE

Sex: The Biological Dimension
- Hermaphrodites/Transsexuals
- Sexual Orientation

Gender: The Cultural Dimension
- The Social Significance of Gender
- Sexism

Gender Stratification in Historical and Contemporary Perspective
- Hunting and Gathering Societies
- Horticultural and Pastoral Societies
- Agrarian Societies
- Industrial Societies
- Postindustrial Societies

Gender and Socialization
- Gender Socialization by Parents
- Peers and Gender Socialization
- Teachers, Schools, and Gender Socialization
- Sports and Gender Socialization
- Mass Media and Gender Socialization
- Adult Gender Socialization

Contemporary Gender Inequality
- Gendered Division of Paid Work
- Pay Equity (Comparable Worth)
- Paid Work and Family Work

Perspectives on Gender Stratification
- Functionalist and Neoclassical Economic Perspectives
- Conflict Perspectives
- Feminist Perspectives

161

Gender Issues in the Future

CHAPTER SUMMARY

It is important to distinguish between **sex**—refers to the biological and anatomical differences between females and males—and **gender**, which refers to the culturally and socially constructed differences between females and males found in the meanings, beliefs, and practices associated with "femininity" and "masculinity." Gender is socially significant because it leads to differential treatment of men and women; sexism (like racism) often is used to justify discriminatory treatment. **Sexism** is linked to patriarchy, a hierarchical system in which cultural, political, and economic structures are male dominated. In most hunting and gathering societies, fairly equitable relationships exist because neither sex has the ability to provide all of the food necessary for survival. In horticultural societies, hoe cultivation is compatible with child care, and a fair degree of gender equality exists because neither sex controls the food supply while in pastoral societies, women have relatively low status. In agrarian societies, male dominance is very apparent; tasks require more labor and physical strength, and women are seen as too weak or too tied to child rearing activities to perform these activities. In industrialized societies, a gap exists between unpaid work performed by women at home and paid work performed by men and women. In postindustrial societies, technology supports a service and information based economy; most adult women are in the labor force and have double responsibilities – those from the labor force and those from the family. The key agents of gender socialization are parents, peers, teachers and schools, sports, and the mass media, all of which tend to reinforce stereotypes of appropriate gender behavior. Gender inequality results from the economic, political, and educational discrimination of women. In most workplaces, jobs are either gender segregated or the majority of employees are of the same gender. Gender segregated occupations lead to a disparity, or **pay gap**, between women's and men's earnings. Even when women are employed in the same job as men, on average they do not receive the same pay. Many women have a "second shift" because of their dual responsibilities for paid and unpaid work. According to functional analysts, husbands perform instrumental tasks of economic support and decision making, and wives assume expressive tasks of providing affection and emotional support for the family. Conflict analysts suggest that the gendered division of labor within families and the workplace results from male control and dominance over women and resources. Although feminist perspectives vary in their analyses of women's subordination, they all advocate social change to eradicate gender inequality.

LEARNING OBJECTIVES

After reading Chapter 11, you should be able to:

1. Distinguish between sex and gender and explain their sociological significance.

2. Explain why sex is not always clear cut; differentiate between hermaphrodites, transsexuals, and transvestites.

3. Describe the relationship between gender roles, gender identity, and body consciousness.

4. Define sexism and explain how it is related to discrimination and patriarchy.

5. Trace gender stratification from early hunting and gathering societies until to contemporary industrial societies.

6. Explain how gender relationships in both the workplace and in families change in postindustrial societies.

7. Describe the process of gender socialization and identify specific ways in which parents, peers, teachers, sports, and mass media contribute to the process.

8. Describe gender bias and explain how schools operate as a gendered institution.

9. Discuss the gendered division of paid work and explain its relationship to the issue of pay equity or comparable worth

10. Trace changes in labor force participation by women and note how these changes have contributed to the "second shift."

11. Describe functionalist and neoclassical economic perspectives on gender stratification and contrast them with conflict perspectives.

12. State the feminist perspective on gender equality and outline the key assumptions of liberal, radical, socialist, and black (African American) feminism.

KEY TERMS

(defined at page number shown and in glossary)

body consciousness 360	patriarchy 362
comparable worth 379	primary sex characteristics 357
feminism 362	secondary sex characteristics 357
gender 359	sex 357
gender bias 372	sexism 362
gender identity 360	sexual harassment 372
gender role 359	sexual orientation 358
hermaphrodite 357	transsexual 358
homophobia 359	transvestite 358
matriarchy 362	wag gap 378

KEY PEOPLE

(identified at page number shown)

Ben Agger 382	Elizabeth Higginbotham 376
Susan Bordo 362	Alice Kemp 376
Paula England and Melissa Herbert 379	Judith Lorber 359
Argie Hochschild 380	Myra Sadker and David Sadker 372
Dorothy Holland and Margaret A. Eisenhart 371	Becky W. Thompson 361

Chapter 11

CHAPTER OUTLINE

I. SEX: THE BIOLOGICAL DIMENSION

    A. **Sex** refers to the biological and anatomical differences between females and males.

        1. **Primary sex characteristics** are the genitalia used in the reproductive process; **secondary sex characteristics** are the physical traits (other than reproductive organs) that identify an individual's sex.

    B. Hermaphrodites/transsexuals are examples of when sex is not always clear-cut.

        1. Hermaphrodites tend to have some combination of male and females genitalia.

        2. Transsexuals often feel they are the opposite sex from their sex organs.

    C. **Sexual orientation** is a preference for emotional sexual relationships with members of the opposite sex (heterosexuality), the same sex (homosexuality), or both (bisexuality).

II. GENDER: THE CULTURAL DIMENSION

    A. **Gender** refers to the culturally and socially constructed differences between females and males found in the meanings, beliefs, and practices associated with "femininity" and "masculinity."

        1. A microlevel analysis of gender focuses on how individuals learn **gender roles** -- the attitudes, behavior, and activities that are socially defined as appropriate for each sex and are learned through the socialization process -- and **gender identity** -- a person's perception of the self as female or male. **Body consciousness**, how a person feels about his or her body, is a part of gender identify

        2. A macrolevel analysis of gender examines structural features, external to the individual, which perpetuate gender inequality, including gendered institutions, that are reinforced by a gendered belief system, based on ideas regarding masculine and feminine attributes that are held to be valid in a society.

    B. The Social Significance of Gender

        1. Gender is a social construction with important consequences in everyday life.

        2. Gender stereotypes hold that men and women are inherently different in attitudes, behavior, and aspirations.

    C. Sexism

        1. **Sexism** -- the subordination of one sex, usually female, based on the assumed superiority of the other sex -- is interwoven with **patriarchy** -- a hierarchical system of social organization in which cultural, political, and economic structures are controlled by men.

        2. **Matriarchy** is a hierarchical system of social organization in which cultural, political, and economic structures are controlled by women; few societies have been organized in this manner.

III. GENDER STRATIFICATION IN HISTORICAL AND COMTEMPORARY PERSPECTIVE

    A. The earliest known division of labor between women and men is in *hunting and gathering societies*; men hunt while women gather for food. A relatively equitable relationship exists because both sexes are necessary for survival.

    B. In *horticultural societies*, women make an important contribution to food production because hoe cultivation is compatible with child care; a fairly high degree of gender

164

equality exists because neither sex controls the food supply; however in *pastoral societies*, herding primarily is done by men; women contribute relatively little to subsistence production and thus have relatively low status.

    C.   Gender inequality increases in *agrarian societies* as men become more involved in food production. Women are secluded, subordinated and mutilated.

    D.   In *industrial societies* -- those in which factory or mechanized production has replaced agriculture as the major form of economic activity -- the status of women tends to decline further; gendered division of labor increases the economic and political subordination of women.

    E.   In *postindustrial societies* technology supports a service — and information — based economy; most adult women are in the work force and have double responsibilities — those from the labor force and those from the family; more households are headed by women with no male present.

IV.   GENDER AND SOCIALIZATION

    A.   Parents as Agents of Gender Socialization

        1.   From birth, parents act toward children on the basis of gender labels; children's clothing and toys reflect their parents' gender expectations.

        2.   Boys are encouraged to engage in gender-appropriate behavior; they are not to show an interest in "girls'" activities.

    B.   Peers and Gender Socialization

        1.   Peers help children learn prevailing gender role stereotypes, as well as gender appropriate and inappropriate behavior.

        2.   During adolescence, peers often are stronger and more effective agents of gender socialization than are adults.

        3.   Among college students, peers play an important role in career choices and the establishment of long term, intimate relationships.

    C.   Teachers and Schools and Gender Socialization

        1.   From kindergarten through college, schools operate as gendered institutions; teachers provide important messages about gender through both the formal content of classroom assignments and informal interactions with students.

        2.   Teachers may unintentionally demonstrate **gender bias** -- the showing of favoritism toward one gender over the other -- toward male students.

    D.   Sports and Gender Socialization

        1.   The type of game played differs with the child's sex: from elementary school through high school, boys play football and other competitive sports while girls are cheerleaders, members of the drill team, and homecoming queens.

        2.   For many males, sports participation and spectatorship is a training ground for masculinity; for females, sports still is tied to the male gender role, thus making it very difficult for girls and women to receive the full benefits of participating in such activities.

    E.   Mass Media and Gender Socialization

1. Gender stereotyping is found in media, ranging from children's cartoons to adult shows.

2. On television, more male than female roles are shown, and male characters typically are more aggressive, constructive, and direct, while females are deferential toward others or use manipulation to get their way.

3. Advertising also plays an important role in gender socialization.

F. Adult Gender Socialization

    1. Men and women are taught gender appropriate conduct in schools and the workplace.

    2. Different gender socialization may occur as people reach their forties and enter "middle age."

V. CONTEMPORARY GENDER INEQUALITY

A. Gendered division of paid work

    1. *Gender-segregated work* refers to the concentration of women and men in different occupations, jobs, and places of work.

    2. *Labor market segmentation* -- the division of jobs into categories with distinct working conditions -- results in women having separate and unequal jobs in the secondary sector of the split or dual labor market that are lower paying, less prestigious, and have fewer opportunities for advancement.

B. Pay Equity (Comparable Worth)

    1. Occupational segregation contributes to a **pay gap** -- the disparity between women's and men's earnings.

    2. **Comparable worth** is the belief that wages ought to reflect the worth of a job, not the gender or race of the worker.

C. Paid Work and family work

    1. Although both men and women profess that working couples should share household responsibilities, researchers find that family demands remain mostly women's responsibility, even among women who hold full time paid employment.

    2. Many women have a "double day" or "second shift" because of their dual responsibilities for paid and unpaid work.

VI. PERSPECTIVES ON GENDER STRATIFICATION

A. Functional and neoclassical economic perspectives on the family view the division of family labor as ensuring that important societal tasks will be fulfilled.

    1. According to the human capital model, individuals vary widely in the amount of education and job training they bring to the labor market.

    2. From this perspective, what individuals earn is the result of their own choices and labor market demand for certain kinds of workers at specific points in time.

    3. Other neoclassical economic models attribute the wage gap to such factors as: (1) the different amounts of energy men and women expend on their work; (2) the occupational choices women make (choosing female dominated occupations so that they can spend more time with their families); and (3) the crowding of too

many women into some occupations (suppressing wages because the supply of workers exceeds demand).

B. According to the conflict perspective, the gendered division of labor within families and the workplace results from male control of and dominance over women and resources.

    1. Although men's ability to use physical power to control women diminishes in industrial societies, they still remain the head of household, control the property, and hold more power through their predominance in the most highly paid and prestigious occupations and the highest elected offices.

    2. Conflict theorists in the Marxist tradition assert that gender stratification results from private ownership of the means of production; some men not only gain control over property and the distribution of goods but also gain power over women.

C. Feminist Perspectives

    1. **Feminism** refers to a belief that women and men are equal and that they should be valued equally and have equal rights.

    2. In **liberal feminism**, gender equality is equated with equality of opportunity.

    3. According to **radical feminists**, male domination causes all forms of human oppression, including racism and classism.

    4. **Socialist feminists** suggest that women's oppression results from their dual roles as paid and unpaid workers in a capitalist economy. In the workplace, women are exploited by capitalism; at home, they are exploited by patriarchy.

    5. **Multicultural feminism** is based on the belief that women of color experience a different world than other people because of multilayered oppression based on race/ethnicity, gender, and class.

VII. GENDER ISSUES IN THE FUTURE

A. During the twentieth century, women have made significant progress in the labor force; laws were passed to prohibit sexual discrimination in the workplace and school; women became more visible in education, the government, and the professional world.

B. Many men have joined feminist movements not only to raise their consciousness about men's concerns, but also about the need to eliminate sexism and gender bias.

C. However, U.S. society still remains far from gender equity in many areas of life.

PRACTICE TESTS

MULTIPLE CHOICE QUESTIONS

Select the response that best answers the question or completes the statement:

1. According to the research of Hesse-Biber:

    a.   women are more dissatisfied with their body weight and shape.

    b.   women diet more than men.

    c.   women express more anxiety about their bodies than men.

    d.   all of the above.

2. Sociologists use the term _____ to refer to the biological attributes of men and women; _____ is used to refer to the distinctive qualities of men and men that are culturally created.

    a.   gender - sex

    b.   sex - gender

    c.   primary sex characteristics - secondary sex characteristics

    d.   secondary sex characteristics - primary sex characteristics

3. A(n) _____ is a person in whom sexual differentiation is ambiguous or incomplete.

    a.   hermaphrodite

    b.   transsexual

    c.   transvestite

    d.   homosexual

4. A person's perception of the self as female or male is referred to as one's:

    a.   self concept.

    b.   gender identity.

    c.   gender role.

    d.   gender belief system.

5. According to historian Susan Bordo, the anorexic body and the muscled body:

    a.   illustrate that eating problems and bodybuilding are unrelated.

    b.   are opposites.

    c.   exist on a continuum.

    d.   are not gendered experiences.

6. All of the following statements are **correct** regarding sexism, **except**:

    a.   sexism, like racism, is used to justify discriminatory treatment.

    b.   evidence of sexism is found in the under-evaluation of women's work.

    c.   women may experience discrimination in leisure activities.

    d.   men cannot be the victims of sexist assumptions.

7. In most hunting and gathering societies:
    a. a relatively equitable relationship exists because neither sex has the ability to provide all of the food necessary for survival.
    b. women are not full economic partners with men.
    c. relationships between women and men tend to be patriarchal in nature.
    d. menstrual taboos place women in subordinate positions by monthly segregation into menstrual huts.

8. Gender inequality and male dominance became institutionalized in _____ societies.
    a. hunting and gathering
    b. horticultural and pastoral
    c. agrarian
    d. industrial

9. Most common in parts of India, suttee refers to the:
    a. custom of thwarting the growth of a female's feet.
    b. seclusion of women, including extreme modesty in apparel.
    c. surgical procedure performed on young girls as a method of sexual control.
    d. sacrificial killing of a widow upon the death of her husband.

10. All of the following statements regarding gender socialization are correct, **except**:
    a. virtually all gender roles have changed dramatically in recent years.
    b. many parents prefer boys to girls because of stereotypical ideas about the relative importance of males and females to the future of the family and society.
    c. parents tend to treat baby boys more roughly than baby girls.
    d. parents' choices of toys for their children are not likely to change in the near future.

11. In their investigation of college women, anthropologists Dorothy C. Holland and Margaret A. Eisenhart determined that:
    a. peer groups on college campuses are not organized around gender relations.
    b. the peer system propelled women into a world of romance in which their attractiveness to men counted most.
    c. the women's peers immediately influenced their choices of majors and careers.
    d. peer pressure did not involve appearance norms.

12. Teachers who devote more time, effort, and attention to boys than to girls in schools are an example of:
    a. gender socialization.
    b. gender identity.
    c. gender role differentiation.
    d. gender bias.

13. A comprehensive study of gender bias in schools suggested that girls' self esteem is undermined in school through all of the following experiences, **except**:

    a. a relative lack of attention from teachers.

    b. sexual harassment from male peers.

    c. an assumption that girls are better in visual spatial ability, as compared with verbal ability.

    d. the stereotyping and invisibility of females in textbooks.

14. Which of the following statements is **true** regarding men and women in higher education?

    a. Men are more likely than women to earn a college degree.

    b. Men tend to have higher grade point averages in college.

    c. Women typically have higher scores on standardized admissions tests like the Scholastic Assessment Test.

    d. Men constitute the majority of majors in architecture, engineering, computer technology, and physical science.

15. According to the text's discussion of gender and athletics:

    a. women who engage in activities that are assumed to be "masculine" (such as bodybuilding) may either ignore their critics or attempt to redefine the activity or its result as "feminine" or womanly.

    b. some women believe they are more likely to win women's bodybuilding competitions if they "overbuild" their bodies.

    c. being active in sports such as gymnastics makes women less likely to be the victims of anorexia and bulimia.

    d. women bodybuilders have learned that they are less likely to win competitions if they look like a fashion model.

16. According to recent research by sociologist Elizabeth Higginbotham, African American professional women:

    a. find themselves limited in employment in certain sectors of the labor market.

    b. are concentrated in public sector employment.

    c. frequently are employed as public school teachers, welfare workers, librarians, public defenders, and faculty members at public colleges.

    d. all of the above.

17. The belief that wages ought to reflect the worth of a job, not the gender or race of the worker, is referred to as:

    a. the earnings ratio.

    b. pay equity.

    c. non comparable worth.

    d. the pay gap.

18. According to the functionalist/human capital model:

    a. what women earn is the result of their own choices and the needs of the labor market.

    b. the gendered division of labor in the workplace results from male control of and dominance over women and resources.

    c. women's oppression results from their dual roles as paid and unpaid workers in a capitalist economy.

    d. none of the above.

19. Critics of functionalist and neoclassical economic perspectives have pointed out that these perspectives:

    a. exaggerate the problems inherent in traditional gender roles.

    b. fail to critically assess the structure of society that makes educational and occupational opportunities more available to some than others.

    c. overemphasize factors external to individuals that contribute to the oppression of white women and people of color.

    d. focus on differences between men and women without taking into account the commonalities they share.

20. A women's group fights for better child care options, women's right to choose an abortion, and the elimination of sex discrimination in the workplace, arguing that the roots of women's oppression lie in women's lack of equal civil rights and educational opportunities. The platform of this group reflects:

    a. black (African American) feminism.

    b. socialist feminism.

    c. radical feminism.

    d. liberal feminism.

TRUE FALSE QUESTIONS

1. Many men compare themselves unfavorably to bodybuilders and believe they need to gain weight or muscularity.
   True or False

2. Most "sex differences" actually are socially constructed "gender differences."
   True or False

3. Gendered belief systems generally do not change over time.
   True or False

4. Sexism is the subordination of one sex, usually female, based on the assumed superiority of the other sex.
   True or False

5. The earliest known division of labor between women and men is in agrarian societies.
   True or False

6. As societies industrialize, the status of women tends to decline further.
   True or False

7. The cult of true womanhood increased white women's dependence on men and became a source of discrimination against women of color.
   True or False

8. In postindustrial societies, gendered segregation in the workforce dramatically decreases.
   True or False

9. Unlike parents in the United States, parents in many other countries do not prefer boys to girls.
   True or False

10. Children's toys reflect their parents' gender expectations.
    True or False

11. Many parents are aware of the effect that gender socialization has on their children and make a conscientious effort to provide nonsexist experiences for them.
    True or False

12. Female peer groups place more pressure on girls to do "feminine" things than male peer groups place on boys to do "masculine" things.
    True or False

13. By young adulthood, men and women no longer receive gender-related messages from peers.
    True or False

14. Research shows the females receive more praise from teachers for their contribution in the class then do males.
    True or False

15. The degree of gender segregation in the professional labor market has declined since the 1970s, but racial-ethnic segregation has remained deeply embedded in the social structures.
    True or False

FILL IN THE BLANK QUESTIONS

1. The word _____ is used to refer to the distinctive qualities of men and women that are culturally created.

2. Aperson in whom sexual differentiation is ambiguous or incomplete is known as a _____ .

3. A _____ is a male who lives as a woman or a female who lives as a man but does not alter the genitalia.

4. Extreme prejudice directed at gays, lesbians, bisexuals, and others who are preceived as not being heterosexual is termed _____ .

5. A person's perceptions of self as female or male is one's _____ .

6. The subordination of one sex, usually female, based on the assumed superiority of the other sex is known as _____ .

7. Gender _____ consists of showing favoritism toward one gender over the other.

8. _____ work refers to the concentration of women and men in different occupations.

9. The beleifs that wages ought to reflect the worth of a job, not the gender or the race of the worker is known as _____ .

10. The disparity between women's and men's earnings is the _____ .

SHORT ANSWER/ESSAY QUESTIONS

1. Why and in what ways do societies differentiate people because of gender?

2. What causes gender inequality in the United States?

3. What are some of the consequences of gender inequality?

4. How do gender relations in both the labor force and in families change in postindustrial societies?

5. How does the nature of work affect gender equality in societies and all over the world?

STUDENT CLASS PROJECTS AND ACTIVITIES

1. Conduct an informal survey of twenty students on your campus about their opinions of the women's movement and feminism. Some suggested guideline questions to ask: (1) What is your name, age, gender, and college major? (2) Do you support women's rights? Why? Why not? (3) What is your opinion of the women's movement in our country? (4) Do you consider yourself a feminist? Why? Why not? (5) Has the women's movement improved your life in any way? If so, how? (6) Is there still a need for a strong women's movement? Why? Why not? (7) Does the present women's movement reflect the view of most women? Explain your answer. (8) Is a woman's place at home with her children, if it is economically feasible? (9) Do women today have more freedom than their mothers did? (10) Do women today enjoy life more than their mothers did? (11) Include any other information they may want to obtain from their respondents. In the writing up of this project, provide the responses to each particular question and a summary of the responses. Provide a conclusion and a personal evaluation of this project and submit it to your instructor at the appropriate time.

2. Research the history of sexual harassment in the United States. You are to research: (1) how the term came to be defined; (2) how it became an issue in our society; (3) how it has affected women in the workplace; (4) some specific examples of how it has affected women in the workplace; (5) the prevalence of sexual harassment in the workplace; (6) some court cases involving charges of sexual harassment and their outcomes. Include any other information in this research project. Provide in your paper a bibliography, a summary of your findings, and a personal evaluation of the project. Submit your paper to your instructor at the appropriate time.

3. This is a project that works best for a coed campus but it could easily be altered to fit your campus. You are to reverse your roles regarding dating on your college campus. The women are to initiate the date invitation either in person or by telephone, invite the young men out, at their expense. Each woman is to drive to her date's residence and pick him up. She should also help him get in and out of the car, open all doors for him, assist with sitting and removing and replacing coats, accept the check and pay for the same. She is, in the meanwhile, to maintain a conversation about normal interests, preferably with reversed themes and roles, such as sports and the stereotyped 'male talk' on campus. The female should initiate all conversation, remain in control of the conversation, interrupt when necessary to maintain control, remain aloof, when necessary, take up more space when sitting, and give all outward appearance of being completely in charge. The women should walk her date to the door and should initiate any signs of affection, if desired. The assignment for the male is this: The males in the class should initiate any activity in order to get asked out by the females, either by females in the class or on campus. The males are to remain rather passive, after making the first move. They are to act dependent and end every statement with a question, such as "What do you think?" "Is this right?" "Is this okay with you?", etc. They are to walk in front of their dates, and ask for assistance with the doors, with the car, and with their coats or hats. They are not to pay for anything, and are to sit quietly and listen politely to their date's conversation. They can never interrupt or take charge of the conversation in any way whatsoever. The females determine all the activity. Following your date, record your specific activities, actions, and reactions and respond, in writing, to the following questions: (1) Were you comfortable? Explain. (2) Did the behaviors seem amusing? (3) What communication problems arose? (4) Did habitual patterns of behavior surface? (5) How did you feel about this activity? (6) What specifically did you

learn? (7) Record any other information, especially an evaluation of the project, and submit your paper to your instructor at the appropriate time.

INTERNET ACTIVITIES

1. Surf these websites in order to compare similarities and differences in the ways that both sexes are defining the issues.

    a. **Men's Studies Websites:**
        *   www.mensstudies.com/
        *   www.menweb.org/throop/index.html
        *   http://topics.practical.org/browse/Men's_Studies_-_General

    b. **Feminist Websites:**
        *   http://vos.ucsb.edu/browse.asp?id=2711
        *   http://bailiwick.lib.uiowa.edu/wstudies/
        *   www.feministstudies.org/

2. This is a giant listing of books related to men's issues. A great starting point for students interested in researching **gender** related topics. www.ncfm.org/read.htm

3. Try and learn as much as you can about **gender** BEFORE you have your first class on this topic. Go to this site in small groups and come back to class and present what you believe to be the most essential aspects of this study. www.trinity.edu/mkearl/gender.html

INFOTRAC EXERCISES

1. Compare research on **Transsexualism**, **Hermaphroditism**, and **Transvestitism**. Search for these terms in the media as well and see how they are portrayed differently.

2. ***Gender differences in undergraduates' body esteem: the mediating effect of objectified body consciousness and actual/ideal weight discrepancy*** Search InfoTrac and read this article. Bring to class three essay questions. You can trade essay questions in class and provide answers in an informal small group discussion.

3. Go to InfoTrac and conduct a general search for the term **Gender**. You will find a multitude of articles in numerous subfields. Come to class with an idea or issue that is new to you. This is a good way to start a class discussion or introduce the topic of **gender**.

4. Look up the keyword **Fatherhood**. Be sure to look at "Fatherhood's Top Ten Films," by Julia Duin in *Insight on the News*, February 15, 1999. What films represent fathers in a positive light?

5. There are over a hundred articles on **Patriarchy** listed on InfoTrac. Write a brief essay on this subject and use at least three sources from this list. The essay should introduce the concept and then demonstrate an important dimension.

175

Solutions

MULTIPLE CHOICE QUESTIONS

1. D p. 356

2. B p. 357-358

3. A p. 357

4. B p. 360

5. C p. 362

6. D p. 362

7. A p. 363

8. C p. 363

9. D p. 364

10. A p. 367-369

11. B p. 37150

12. D p. 372

13. C p. 372

14. D p. 373

15. A p. 374

16. D p. 376-377

17. B p. 379

18. A p. 380

19. B p. 381

20. D p. 382

TRUE FALSE QUESTIONS

1. T p. 356

2. T p. 359

3. F p. 361

4. T p. 362

5. F p. 363

6. T p. 365

7. T p. 365

8. F p. 366

9. F p. 367

10. T p. 368

11. T p. 370

12. F p. 370

13. F p. 371

14. F p. 372

15. T p. 376-377

FILL IN THE BLANK QUESTIONS

1. gender

2. hermaphodite

3. transvestite

4. homophobic

5. gender identity

6. sexism

7. bias

8. Gender-segregated

9. comparable worth

10. wage gap

Chapter 12

AGING AND INEQUALITY BASED ON AGE

BRIEF CHAPTER OUTLINE

The Social Significance of Age

- Trends in Aging
- Age in Historical and Contemporary Perspective

Age in Global Perspective

- Hunting and Gathering Societies
- Horticultural, Pastoral, and Agrarian Societies
- Industrial and Postindustrial Societies
- A Case Study: Aging, Gender, and Japanese Society

Age and the Life Course in Contemporary Society

- Infancy and Childhood
- Adolescence
- Young Adulthood
- Middle Adulthood
- Late Adulthood

Inequalities Related to Aging

- Ageism
- Wealth, Poverty, and Aging
- Age, Gender and Inequality
- Age and Race/Ethnicity
- Older People in Rural Areas
- Elder Abuse

Living Arrangements for Older Persons

- Support Services, Homemaker Services, and Day Care
- Housing Alternatives
- Nursing Homes

Sociological Perspectives on Aging

- Functionalist Perspectives on Aging
- Symbolic Interactionist Perspectives on Aging

- Conflict Perspectives on Aging

Death and Dying

Aging in the Future

CHAPTER SUMMARY

Aging is the physical, psychological, and social processes associated with growing older. Over the past two decades, the older U.S. population has been increasing, while the proportion of young people is decreasing. As a result of these changing population trends, research on aging has grown dramatically according to the discipline of **gerontology**, the study of aging and older people. People are assigned roles and positions based on the age structure and role structure in a particular society. In hunting and gathering societies, people typically have shorter life expectancies and all are expected to work. Young people are valuable assets and older people may be perceived as being less productive. In horticultural, pastoral, and agrarian societies, people begin to live longer and begin to accumulate a surplus. However, life is still very hard for most people. In industrial societies, living standards improve and advances in medicine contribute to greater longevity for more people. In postindustrial societies, a shift from a primarily young society to an older society brings about major changes in societal patterns and in the needs of the population. According to a case study, the graying of the Japanese population has taken only 25 years, whereas it took almost a century in North America and Europe. This "graying" of the Japanese population may be bringing about a gradual change in the social importance of the elderly in that nation. Age differentiation in the United States produces **age stratification**: the inequalities, differences, segregation, or conflict between age groups. In contemporary society, various strata of the life course present unique problems at each level. The strata range from infancy and childhood, adolescence, young adulthood, middle adulthood, and late adulthood. **Ageism** -- prejudice and discrimination against people on the basis of age -- is reinforced by stereotypes based on one sided and exaggerated images of older people. Age, gender, and inequality are intertwined. Older women who retire from the work force do not garner economic security for their retirement years at the same rate that many men do. Age, race/ethnicity, and economic inequality are also closely intertwined; the lower income status of older American ethnic minority group members can be traced to patterns of limited economic opportunities throughout their lives. Older people in rural areas are more likely to have lower incomes and tend to be classified as poor. **Elder abuse** includes physical abuse, psychological abuse, financial exploitation, and medical abuse or neglect of people age 65 or older. In examining the living arrangements for older adults, relatives provide most of the care, although support services help older individuals cope with their daily problems. Either by choice or necessity, some older adults move to smaller housing units or apartments. The most restrictive environment for older persons is the nursing home setting, even in a best case scenario. Functionalist explanations of aging -- such as **disengagement theory** -- focus on how older persons adjust to their changing roles in society by detaching themselves from their social role and prepare for their eventual death. **Activity theory** – a symbolic interactionist perspective -- states that people change in late middle age and find substitutes for previous statuses, roles, and activities. Conflict theorists link the loss of status and power experienced by many older persons to their lack of ability to produce and maintain wealth in a capitalist economy. The association of death with the aging process contributes to ageism in our society. Three well-known frameworks explain how people cope with the process of dying: the *stage-based approach*, the *dying trajectory*, and the *task-based approach*. How a person dies is shaped by many social and cultural factors. A **hospice** is an organization that provides a home-like facility or home-based care for people who are terminally ill. Over time, hospice care has moved toward hospital standards. In examining aging in the future, advances in medical technology may lead to a more positive outlook on aging, however with the increase of the aged population and the decrease of the birth rate, concerns over entitlements and other governmental assistance for the aged continue. Classism, racism, sexism, and ageism all restrict individual's access to valued goods and services in society. Older people continue to resist ageism through organizations, such as the Grey Panthers, AARP, and the Older Women's League.

LEARNING OBJECTIVES

After reading Chapter 12, you should be able to:

1. Define aging and explain why research on aging has recently increased.

2. Differentiate between chronological age and functional age and note the social significance of each.

3. Trace recent trends in aging and explain how life expectancy has changed in the United States during the twentieth century.

4. Compare historical and contemporary perspectives on age.

5. Explain the life experiences of older people in hunting and gathering societies and in horticultural, pastoral, and agrarian societies.

6. Describe the changes in industrial and postindustrial societies and how these changes affect older people.

7. Trace the process of aging through the life course, noting the social consequences of age at each stage.

8. Discuss ageism and describe the negative stereotypes associated with older persons.

9. Describe the relationship of wealth, poverty and aging.

10. Describe the relationship between aging and inequality, age, race/ethnicity, and gender.

11. Describe and provide explanations for elder abuse.

12. Explain the typical living arrangements for older persons in the United States.

13. List and describe support services for older persons.

14. Distinguish between functionalist, interactionist, and conflict perspectives on aging.

15. Identify the three major frame works that explain how people cope with death and dying.

KEY TERMS

(defined at page number shown and in glossary)

activity theory 411
age stratification 397
ageism 402
aging 389
chronological age 390
cohort 391
disengagement theory 411

elder abuse 408
entitlements 406
functional age 390
gerontology 392
hospice 415
life expectancy 391

KEY PEOPLE

(identified at page number shown)

Elaine C. Cumming and William E. Henry 411
Anne Fausto Sterling 399
Melissa A. Hardy and Lawrence E. Hazelrigg 405
Madonna Harrington Meyer 410

Elisabeth Kubler Ross 414
William C. Levin 404
Patricia Moore 404
William J. Wilson 399

CHAPTER OUTLINE

I. THE SOCIAL SIGNIFICANCE OF AGE

    A. **Aging** is the physical, psychological, and social processes associated with growing older.

    B. **Chronological age** is a person's age based on date of birth; functional age is observable physical attributes (physical appearance, mobility, etc.) that are used to assign people to age categories.

    C. There are significant differences in **life expectancy** -- the average length of time a group of individuals of the same age will live -- based on racial ethnic and sex differences.

    D. Social gerontology is the study of the social (non physical) aspects of aging; gerontology is the study of aging and older people.

    E. While young persons historically were considered "little adults" and were expected to do adult work, today the skills necessary for many roles are more complex and the number of unskilled positions is more limited.

    F. **Age stratification** refers to the inequalities, differences, segregation, or conflict between age groups.

II. AGE IN GLOBAL PERSPECTIVE

    A. In hunting and gathering societies, people typically have shorter life expectancies and all people are expected to work.

        1. Young people are assets in the nomadic lifestyle involved in hunting wild game.

        2. Older people may be perceived as being less productive.

    B. In horticultural, pastoral, and agrarian societies, death rates begin to decline.

1.   More people reach older ages, but life is still very hard.

2.   Accumulating a surplus becomes possible and older individuals, especially men, are often the most privileged in society.

3.   In agrarian societies, food surplus, because of farming, makes it possible for more people to live to adulthood and old age; in these societies, most older people live with the other family members.

C.   In industrial societies, living standards improve and advances in medicine contribute to greater longevity for more people while in postindustrial societies, a shift from a primarily young society to an older society brings about major changes in societal patterns and in the needs of the population.

D.   The graying of the Japanese population has taken only twenty-five years, whereas it took almost a century in North America and Europe.

1.   The sociocultural change and population shift may bring about gradual change in the social importance of the elderly in Japan.

2.   With over 60 percent of Japanese women in the labor force, greater pressure is being placed on Japanese policy makers to consider how the government can play a larger role in the care of the aging population rather than that care placed completely on the family, especially women.

III.   AGE AND THE LIFE COURSE IN CONTEMPORARY SOCIETY

A.   Infancy and childhood are typically thought of as carefree years; however children are among the most powerless and vulnerable people in society.

1.   Early socialization plays a significant part in children's experiences and their quality of life.

2.   Two-thirds of all childhood deaths are caused by injury; far too many children lose their lives at an early age due to the abuse, neglect, or negligence of adults.

B.   Adolescence roughly spans the teenage years; today it is a period in which young people are expected to continue their education and perhaps hold a part-time job.

1.   A variety of reports have labeled contemporary U.S. teenagers as a "generation at risk" because of many social problems, including crime and violence, teenage pregnancy, suicide, drug abuse and peer pressure.

2.   One way to save the adolescent generation of today is to reduce poverty among them and their families.

C.   Young Adulthood follows adolescence and lasts to about age 39.

1.   During this time, people are expected to get married, have children, and get a job.

2.   People who are unable to earn income and pay into social security or other retirement plans in early adulthood become disadvantaged in later life.

D.   Middle Adulthood--roughly the ages of 40 to 65--did not exist in the United States until recently.

1.   The process of *senescence*, primary aging, occurs at this time.

2.   Women under go *menopause* (the cessation of the menstrual cycle); men undergo a *climacteric* in which the production of the "male" hormone levels produces nervousness and depression.

3.   On the positive side, for some people, middle adulthood represents the time period of having the highest levels of income and prestige.

E.   Late adulthood is generally considered to begin at age 65--the "normal" retirement age.

1.   *Retirement* is the institutionalized separation of an individual from an occupational position, with continuation of income through a retirement pension based on prior years of service.

2.   Some gerontologists subdivide late adulthood into three categories: (1) the "young-old (ages 65-74); (2) the "old-old (ages 75-85); and (3) the "oldest-old" (over age 85).

3.   The rate of biological and psychological changes in older persons may be as important as their chronological age in determining how they are perceived by themselves. A loss of height, impaired ability to function, heart attacks, strokes, and cancer are not uncommon at this stage of life; these changes can cause stress.

4.   Late adulthood may turn into a time of despair or one of integrity.

IV.   INEQUALITIES RELATED TO AGING

A.   **Ageism** -- prejudice and discrimination against people on the basis of age, particularly when they are older persons -- is reinforced by stereotypes of older persons as cranky, sickly, and lacking in social value.

B.   If we compare wealth (all economic resources of value) with income (available money or its purchasing power), we find that older people tend to have more wealth but less income than younger people; among older people, there is a wider range of assets and income than in other age categories.

C.   Age, gender, and inequality are intertwined; although middle-aged and older women make up an increasing portion of the work force, they are paid much less than men their age, receive raises at a slower rate, and still work largely in gender-segregated jobs.

D.   Ninety percent of all retired people in the U.S. draw Social Security benefits, which are a form of **entitlements** -- benefits paid by the government. Supplemental Social Income, Medicaid, civil service pensions, and Medicare are among the primary entitlements for those over the age of 65. Medicare is a nationwide health care program for persons age 65 and over who participate in Social Security or "buy into" the program.

E.   Age, race/ethnicity and economic inequality are closely intertwined.

1.   The lower income states of old American ethnic minority group members can be traced to patterns of limited economic opportunities throughout their lives.

F.   Older people in rural areas are more likely to have lower incomes and tend to be classified as poor.

1.   The rural elderly have lower lifetime earnings, limited savings, and fewer opportunities for part-time work.

2.   The homes of the rural elderly have lower value and are in greater need of repair.

G.   **Elder abuse** refers to physical abuse, psychological abuse, financial exploitation, and medical abuse or neglect of people age 65 or over.

V.   LIVING ARRANGEMENTS FOR OLDER ADULTS

A.   Support services, homemaker services and day care centers help older people cope with the problems of daily care.

B.   Nursing homes are the most restrictive environments for older persons.

　　1.   Financing of long-term care is a problem for most older persons.

　　2.   Medicare excludes most long-term care; most private insurance policies also exclude long-term care.

　　3.   Even the best-run nursing homes deny the personhood of age.

VI.   SOCIOLOGICAL PERSPECTIVES ON AGING

A.   Functionalists examine how older persons adjust to their changing roles. According to **disengagement theory**, older persons make a normal and healthy adjustment to aging when they detach themselves from their social roles and prepare for their eventual death.

B.   **Activity theory** – a symbolic interactionist perspective on aging -- states that people tend to shift gears in later life and find substitutes for previous statuses, roles, and activities.

C.   Conflict theorists note that, as people grow older, their power tends to diminish unless they are able to maintain their wealth. Consequently, those who have been disadvantaged in their younger years become even more so in late adulthood.

VII.   DEATH AND DYING

A.   In contemporary industrial societies, death is looked on as unnatural because it has been removed from everyday life: most deaths occur among older persons and in institutionalized settings.

B.   Three well-known frameworks provide explanations of how people cope with the process of dying.

　　1.   The *stage-based approach*, popularized by Elizabeth Kubler-Ross, who proposed five stages in the dying process:

　　　　a.   denial ("Not me!");

　　　　b.   anger ("Why me?");

　　　　c.   bargaining ("Yes me, but....");

　　　　d.   depression and sense of loss; and

　　　　e.   acceptance.

　　2.   The *dying trajectory*, which focuses on the perceived course of dying and the expected time of death.

　　3.   The *task-based approach* is based on the assumption that the dying person can and should go about daily activities and completing physical, social, or spiritual tasks.

C.   A **hospice** is a homelike facility that provides supportive care for patients with terminal illnesses; over time hospice care has moved toward hospital standards.

VIII.   AGING IN THE FUTURE

A.   By the year 2050, there will be approximately 80 million persons age 65 and over, as compared with 35 million in 2000. More people will survive to age 85 -- or even 95 and over.

B. A 1994 report warned that this increase (coupled with a decreasing birth rate) may result in entitlements consuming nearly all federal tax revenues by the year 2012, leaving the government with no money for anything else.

C. New biomedical research discoveries may lead to more positive aging; however, many of the benefits and opportunities of living in a highly technological, affluent society are not available to all.

PRACTICE TESTS

MULTIPLE CHOICE QUESTIONS

Type Question Instructions

1. All of the following statements regarding aging are correct, **except**:

    a. Aging is the physical, psychological, and social processes associated with growing older.

    b. Aging is an inevitable consequence of living.

    c. Aging is a socially significant process.

    d. In the United States, aging is valued status.

2. _____ age refers to a person's age based on date of birth; by contrast, _____ age refers to observable individual attributes such as physical appearance, mobility, strength, coordination, and mental capacity that are used to assign people to age categories.

    a. Obvious - subjective

    b. Subjective - obvious

    c. Chronological - functional

    d. Functional - chronological

3. The median age of the U.S. population is:

    a. increasing due to an increase in life expectancy combined with a decrease in birth rates.

    b. decreasing due to an increase in birth rates.

    c. roughly the same as it had been for most of the twentieth century due to stabilization of both birth and death rates.

    d. unaffected by the aging of the Baby Boomers.

4. Two hundred years ago, the age spectrum was divided into:

    a. babyhood and adulthood.

    b. babyhood, a very short childhood, and adulthood.

    c. babyhood, childhood, adulthood, and old age.

    d. infancy, childhood, adolescence, adulthood, and old age.

5. In postindustrial societies, the largest employers are in the fields of _____ and _____ which may benefit older people.

    a.   health; agriculture

    b.   education; health

    c.   education; textile production

    d.   textile production; service industries

6. In the USA most of all childhood deaths today are caused by:

    a.   HIV/AIDS.

    b.   injuries.

    c.   communicable diseases.

    d.   birth defects.

7. According to the text, middle adulthood represents the time when many people:

    a.   are strapped for cash because their children are in college.

    b.   may have grandchildren who give them another tie to the future.

    c.   have a decline in income as they approach their retirement years.

    d.   grow discontented with their spouse of many years.

8. Which of the following statements is **correct** regarding Alzheimer's disease?

    a.   Most older people suffer from Alzheimer's disease.

    b.   Most people with Alzheimer's disease have an extremely short life expectancy.

    c.   About 55 percent of all organic mental disorders in the older population are caused by Alzheimer's disease.

    d.   In 1995, researchers found a possible cure for Alzheimer's disease.

9. According to Erik Erikson, older people must resolve a tension of _____ versus _____ in their lives.

    a.   integrity - despair

    b.   activity - disengagement

    c.   stability - change

    d.   autonomy - entitlements

10. Ageism is:

    a.   prejudice and discrimination against people on the basis of age, particularly when they are younger persons.

    b.   prejudice and discrimination against people on the basis of age, particularly when they are older persons.

    c.   gradually being overcome by positive depictions of older persons in the media.

    d.   experienced equally by both women and men.

11. When Patricia Moore, at age 27, disguised herself as an 85-year-old woman and went to a grocery store, she learned that:

    a. people permitted her to go to the head of the checkout line because of her age.

    b. grocery store clerks treated her as a preferred customer.

    c. people tried to have as little to do with her as possible.

    d. other people's reactions to her changed when she played the role of an older person.

12. In a recent study, gerontologists Melissa H. Hardy and Lawrence E. Hazelrigg found that:

    a. gender is more directly related to poverty in older persons than is race/ethnicity, educational background, or occupational status.

    b. race/ethnicity is more directly related to poverty in older persons than is gender, educational background, or occupational status.

    c. educational background is more directly related to poverty in older persons than is gender, race/ethnicity, or occupational status.

    d. occupational status is more directly related to poverty in older persons than is gender, race/ethnicity, or educational background.

13. **All** of the following statements are **correct** regarding elder abuse, **except**:

    a. abuse and neglect of older persons has received increasing public attention in recent years.

    b. financial exploitation is a form of elder abuse.

    c. more than 1.6 million older people in the United States are victims of elder abuse.

    d. nursing home personnel are the most frequent abusers of older persons.

14. In her analysis of the financing of nursing home care, sociologist Madonna Harrington Meyer concluded that the United States has a long-term care system that is based on and perpetuates:

    a. racial inequality.

    b. class inequality.

    c. gender inequality.

    d. all of the above.

15. Functionalist perspectives on aging focus on:

    a. how older persons adjust to their changing roles in society.

    b. the connection between personal satisfaction in a person's later years and a high level of activity.

    c. reasons why aging is especially problematic in contemporary capitalist societies.

    d. how people are consigned to the sick role.

16. _____ theory states that people tend to shift gears in late middle age and find substitutes for previous statuses, roles, and activities.

    a. Continuity

    b. Disengagement

    c. Activity

    d. Engagement

17. _____ theorists view aging as problematic in contemporary capitalistic societies.
    a. Functionalist
    b. Activity
    c. Conflict
    d. Symbolic Interactionalists

18. The _____ framework focuses on the perceived course of dying and the expected time of death.
    a. Dying trajectory
    b. Stage-based approach
    c. Task-based approach
    d. Kubler-Ross approach

19. All of the following about hospice care are true **except**:
    a. a hospice provides care for the terminally ill.
    b. overtime, hospice care has moved away from hospital standards.
    c. hospice philosophy asserts that people should participate in their own care and control.
    d. the approach is family based.

20. All of the following are organizations fighting ageism except:
    a. Gray Panthers.
    b. Aged United.
    c. Older Women's League.
    d. American Association of Retired Persons.

TRUE FALSE QUESTIONS

1. A group of people born within a specific period in time is known as a cohort.
   True or False

2. As men age, they are believed to become less powerful when compared to women.
   True or False

3. About 4 percent of the U.S. population was over age 65 in 1993; by 2000, that population increased by 15 percent.
   True or False

4. Gerontology is the study of the non physical aspects of aging.
   True or False

5. In hunting and gathering societies, the elderly have great prestige because they accumulate a surplus of goods.
   True or False

6. The graying of Japan has taken longer than in North America and Europe.
   True or False

7. Adolescence is a twentieth century concept.
   True or False

8. In the USA, young adulthood lasts to about age 39.
   True or False

9. Few of the wealthiest people in the United States are over 65 years of age.
   True or False

10. Age, race/ethnicity, gender, and economic inequality are interrelated.
    True or False

11. Nearly half of all women over age sixty-five are widowed and living alone on fixed incomes.
    True or False

12. According to analysts, Social Security keeps more white men out of poverty than it does white women and people of color.
    True or False

13. Older Native Americans are among the most disadvantaged of all categories.
    True or False

14. The most restrictive environment for older persons is the nursing home setting.
    True or False

15. Over time, the hospice movement has moved away from hospital standards to more home-based care.
    True or False

FILL IN THE BLANK QUESTIONS

1. A person's age based on date of birth is one's _____ age, while observable individual attributes is one's _____ age.

2. The average number of years that a group of people born in the same year could be expected to live is known as _____ .

3. A group of people born within a specific period of time is known as a _____ .

4. The study of aging and older people is known as _____ .

5. The inequalities differences, segregation, or conflict between age groups is known as _____ .

6. Prejudice and discrimination against people on the basis of age is termed _____ .

7. Certain benefit payments paid by the government are known as _____ .

8. A _____ is a document stating people's wishes about the medical circumstances under which their lives might end.

9. Phyciatrist _____ proposed a five stage theory of the process of dying.

10. A _____ is an organization that provides home-based or a home like facility care for terminally-ill people.

SHORT ANSWER/ESSAY QUESTIONS

1. Is the United States graying? If so, what is the significance of this graying?

2. How are race, class, gender, and aging related?

3. What is the typical living arrangement for older adults in the United States?

4. What are some examples of ageism in the United States?

5. What are some examples of problems of the elderly, primarily problems of elderly women?

STUDENT CLASS PROJECTS AND ACTIVITIES

1. Conduct research on the history of the original Social Security legislation in our country. In your research, examine these issues and provide responses to the following questions: (1) What was the original purpose of the act, and what were the major provisions of the act? (2) Did most legislators support the act? Why? (3) What groups were opponents of the act? (4) What was the political position of the President toward the act? (5) What year did the legislation become law? (6) Why? (7) Why was the United States one of the last industrialized nations in the world to provide its elderly citizens with old-age insurance? (8) What western country was the first to enact old-age benefits? (9) List at least ten different countries that had some type of old-age insurance programs before the United States. (10) How was the program originally funded? What did the employer contribute? (11) How did workers become eligible for full benefits? (12) Evaluate the effectiveness of this legislation. Did it meet its goals? Why? Why not? (13) Personally critique this act. Do you agree with the premises of Social Security? Why? Why not? Submit your written paper to your instructor at the appropriate time, following any instructions given to you by your instructor.

2. You should conduct research of an old-age insurance program found in one other country for the purpose of comparing the current state of its program with the current "crisis" of Social Security in the United States. Some possible choices: Germany, Denmark, Sweden, United Kingdom, Austria, France, Ireland, Italy, Spain, Belgium, Greece, the Netherlands, New Zealand, Australia, and Japan. Examine the history of the legislation, and answer the following questions: (1) What was the purpose of the act, and what were the major provisions of the act? (2) What groups supported the act? Why? (3) What groups opposed the act? Why? (4) What was the political climate of the time; did the leader of the country support the act? Why? (5) When did the act become law? (6) How is the program financed? (7) How do people qualify for the program? (8) What is its current status? Are there any indications of a financial crisis for the program? (9) Briefly compare this country's program with that of the Social Security program in the United States. Are there any similarities? Some differences? (10) Provide any other information that will enhance the research, including a conclusion and a personal evaluation. Submit your paper, following your instructor's guidelines, at the appropriate time.

3. Choose at least two elderly people who are accessible to you (such as grandparents, neighbors, retired faculty, etc.) and interview them about their experiences in aging. If they do not object, you may use a tape recorder to record the interview. In the interview, ask them to describe some of the important events that occurred in their childhood, adolescence, adulthood, and most recently, in the past several years. For consistency in your interviews and written papers, answer the each of these questions: (1) How do they describe themselves? (2) What has been some of the most important events in their lives? Remember to cover childhood, adolescence, and adulthood. (3) How do members of their family, friends, and other people treat them? Is this different from previous times? How? (4) Do they think of themselves as old? Why? Why not? (5) What is one thing that they like about their lives today? (6) What is one thing that they liked about their yesteryear life? (7) What type of celebrations was most important in their lives? Describe them. (8)What was the most significant event in their life up to this point? (9) What is one thing they would change if they could? (10) What is one thing they would never change? (11) How do they think the majority of society views them today? How do they feel about this view? (12) Do they have any additional statements or thoughts they would like to make? Summarize the major points of the interviews and present this information in a written paper. Submit your paper to your instructor at the appropriate time.

INTERNET ACTIVITIES

1. To learn more about research being conducted on **aging**, go the site for the National Institute on Aging. Click on *Research Programs* (behavioral and social research) to read about current research on **aging**. Look for research on myths about **aging** and how drug costs affect the elderly. www.nia.nih.gov/

2. A very powerful interest group is the AARP (The American Association of Retired Persons). Click on *AARP* in your state and then select either a region or your state specifically to read about the services that are provided by the AARP to members. Next, select some other states for purposes of comparison-e.g., Florida and Arizona have large older populations-does the AARP have a stronger presence in those states, or offer more services? www.aarp.org

3. The Administration on Aging also provides extensive information on **aging** for professionals in the field of **aging**, service providers, and policy makers, as well as older Americans themselves. www.aoa.dhhs.gov

4. You can calculate your own **life expectancy** from the *Living to 100 Life Expectancy Calculator* web site. www.livingto100.com/

5. To find health related research, e.g., research on Alzheimer's, go to the National Institute of Health website and do a search for **aging** research. www.nih.gov/

INFOTRAC EXERCISES

1. Look for newspaper articles on **Age Discrimination**. Compare these with research articles on the same topic. Does it appear that the general public really understands this issue?

2. Examine research on **Elder Abuse** in the home and in nursing homes. Take a look at the *California Elder Abuse and Dependent Adult Civil Protection Act*. What factors seem to contribute to **elder abuse**?

3. Write an essay on the **Social Aspects of Aging**. There are a number of journal and news articles on this sub field.

4. Look for articles that explore **Aging** in other countries, especially Asian countries.

Chapter 12

Solutions

MULTIPLE CHOICE QUESTIONS

1. D p. 389

2. C p. 391

3. A p. 391

4. B p. 392

5. B p. 395

6. B p. 398

7. B p. 400

8. C p. 401

9. A p. 402

10. B p. 402

11. C p. 405

12. A p. 405

13. D p. 408

14. D p. 410

15. A p. 411

16. C p. 411

17. C p. 413

18. A p. 414

19. A p.415

20. B p. 416

TRUE FALSE QUESTIONS

1. T p. 391

2. F p. 390

3. F p. 391

4. T p. 392

5. F p. 394

6. F p. 395

7. T p. 398

8. T p. 399

9. F p. 405

10. T p. 408

11. T p. 406

12. T p. 406

13. T p. 407

14. T p. 410

15. F p. 415

FILL IN THE BLANK QUESTIONS

1. chronological , functional

2. life expectancy

3. cohort

4. gerontology

5. age stratification

6. agism

7. entitlement

8. living will

9. Elizabeth Kübler-Ross

10. hospice

Chapter 13

THE ECONOMY AND WORK IN GLOBAL PERSPECTIVE

BRIEF CHAPTER OUTLINE

Comparing the Sociology of Economic Life with Economics

Economic Systems in Global Perspective

- Preindustrial Economies

- Industrial Economies

- Postindustrial Economies

Contemporary Economic Systems

- Capitalism

- Socialism

- Mixed Economies

Perspectives on Economy and Work in the United States

- Functionalist Perspective

- Conflict Perspective

- Symbolic Interactionist Perspective

The Social Organization of Work

- Occupations

- Professions

- Managers and the Managed

- The Lower Tier of the Service Sector and Marginal Jobs

- Contingent Work

Unemployment

Worker Resistance and Activism

- Labor Unions

- Absenteeism, Sabotage, and Resistance

Employment Opportunities for Persons with a Disability

The Global Economy in the Future

- The U.S. Economy

- Global Economic Interdependence and Competition

CHAPTER SUMMARY

While economists attempt to explain how the limited resources and efforts of a society are allocated among competing ends, sociologists focus on interconnections among the economy, other social institutions, and the social organization of work, at both the microlevel and the macrolevel of analysis. The **economy** is the social institution that ensures the maintenance of society through the production, distribution, and consumption of goods and services. Preindustrial economies are characterized by **primary sector production** in which workers extract raw materials and natural resources from the environment and use them without much processing. Industrial economies engage in **secondary sector production**, which is based on the processing of raw materials (from the primary sector) into finished goods. The economic base in postindustrial economies shifts to **tertiary sector production** -- the provision of services rather than goods. As an ideal type, **capitalism** has four distinctive features: private ownership of the means of production, pursuit of personal profit, competition, and lack of government intervention. **Socialism** is characterized by public ownership of the means of production, the pursuit of collective goals, and centralized decision making. In a **mixed economy**, elements of a capitalist, market economy are combined with elements of a command, socialist economy. Mixed economies are often referred to as **democratic socialism** -- an economic and political system that combines private ownership of some of the means of production, governmental distribution of some essential goods and services, and free elections. For many people, jobs and professions are key sources of identity. Functionalists, conflict theories, and symbolic interactionists view the economy and the nature of work from a variety of perspectives. In examining how societies organize work, analysts find that as societies grow larger in population and more complex in their division of labor, different categories of work are identified. **Occupations** are categories of jobs that involve similar activities at different work sites. **Professions** are high status, knowledge based occupations characterized by abstract, specialized knowledge, autonomy, authority over clients and subordinate occupational groups, and a degree of altruism. Those in managerial occupations typically are responsible for workers, physical plants, equipment, and the finances of a bureaucratic organization. **Marginal jobs** are those that do not comply with the following employment norms: job content should be legal, jobs should be covered by government regulations, jobs should be relatively permanent, and jobs should provide adequate hours and pay in order to make a living. **Contingent work** is part time work, temporary work, and **subcontracted work** that offers advantages to employers but may be detrimental to workers. **Unemployment** remains a problem for many workers. There are three types of unemployment – cyclical, seasonal, and structural. The **unemployment rate** is the percentage of unemployed persons in the labor force actively seeking jobs. U.S. labor unions have been credited with improving their work environment and gaining some measure of control over their work-related activities. Many workers have joined unions in order to gain strength through collective actions. The number of persons in the U.S. having physical or mental disabilities is increasing. In 1990, the United States became the first nation to formally address the issue of equality for persons with a disability. Future trends of the U.S. economy and the global economy all indicate that the U.S. will remain a major player in the world economy and that transnational corporations will become even more significant. A global workplace is emerging in which telecommunications networks will link workers in distant location; however, the prospects for greater income equality do not appear hopeful.

LEARNING OBJECTIVES

After reading Chapter 13, you should be able to:

1. Describe the purpose of the economy and distinguish between sociological perspectives on the economy and the study of economics.

2. Trace the major global historical changes that have occurred in economic systems and note the most prevalent form of production found in each.

3. Describe the four distinctive features of "ideal" capitalism and explain why pure capitalism does not exist.

4. Discuss socialism and describe its major characteristics.

5. Compare and contrast capitalism, socialism, and mixed economies.

6. Distinguish between the functionalist, conflict, and symbolic interactionist perspectives on the economy and work in the United States.

7. Describe job satisfaction and alienation, and explain the impact of each on workers.

8. Distinguish between the primary and secondary labor markets and describe the types of jobs found in each.

9. Discuss the major characteristics of professions and describe the process of deprofessionalization.

10. Compare scientific management (Taylorism) with mass production through automation (Fordism), noting the strengths and weaknesses of each.

11. Identify the occupational categories considered to be marginal jobs and explain why they are considered to be marginal.

12. Discuss contingent work and identify the role subcontracting often plays in contingent work.

13. Distinguish between the various types of unemployment and explain why the unemployment rate may not be a true reflection of unemployment in the United States.

14. Trace the development of labor unions and describe some of the means by which workers resist working conditions they consider to be oppressive.

15. Examine employment opportunities for persons with a disability and explain why the numbers of persons with a disability continue to increase.

16. Describe the U.S. and the global economy in the future.

KEY TERMS

(defined at page number shown and in glossary)

KEY PEOPLE

(identified at page number shown)

CHAPTER OUTLINE

I. COMPARING THE SOCIOLOGY OF ECONOMIC LIFE WITH ECONOMICS
   A. Economists attempt to explain how the limited resources and efforts of a society are allocated among competing ends; sociologists focus on interconnections between the economy, other social institutions, and the social organization of work.
   B. At the macrolevel, sociologists may study the impact of transnational corporations on industrial and low-income nations; at the microlevel, they may study people's satisfaction with their jobs.

II. ECONOMIC SYSTEMS IN GLOBAL PERSPECTIVES
   A. The **economy** is the social institution that ensures the maintenance of society through the production, distribution, and consumption of goods and services.
   B. In preindustrial societies, most workers engage in **primary sector production** -- the extraction of raw materials and natural resources from the environment.
   C. Industrialization brings sweeping changes to the economy as new forms of energy and machine technology proliferate as the primary means of producing goods and most workers engage in **secondary sector production** -- processing raw materials into finished goods.

D.   A postindustrial economy is based on tertiary sector production -- the provision of services (such as food service, transportation, communication, education, and entertainment) rather than goods.

III.   CONTEMPORARY ECONOMIC SYSTEMS

A.   **Capitalism** is an economic system characterized by private ownership of the means of production, from which personal profits can be derived through market competition and without government intervention.

B.   "Ideal" capitalism has four distinctive features:

1.   Private ownership of the means of production

2.   Pursuit of personal profit

3.   Competition; and

4.   Lack of government intervention.

C.   However, ideal capitalism does not exist in the U.S. for a number of reasons, including the presence of:

1.   **Oligopolies** -- where several companies control an entire industry.

2.   **Shared monopolies** -- where four or fewer companies supply 50 percent or more of a particular market.

3.   Mergers and acquisitions across industries create **conglomerates** -- combinations of businesses in different commercial areas, all owned by one holding company.

4.   Competition also is reduced by **interlocking corporate directorates** -- members of the board of directors of one corporation who also sit on the board(s) of other corporations.

5.   Government intervention often occurs in the form of regulations after some individuals and companies in pursuit of profits have run roughshod over weaker competitors; however, much "government intervention" has been in the form of aid to business (tax credits, loan guarantees, etc.).

D.   **Socialism** is an economic system characterized by public ownership of the means of production, the pursuit of collective goals, and centralized decision making.

E.   "Ideal" socialism has three distinctive features:

1.   Public ownership of the means of production

2.   Pursuit of collective goals; and

3.   Centralized decision making.

F.   A **mixed economy** combines elements of a market economy (capitalism) with elements of a command economy (socialism).

IV.   PERSPECTIVES ON ECONOMY AND WORK IN THE UNITED STATES

A.   From a functionalist perspective, the economy is a vital social institution because it is the means by which goods and services are produced and distributed.

1.   When the economy runs smoothly, other parts of society function more effectively; however, if the system becomes unbalanced, a maladjustment occurs.

2.   The business cycle is the rise and fall of economic activity relative to long term growth in the economy.

B. From a conflict perspective, business cycles are the result of capitalist greed; in order to maximize profits, capitalists suppress the wages of workers.
   1. As the prices of the products increase, the workers are not able to purchase them in the quantities that have been produced.
   2. Consequently, surpluses occur that cause capitalists to reduce production, close factories, lay off workers, and thus contribute to the growth of the reserve army of the unemployed which then helps to reduce the wages of the remaining workers. In some situations, workers are replaced with machines or nonunionized workers.
C. Symbolic interactionists examine factors that contribute to worker satisfaction.
   1. Work is an important source of self-identity for many people.
   2. Work can help people feel positive about themselves or it can cause them to feel alienated.
   3. Job satisfaction is highest when employees have some degree of control over their work, when they feel that they are part of the decision-making process, when they are not too closely supervised, and when they fell they play an important part in the outcome.

V. THE SOCIAL ORGANIZATION OF WORK
   A. Sociologists who focus on microlevel analysis are interested in how the economic system and the social organization of work affect people's attitudes and behavior. Interactionists examine factors that contribute to job satisfaction or feelings of alienation.
   B. Job Satisfaction and Alienation
      1. Job satisfaction refers to an attitude that people experience about their work, which results from (a) their job responsibilities, (b) the organizational structure in which they work, and (c) their individual needs and values.
      2. Self actualization occurs when people feel a sense of accomplishment and fulfillment as a result of their work. Studies have found that worker satisfaction is highest when employees have some degree of control over their work and are not too closely supervised.
      3. Alienation occurs when workers' needs for identity and meaning are not met, and when work is done strictly for material gain, not a sense of personal satisfaction.
   C. **Occupations** are categories of jobs that involve similar activities at different work sites.
      1. The **primary labor market** is comprised of high paying jobs with good benefits that have some degree of security and the possibility for future advancement.
      2. The **secondary labor market** is comprised of low paying jobs with few benefits and very little job security or possibility for future advancement.
   D. **Professions** are high-status, knowledge-based occupations that have five major characteristics:
      1. Abstract, specialized knowledge
      2. Autonomy
      3. Self-regulation
      4. Authority
      5. Altruism.

E.   The term "manager" often is used to refer to executives, managers, and administrators who typically have responsibility for workers, physical plants, equipment, and the financial aspects of a bureaucratic organization.

1.   Scientific Management (Taylorism) was developed by industrial engineer **Frederick Winslow Taylor** to increase productivity in factories by teaching workers to perform a task in a concise series of steps; paying workers only for the number of units they produced also contributed to the success of Taylorism.

2.   Mass Production through Automation (Fordism) incorporated hierarchical authority structures and scientific management techniques into the manufacturing process. Assembly lines, machines, and robots became a means of technical control over the work process.

F.   Lower Tier of the Service Sector and Marginal Jobs.

1.   Positions in the lower tier of the service sector are part of the **secondary labor market**, characterized by low wages, little job security, few chances for advancement, higher unemployment, and very limited (if any) unemployment benefits.

2.   Examples include janitors, waitresses, messengers, lower-level sales clerks, typists, file clerks, migrant laborers, and textile workers.

3.   Many jobs in this sector are **marginal jobs** that differ from the employment norms of the society in which they are located. In the U.S., these norms are: (a) job content is legal; (b) the job is covered by government work regulations; (c) the job is relatively permanent; and (d) the job provides adequate pay with sufficient hours of work each week to make a living.

4.   More than 11 million workers are employed in personal service industries, such as eating and drinking places, hotels, laundries, beauty shops, and household service, primarily maid service.

G.   **Contingent work** is part time work, temporary work, and subcontracted work that offers advantages to employers but often is detrimental to the welfare of workers.

1.   Employers benefit by hiring workers on a part time or temporary basis; they are able to cut costs, maximize profits, and have workers available only when they need them.

2.   **Subcontracting** -- a form of economic organization in which a larger corporation contracts with other (usually smaller) firms to provide specialized components, product, or services -- is another form of contingent work that cuts employers costs but often at the expense of workers.

VI.   UNEMPLOYMENT

A.   There are three major types of unemployment: (1) cyclical unemployment occurs as a result of lower rates of production during recessions in the business cycle; (2) seasonal unemployment results from shifts in the demand for workers based on conditions such as weather or seasonal demands such as holidays and summer vacations; and (3) structural unemployment which arises because the skills demanded by employers do not match the skills of the unemployed or because the unemployed do not live where the jobs are located.

B. The **unemployment rate** is the percentage of unemployed persons in the labor force actively seeking jobs.

C. Unemployment compensation provides unemployed workers with short term income while they look for other jobs.

VII. WORKER RESISTANCE AND ACTIVISM

    A. Labor Unions

        1. U.S. labor unions have been credited with gaining an eight hour work day, a five day work week, health and retirement benefits, sick leave and unemployment insurance, and workplace health and safety standards for many employees through **collective bargaining** -- negotiations between labor union leaders and employers on behalf of workers.

        2. Although the overall number of union members in the United States has increased since the 1960s, the proportion of all employees who are union members has declined.

    B. Absenteeism, Sabotage, and Resistance

        1. Absenteeism is one means by which workers resist working conditions they consider to be oppressive.

        2. Other workers use sabotage to bring about informal work stoppages, such as "throwing a monkey wrench in the gears" to halt the movement of the assembly line.

        3. While most workers do not sabotage machinery, a significant number do resist what they perceive to be oppression from supervisors and employers.

VIII. EMPLOYMENT OPPORTUNITIES FOR PERSONS WITH A DISABILITY

    A. The number of persons in the United States having physical or mental disabilities is increasing because:

        1. Advances in medical technology now make survival possible.

        2. As people live longer they are more likely to experience disabling diseases.

        3. Persons born with serious disabilities are more likely to survive infancy.

    B. In 1990, the United States passed the Americans with Disabilities Act.

        1. The ADA forbids discrimination on the basis of disability.

        2. Despite the law, about two-thirds of working-age persons with a disability in the U.S.A. are unemployed today.

IX. THE GLOBAL ECONOMY IN THE FUTURE

    A. The U.S. economy will experience dramatic changes in the next century as workers may find themselves fighting for a larger piece of an ever shrinking economic pie which includes trade deficit and a large national debt.

    B. Workers increasingly may be fragmented into two major divisions -- those who work in the innovative, primary sector and those whose jobs are located in the growing secondary, marginal sector of the labor market.

    C. Most futurists predict that economic interdependence and competition will become even more significant in the global economy of the future, and multinational corporations will become even less aligned with the values of any one nation.

PRACTICE TESTS

MULTIPLE CHOICE QUESTIONS

Select the response that best answers the question or completes the statement:

1. The _____ is the social institution that ensures the maintenance of society through the production, distribution, and consumption of goods and services.

    a. economy

    b. government

    c. state

    d. political arena

2. The owner of a large corporation has amassed several million dollars that she utilizes in expanding her enterprise. This wealth is referred to as:

    a. services.

    b. labor.

    c. goods.

    d. capital.

3. Most of sub-Saharan Africa is highly dependant on _____ sector production.

    a. primary

    b. secondary

    c. tertiary

    d. quartiary

4. Industrial economies are characterized by _____ sector production.

    a. primary

    b. secondary

    c. tertiary

    d. quartiary

5. According to Census 2000, the majority of U.S. jobs are in:

    a. service occupations.

    b. sales and office occupations.

    c. management, professional, and related occupations.

    d. production, transportation, and material moving occupations.

6. According to the text, all of the following are features of capitalism, **except**:

    a. private ownership of the means of production.

    b. pursuit of personal profit.

    c. competition.

    d. governmental intervention in the marketplace.

7. Huge corporations developed during the period of:

    a. early capitalism.

    b. early monopoly capitalism.

    c. advanced monopoly capitalism.

    d. post capitalism.

8. If Sony, Philips, Time Warner, and only a few other companies control the entire music industry, this arrangement would be a(n):

    a. oligopoly.

    b. monopoly.

    c. conglomerate.

    d. amalgamation.

9. _____ is an economic system characterized by public ownership of the means of production, the pursuit of collective goals, and centralized decision making.

    a. Capitalism

    b. Communism

    c. Socialism

    d. Communitarianism

10. Democratic socialism is characterized by:

    a. extensive government action to provide support and services to its citizens.

    b. private ownership of the means of production, from which personal profits can be derived through market competition and without government intervention.

    c. public ownership of the means of production, the pursuit of collective goals, and centralized decision making.

    d. private ownership of some of the means of production, governmental distribution of some essential goods and services, and free elections.

11. According to the _____ perspective, when the economy runs smoothly, other parts of society function more effectively.

    a. conflict

    b. functionalist

    c. interactionist

    d. neo Marxist

12. Job satisfaction refers to people's attitudes toward their work, based on:

    a. their job responsibilities.

    b. the organizational structure in which they work.

    c. their individual needs and values.

    d. all of the above.

13. Studies have found that job satisfaction is highest when workers:
    a. have some degree of control over their work.
    b. are removed from the decision making process.
    c. know that their supervisors closely watch all aspects of their work.
    d. do not feel the pressure of playing an important part in the outcome.

14. All of the following are characteristics of professions, **except**:
    a. broad based knowledge on a wide variety of topics.
    b. authority.
    c. concern for others, not just self interest.
    d. self regulation.

15. Scientific management (Taylorism) is characterized by:
    a. mass production.
    b. automation.
    c. time and motion studies.
    d. Fordism.

16. Fast food restaurants like McDonald's and Burger King illustrate:
    a. the industrial society.
    b. the piece rate system.
    c. Fordism.
    d. robotics.

17. According to the text, _____ jobs differ from employment norms of the society in which they are located.
    a. primary tier
    b. marginal
    c. peripheral
    d. criminal

18. Studies of immigrant women workers in the Silicon Valley have concluded that:
    a. capitalist economic development in the past decade has been relatively free of racism as a method of labor division and control.
    b. these workers recently have joined unions and are now demanding higher wages.
    c. women currently make up nearly 100 percent of the high tech workforce in California.
    d. gender segregation is apparent on high tech assembly lines.

19. Which one of these is <u>not</u> a major type of unemployment?
    a. Vertical .
    b. Seasonal.
    c. Cyclical.
    d. Structural.

20. Despite the Americans with Disabilities Act, about _____ of working-age persons with a disability are unemployed today.

    a. one-fourth

    b. one-third

    c. two-thirds

    d. two-fifths

TRUE FALSE QUESTIONS

1. The economy is the social institution responsible for the production, distribution, and consumption of goods and services.
    True or False

2. Preindustrial economies typically are based on the extraction of raw materials and natural resources from the environment.
    True or False

3. U.S. labor unions came into existence in the twentieth century when workers became tired of toiling for the benefit of capitalists.
    True or False

4. A conglomerate exists when four or fewer companies supply 50 percent or more of a particular market.
    True or False   .

5. According to Karl Marx, socialism and communism are virtually identical.
    True or False

6. According to a functionalist perspective, some problems in society are linked to peaks and troughs in the business cycle.
    True or False

7. Conflict theorists view capitalism as the solution to society's problems.
    True or False

8. Primary labor market consists of low-paying jobs with few benefits .
    True or False

9. Sociologists categorize most doctors, engineers, lawyers, professors, computer scientists, and certified public accounts as "professionals."
    True or False

10. Children whose parents are professionals are more likely to become professionals themselves.
    True or False

11. Scientific management increased worker satisfaction.
    True or False

12. Positions in the lower tier of the service sector are part of the secondary labor market, characterized by low wages, little job security, few chances for advancement, higher unemployment rates, and very limited unemployment benefits.
    True or False

13. Private household workers are among the most powerless because they cannot rely on any resources to protect them from abuse.
    True or False

14. Temporary workers are one of the slowest growing segments of the contingent work force.
    True or False

15. The United States is the first nation to formally address the issue of equality for persons with a disability.
    True or False

FILL IN THE BLANK QUESTIONS

1. The extraction of raw materials and natural resources is known as _____ production.

2. Postindustrial economics are characterized by _____ production.

3. A _____ is group of employees who join together to bargain with an employer over wages, benefits, and working conditions.

4. Large corporations that are headquartered in one country but sell and produce goods and services in many countries are known as _____ .

5. An _____ exists when several companies overwhelmingly control an entire industry.

6. Economist _____ wrote the classical book *An Inquiry in to the Nature and Causes of the Wealth of Nations*.

7. Karl Marx described _____ as a temporary stage en route to an ideal communist society.

8. _____ revolutionized management with a system called _____ .

9. Fordism is named for _____ who used _____ technique in his manufacturing of automobiles.

10. In 1990, the United States became the first nation to formally address the issue of _____ .

SHORT ANSWER/ESSAY QUESTIONS

1. How far has the United States moved into postindustrialization? What are some of the fastest growing U.S. occupations?

2. What are the occupational categories considered to be marginal jobs in the United States? What are considered to be marginal? What is it meant by internationalization of marginal jobs?

3. What are the three major contemporary economic systems? How do they differ?

4. What are some similarities, and differences in scientific management and mass production?

5. How do the functionalists, conflict, and symbolic interactionists explain work in the United States?

STUDENT CLASS PROJECTS AND ACTIVITIES

1. This project calls for you to compare the U.S.A. budget deficit today to that for the years 1980-2002. During the years 1980-1992, the federal budget deficit shot up to between 3% and 7% of the gross domestic product. In the years of Presidents Kennedy, Johnson and Nixon, the deficits generally hovered at a relatively harmless 1% or 2% of the GDP, except for a very brief increase to 3% at the end of the Johnson Administration to help pay for the Vietnam War. You are to research the reasons that federal spending outstripped revenues at such as astonishing rate of increase during the Reagan-Bush years. Analyze the effectiveness of "supply-side" economics during these years (the idea that the U.S. could cut income taxes while simultaneously pay for massive increases in defense and certain highly popular domestic programs). Depict the federal budget deficit by presentation of graphs (probably a bar graph would serve best here) from the years 1972 to 2002. Then compare the federal budget deficit of the mid 1990's to today's deficit. Present at least four well thought out solutions for cutting the deficit. Critique some of the present policies enacted in order to cut the deficit. Some research sources for this project would be in the government documents section of your library, or from the Office of Management and Budget, U.S. Government. In the writing up of this paper, present a bibliography, as well as a well-written paper.

2. This project calls for you to conduct interviews. You are to interview one person who is employed in the primary labor market, one in the secondary labor market, and one in the tertiary labor market. You are to provide the names, company address, sex, race, and age of the workers. You are to ask questions about (1) the worker's family and educational background; (2) training requirements for the job; (3) how and why they entered this particular segment of the labor market; (4) their typical day of work; (5) employment benefits such as paid vacations, paid holidays, sick leave, health insurance, etc.; (6) job security and advancement possibilities; and (7) worker satisfaction. In the writing up of this project, include a summary of the responses to each specific question

and an evaluation of this project. Submit your paper to your instructor at the appropriate time; following any other directions you have been given.

3. Trace the history (including the origin and the growth) of labor unions in the United States, for both male and female workers. Include in your research a statement of the present status of labor unions in the present American marketplace.

4. Trace the growth, development, and change of blue-collar and white-collar jobs in the American work force. Include in your research the present status of blue-collar versus white-collar jobs. Some possible sources are: the Economic Policy Institute (a think-tank in Washington D.C.) and in government documents such as the *Historical Statistics of the United States*. Include, when feasible, any charts and graphs, and provide a summary and conclusion of your research.

INTERNET ACTIVITIES

1. For examples of worker activism, go the Retail Workers site. Once there, click on *McDonald's Union Busting in Russia*, for a report on Russian workers who tried to organize a union and met with resistance and layoffs. www.retailworker.com/archive.html

2. *Walmartyrs* is a site developed to foster interaction and communication among Wal-Mart workers. Students can access behind the scenes information about the largest corporation in the United States. www.walmartyrs.com/

3. To read about one of the most powerful labor organizations in the United States, go to the *AFL-CIO* web site. Once there, click on unions affiliated with the AFL-CIO. As you can see, a very large number of unions are associated with this organization. www.aflcio.org

4. To read some frequently asked questions about **capitalism**, go to the *Capitalism: Frequently Asked Questions* site. Look at questions about the relationship between **capitalism** and democracy, and is **capitalism** a just social system. http://lilt-vetri.lilt.ilstu.edu/rrpope/rrpopepwd/articles/capitalism.html

5. Check out *Forbes* listing of the richest people in the world. Do a web search for some of these people and see what businesses they are associated with. www.forbes.com/2002/02/28/billionaires.html

INFOTRAC EXERCISES

1. Search for articles on both **Seasonal** and **Structural Unemployment**. Bring to class a brief summary that compares and contrasts what we know about these two forms of unemployment.

2. **The Virtual Seminar in Global Political Economy** - The Virtual Seminar is a true international college of the Internet, with on-line classes for college credit exploring questions such as the Third World Debt crisis and international social movements.

3. Look up articles on **Economic Interdependence**. Scan these articles and make a list of related issues to understand in order to get the full picture of this growing phenomenon.

Solutions

MULTIPLE CHOICE QUESTIONS

1. A p. 420

2. D p. 421

3. A p. 421

4. B p. 424

5. A p.425

6. D p. 431

7. B p. 430

8. A p. 430

9. C p. 432

10. D p. 434

11. B p. 434

12. D p. 435

13. A p. 435

14. A p. 438

15. C p. 440

16. C p. 440-441

17. B p. 441

18. D p. 443

19. A p. 445

20. C p. 448

TRUE FALSE QUESTIONS

1. T p. 420

2. T p. 421

3. T p. 428

4. F p. 431

5. F p. 432

6. T p. 434

7. F p. 435

8. F p. 436

9. T p. 437

10. T p. 438

11. F p. 440

12. T p. 441

13. T p. 441

14. F p. 443

15. T p. 448

FILL IN THE BLANK QUESTIONS

1. primary sector

2. tertiary sector

3. labor union

4. transnational corporations

5. oligarchy

6. Adam Smith

7. socialism

8. Frederick Winslow Taylor, scientific management

9. Henry Ford, scientific management

10. disability

Chapter 14

POLITICS AND GOVERNMENT IN GLOBAL PERSPECTIVE

BRIEF CHAPTER OUTLINE

Politics, Power, and Authority

- Political Science and Political Sociology
- Power and Authority
- Ideal Types of Authority

Political Systems in Global Perspective

- Monarchy
- Authoritarianism
- Totalitarianism
- Democracy

Perspectives on Power and Political Systems

- Functionalist Perspectives: The Pluralist Model
- Conflict Perspectives: Elite Models
- Critique of Pluralist and Elite Models

The U.S Political System

- Political Parties and Elections
- Political Participation and Voter Apathy

Governmental Bureaucracy

- Characteristics of the Federal Bureaucracy
- The Iron Triangle and the Military-Industrial Complex

The Military and Militarism

- Explanations for Militarism
- Gender, Race and the Military

Terrorism and War

- Types of Terrorism
- Terrorism in the United States
- War

Politics and Government in the Future

CHAPTER SUMMARY

The relationship between politics, power and authority is a strong one in all countries. **Politics** is the social institution through which power is acquired and exercised by some people or groups. **Power** -- the ability of persons or groups to carry out their will even when opposed by others -- is a social relationship involving both leaders and followers. Most leaders seek to legitimate their power through **authority** -- power that people accept as legitimate rather than coercive. **Government** is the formal organization that regulates relationships among members of a society and those outside its borders. Some social analysts refer to the government as the **state** — the political entity that possesses a legitimate monopoly of the use of force within its territory to achieve its goals. According to Max Weber, there are three ideal types of authority: (1) **traditional**, (2) **charismatic**, and (3) **rational legal** (**bureaucratic**). There are four main types of contemporary political systems: monarchy, authoritarianism, totalitarianism, and democracy. In a democracy the people hold the ruling power either directly or through elected representatives. There are two key perspectives on how power is distributed in the United States. According to the **pluralist model**, power is widely dispersed throughout many competing interest groups. According to the **elite model**, power is concentrated in a small group of elites and the masses are relatively powerless. The **power elite** is comprised of influential business leaders, key government leaders, and the military. **Political parties** are organizations whose purpose is to gain and hold legitimate control of government. The Democrats and the Republicans have dominated the U.S. political system since the mid nineteenth century, although party loyalties have been declining in recent years. People learn political attitudes, values, and behaviors through **political socialization**. The vast governmental bureaucracy is a major source of power and carries out the actual functioning of the government. One way that special interest groups exert powerful influence on the bureaucracy is through the iron triangle of power — a three-way arrangement in which a private interest group of a congressional committee and bureaucratic agency make the final decision on a political issue. The military bureaucracy is so wide ranging that it encompasses the **military-industrial complex** -- the mutual interdependence of the military establishment and private military contractors. This complex is supported by **militarism** -- a societal focus on military ideals and an aggressive preparedness for war. **Terrorism**, the use of calculated, unlawful physical force or threats of violence against a government, organization, or individual to gain some political, religious, economics or social objective, has recently created world-wide fear. Three types of terrorism—revolutionary terrorism, state-sponsored terrorism, and repressive terrorism—all extract a massive toll by producing rampant fear, widespread loss of human life, and extensive destruction of property. Recent acts of terrorism directed against the United States have been facts of life in some other countries for many years. **War**, an organized, armed conflict between nations or distinct political factions, has both directed and indirect effects. In examining politics and government in the future, one group of analysts view the U.S. as becoming less democratic. Other analysts focus more narrowly on specific questions of concern. Our response to these concerns will have a profound effect on people and governments all around the globe.

LEARNING OBJECTIVES

After reading Chapter 14, you should be able to:

1. Explain the relationship between politics, power and authority, and note how political sociology differs from political science.

2. Distinguish between power and authority.

3. Identify the three ideal types of authority.

4. Compare and contrast governments characterized by monarchy, authoritarianism, totalitarianism, and democracy.

5. State the major elements of the pluralist (functionalist) model of power and political systems.

6. State the major elements of elite (conflict) models of power and political systems, and note how they differ from pluralist (functionalist) models.

7. Describe the purpose of political parties and analyze how well U.S. parties measure up to the ideal type characteristics of political parties.

8. Explain the relationship between political socialization, political attitudes, and political participation.

9. Discuss the characteristics of the federal bureaucracy and explain what is meant by the "permanent government."

10. Describe the military industrial complex and explain why it is called an iron triangle.

11. Discuss militarism and explain why support for this ideology has been so strong in the United States.

12. Define terrorism and list and discuss the three types of terrorism.

13. Describe the terrorism, past and present, in the United States.

14. Define "war" and the costs and effects of war.

15. Analyzed varied concerns about politics and government in the future.

KEY TERMS

(defined at page number shown and in glossary)

authoritarianism 462

authority 459

charismatic authority 459

democracy 464

elite model 467

government 456

militarism 480

military-industrial complex 477

monarchy 461

pluralist model 465

political action committees 467

political party 470

political socialization 473

political sociology 457

politics 456

power 457

power elite 468

rational-legal authority 460

routinization of charisma 460

special interest groups 466

state 456

terrorism 481

totalitarianism 463

traditional authority 457

war 482

KEY PEOPLE

(identified at page number shown)

G. William Domhoff 468

Emile Durkheim 465

Thomas Dye 465

Zillah R. Eisenstein 459

Joe Feagin 477

Karl Marx 470

C. Wright Mills 468

Max Weber 459

CHAPTER OUTLINE

I.   POLITICS, POWER, AND AUTHORITY

    A.   **Politics** is the social institution through which power is acquired and exercised by some people and groups.

    B.   In contemporary societies, the primary political system is the **government** -- the formal organization that has the legal and political authority to regulate the relationships among members of a society and between the society and those outside its borders.

    C.   Sociologists often refer to the government as the **state** -- the political entity that possesses a legitimate monopoly over the use of force within its territory to achieve its goals.

    D.   While political science primarily focuses on power and the distribution of power in different types of political systems, **political sociology** examines the nature and consequences of power within or between societies and focuses on the social circumstances of politics and the interrelationships between politics and social structures.

    E.   Power and Authority

        1.   **Power** is the ability of persons or groups to achieve their goals despite opposition from others.

        2.   **Authority** is power that people accept as legitimate rather than coercive.

F.   Ideal Types of Authority

    1.   According to Max Weber, there are three ideal types of authority:

       a.   **Traditional authority** is power that is legitimized on the basis of long standing custom.

       b.   **Charismatic authority** is power legitimized on the basis of a leader's exceptional personal qualities or the demonstration of extraordinary insight and accomplishment that inspire loyalty and obedience from followers.

       c.   **Rational-legal authority** is power legitimized by law or written rules and regulations.

    2.   These three types of authority demonstrate how different bases of legitimacy are tied to societies' economy.

II. POLITICAL SYSTEMS IN GLOBAL PERSPECTIVE

    A.   Emergence of Political Systems

       1.   Hunting and gathering societies do not have political institutions as such because they have very little division of labor or social inequality.

       2.   Political institutions first emerge in agrarian societies as they acquire surpluses and develop greater social inequality.

       3.   Nation-states -- political organizations that have recognizable national boundaries within which their citizens possess specific legal rights and obligations -- developed first in Spain, France, and England between the twelfth and fifteenth centuries.

    B.   **Monarchy** is a political system in which power resides in one person or family and is passed from generation to generation through lines of inheritance.

    C.   **Authoritarianism** is a political system controlled by rulers who deny popular participation in government.

    D.   **Totalitarianism** is a political system in which the state seeks to regulate all aspects of people's public and private lives.

    E.   **Democracy** is a political system in which the people hold the ruling power either directly or through elected representatives.

III. PERSPECTIVES ON POWER AND POLITICAL SYSTEMS

    A.   Functionalist Perspectives: According to the **pluralist model**, power in political systems is widely dispersed throughout many competing **special interest groups** -- political coalitions comprised of individuals or groups that share a specific interest they wish to protect or advance with the help of the political system.

       1.   Functionalist Perspectives: According to the pluralist model, power in political systems is widely dispersed throughout many competing special interest groups -- political coalitions comprised of individuals or groups that share a specific interest they wish to protect or advance with the help of the political system.

         a.   Decisions are made on behalf of the people by leaders who engage in a process of bargaining, accommodation, and compromise.

         b.   Competition among leadership groups (such as leaders in business, labor, education, law, medicine, consumer groups, and government) protects people by making the abuse of power by any one group more difficult.

      c.   People can influence public policy by voting in elections, participating in existing special interest groups, or forming new ones to gain access to the political system.

      d.   Power is widely dispersed in society; leadership groups that wield influence on some decisions are not the same groups, which may be influential in other decisions.

      e.   Public policy is not always based on majority preference; it is the balance between competing interest groups.

  2.   Over the last two decades, special interest groups have become more involved in "single issue politics," such as abortion, gun control, gay and lesbian rights, or environmental concerns.

  3.   **Political action committees (PACs)** are organizations of special interest groups that fund campaigns to help elect (or defeat) candidates based on their stances on specific issues.

B.   Conflict Perspectives: According to the **elite model**, power in political systems is concentrated in the hands of a small group of elites and the masses are relatively powerless.

  1.   Key elements of this model:

      a.   Decisions are made by the elite, possessing greater wealth, education, status, and other resources than does the "masses" it governs.

      b.   Consensus exists among the elite on the basic values and goals of society; however, consensus does not exist among most people in society on these important social concerns.

      c.   Power is highly concentrated at the top of a pyramid shaped social hierarchy; those at the top of the power structure come together to set policy for everyone.

      d.   Public policy reflects the values and preferences of the elite, not the preferences of the people.

  2.   According to C. Wright Mills, the **power elite** is comprised of leaders at the top of business, the executive branch of the federal government, and the military (especially the "top brass" at the Pentagon). The elites have similar class backgrounds and interests.

      a.   The corporate rich are the most powerful because of their unique ability to parlay the vast economic resources at their disposal into political power.

      b.   At the middle level of the pyramid, Mills placed the legislative branch of government, interest groups, and local opinion leaders.

      c.   The bottom (and widest layer) of the pyramid is occupied by the unorganized masses that are relatively powerless and vulnerable to economic and political exploitation.

  3.   G. William Domhoff referred to elites as the *ruling class* -- a relatively fixed group of privileged people who wield sufficient power to constrain political processes and serve underlying capitalist interests.

      a.   Individuals in the upper echelon are members of a business class based on the ownership and control of large corporations.

  b.   The intertwining of the upper class and the corporate community produces cohesion at both the economic and social levels.

  c.   Members of the ruling class also are linked though exclusive social clubs, expensive private schools, debutante parties, listings in the Social Register, and other upper class indicators.

  d.   The corporate rich and their families influence the political process in three ways:

   i.   they influence the candidate selection process by helping to finance campaigns and providing favors to political candidates;

   ii.   through participation in the special interest process, they are able to gain favors, tax-breaks, regulatory rulings, and other governmental supports;

   iii.   they gain access to the policy-making process by holding prestigious positions on governmental advisory committees, presidential commissions, and other governmental appointments.

4. Class Conflict Perspectives

  a.   Most contemporary elite models are based on the work of Karl Marx; however, there are divergent viewpoints about the role of the state within this perspective.

  b.   While instrumental Marxists argue that the state acts invariably to perpetuate the capitalist class, structural Marxists contend that the state is not simply a passive instrument of the capitalist class.

5. Critique of Pluralist and Elite Models

  a.   The Pluralist model emphasizes that many different groups compete for power and advantage in society.

  b.   Domhoff argues U.S. society appears to be pluralist when actually it is elitist

  c.   Mills suggests that the economic, political, and military elite may be a relatively cohesive group.

IV. THE U.S. POLITCIAL SYSTEM

  A. Political Parties and Elections

   1. A **political party** is an organization whose purpose is to gain and hold legitimate control of government; they affect elections.

     a.   Parties develop and articulate policy positions; educate voters about the issues and simplify the choices for them; recruit candidates who agree with those policies, and help those candidates win office; and, when elected, hold the candidates responsible for implementing the party's policy positions.

     b.   Since the Civil War, two political parties -- the Democratic and the Republican -- have dominated the political system in the United States and confronted two broad types of concerns.

      i.   Social issues are those relating to moral judgments or civil rights.

215

          ii.   Economic issues involve the amount that should be spent on government programs and the extent to which these programs should encourage a redistribution of income and assets.

   B.   Political Participation and Voter Apathy

      1.   **Political socialization** is the process by which people learn political attitudes, values, and behavior. For young children, the family is the primary agent of political socialization.

      2.   Socioeconomic status affects people's political attitudes, values, and beliefs.

      3.   Political participation occurs at four levels:

          a.   voting

          b.   attending and taking part in political meetings

          c.   actively participating in political campaigns

          d.   running for or holding political office.

      4.   At most, about 10 percent of the voting age population in this country participates at a level higher than simply voting, and less than 51 percent of the voting age population voted in the 2000 presidential election.

V.   GOVERNMENTAL BUREAUCRACY

   A.   Characteristics of the Federal Bureaucracy

      1.   The size and scope of government has grown in recent decades partially because of dramatic increases in technology and in demands from the public that the government "do something" about various problems facing society.

      2.   Much of the actual functioning of the government is carried on by the permanent government in Washington that is made up of top tier, civil service bureaucrats who have built a major power base.

      3.   The governmental bureaucracy has been able to perpetuate itself and expand because it has many employees with highly specialized knowledge and skills who cannot easily be replaced by those from the "outside."

   B.   The Iron Triangle and the Military Industrial Complex

      1.   The *iron triangle* is a three-way arrangement in which a private-interest group (usually a business corporation), a congressional committee or subcommittee, and a bureaucratic agency make the final decision on a political issue that is to be decided by that agency.

      2.   A classic example of the iron triangle is an arrangement referred to as the **military-industrial complex** -- the mutual interdependence of the military establishment and private military contractors that started during World War II and has continued to the present.

          a.   Between 1945 and early 1990's, the U.S. government spent an estimated $10.2 trillion for national defense (in constant 1987 dollars). In the 1990's, the U.S. spent more than $270 billion per year on the U.S. military budget.

          b.   Several of the largest multinational corporations are among the largest defense contractors, and the defense divisions of these companies have a virtual monopoly over defense contracts. The military budgets for 2003 and 2004 were almost $400 billion per year.

    c.   Some members of Congress have actively supported the military industrial complex because it provided a unique chance for them to provide economic assistance for their local, voting constituencies in the form of funding for defense related industries, military bases, and space centers in their home state. These activities are known as *pork* or *pork barrel projects*.

VI.   THE MILITARY AND MILITARISM

    A.   **Militarism** is a societal focus on military ideals and an aggressive preparedness for war; militarism is supported by core U.S. values such as patriotism, courage, reverence, loyalty, obedience, and faith in authority. Sociologists have proposed several reasons for militarization:

        1.   The economic interests of capitalists, college and university faculty and administrators who are recipients of research grants, workers, labor union members, and others who depend on military spending.

        2.   The role of the nation and its inclination toward coercion in response to perceived threats.

        3.   The relationship between militarism and masculinity.

    B.   Gender, Race and the Military

        1.   The introduction of the all-volunteer force in the early 1970's and the end of the draft shifted the focus of the military from training "good citizen soldiers" to an image of the "economic person" -- one who enlists in the military in the same way that a person might take a job in the private sector.

        2.   Considerable pressure has been placed on the military to recruit women; in 2002 women made up approximately 15 percent of the total uniformed force.

        3.   Militarization uses and affects women differently based on their ethnic or racial group; by 2001, African American women made up 47 percent of all enlisted (non-officer) women in the United States Army, a percentage four times their proportion compared with all United States women.

        4.   People of color may enlist in the military, not because of their militaristic tendencies, but because of the more limited options available to them in society at large, especially if they come from lower income family backgrounds.

VII.   TERRORISM and WAR

    A.   **Terrorism** is the use of calculated, unlawful physical force or treats of violence against a government, organization, or individual to gain some political, religious, economic, or social objective.

    B.   Types of Terrorism

        1.   *Political terrorism* uses intimidation, coercion, treats of harm, and other violence that attempts to bring about a significant change in or overthrow an existing government. There are three types of political terrorism.

            a.   *Revolutionary terrorism* refers to acts of violence against civilians that are carried out by enemies of the government who want to bring about political change.

b. *State sponsored terrorism* occurs when a government provides financial resources for terrorists who conduct their activities in other nations.

c. *Repressive terrorism* is conducted by a government against its own citizens for the purpose of protecting an existing political order.

C. Terrorism in the United States

1. The years 1995 and 2001 stand out in recent U.S. history as the two worst terrorist attacks that ever occurred in the continental United States.

2. Bombings, biological and chemical attacks are now reality in the United States.

3. Many people now rely on government officials to calm their fears.

D. War

1. **War**—organized, armed conflict between nations or distinct political factions—includes both declared and undeclared wars.

2. Casualties in conventional warfare pales when compared to biological or chemical warfare.

3. Patriotism, even when temporary, causes a renewed interest in how the government is run, and affords an expression of loyalty to the exiting order, although some criticism remains.

VIII. Politics and Government in the Future

A. One group of analysts provides a distressed view about the future of the U.S.A.

B. Other views focus more narrowly on specific questions of concern seeking solutions.

PRACTICE TESTS

MULTIPLE CHOICE QUESTIONS

Select the response that best answers the question or completes the statement:

1. The social institution through which power is acquired and exercised by some people and groups is known as:

   a. government.

   b. politics.

   c. the state.

   d. the military.

2. According to the text, the state is:

   a. the social institution through which power is acquired and exercised by some people and groups.

   b. the formal organization that has the legal and political authority to regulate the relationships among members of a society and between the society and those outside its borders.

   c. the political entity that possesses a legitimate monopoly over the use of force within its territory to achieve its goals.

   d. the political entity that seeks to regulate all aspects of people's public and private lives.

3. _____ is the power that people accept as legitimate rather than coercive.
   a. Influence
   b. Clout
   c. Authority
   d. Legitimation

4. Traditional authority is based on:
   a. a leader's exceptional personal qualities.
   b. written rules and regulations of law.
   c. documents such as the U.S. Constitution.
   d. long-standing custom.

5. Napoleon, Julius Caesar, Martin Luther King, Jr., Caesar Chavez, and Mother Teresa are examples of:
   a. charismatic authority.
   b. traditional authority.
   c. rational-legal authority.
   d. nontraditional authority.

6. All of the following statements regarding racialized patriarchy are correct, **except**:
   a. Zillah R. Eisenstein coined the term "racialized patriarchy."
   b. Racialized patriarchy is closely intertwined with rational-legal authority.
   c. Racialized patriarchy is the continual interplay of race and gender.
   d. Racialized patriarchy remains a reality in both preindustrial and industrialized nations.

7. A unit of political organizations that has recognizable national boundaries where citizens possess legal rights and obligations is a:
   a. bureaucracy
   b. government
   c. nation-state
   d. city-state

8. A hereditary right to rule or a divine right to rule is most likely to be found in a(n):
   a. monarchy.
   b. authoritarian regime.
   c. totalitarian regime.
   d. democracy.

9. The National Socialist (Nazi) party in Germany during World War II is an example of a(n):
   a. monarchy.
   b. authoritarian regime.
   c. totalitarian regime.
   d. democracy.

10. All of the following statements regarding democracy are true, except:

    a. Democracy is a political system in which the people hold the ruling power either directly or through elected representatives.

    b. The United Kingdom and Canada have recently attempted direct democracy at the national level.

    c. Representative democracy is not always equally accessible to all people in a nation.

    d. The framers of the Constitution established a system of representative democracy in the United States.

11. According to the pluralist model, power in political systems is:

    a. widely dispersed throughout many competing interest groups.

    b. concentrated in the hands of a small group of elites.

    c. comprised of leaders at the top of business, the executive branch of the federal government, and the military.

    d. controlled by members of the ruling class.

12. Special interest groups who put political pressure on leaders in order to influence legislation are known as

    a. power elites

    b. elite groups

    c. special interest groups

    d. PACs

13. Political action committees:

    a. generally have been abolished by reforms in campaign finance laws.

    b. are comprised of people who volunteer their time but not money to political candidates and parties.

    c. are organizations of special interest groups that fund campaigns to help elect candidates based on their stances on specific issues.

    d. encourage widespread political participation by citizens at the grassroots level.

14. The power elite model was developed by:

    a. Emile Durkheim.

    b. Thomas R. Dye and Harmon Zeigler.

    c. Joseph Steffan.

    d. C. Wright Mills.

15. The organizations responsible for developing and articulating policy positions, educating voters about issues, and recruiting candidates to run for office are known as:

    a. political parties.

    b. political action committees.

    c. interest groups.

    d. federal election committees.

16. _____ is the process by which people learn political attitudes, values, and behavior.
    a. Indoctrination
    b. Military training
    c. Resocialization
    d. Political socialization

17. According to the text, most of the actual functioning of the U.S. government is carried on by:
    a. political action committees.
    b. the federal bureaucracy.
    c. the criminal justice system.
    d. political parties.

18. The three-way arrangement in which a private interest group, a congressional committee, and a bureaucratic agency make the final decision on a political issue that is to be decided by that agency is known as:
    a. political subversion.
    b. the iron law of oligarchy.
    c. the iron triangle of power.
    d. the power elite.

19. _____ is a societal focus on military ideals and an aggressive preparedness for war.
    a. Militarism
    b. Authoritarianism
    c. Totalitarianism
    d. Warmongerism

20. Which of the following statements is **correct** regarding the U.S. military?
    a. As more women have moved into the ranks of officers in the military, sexual harassment largely has been eliminated.
    b. Women's roles in the military have disturbed the existing world of male militarism.
    c. The percentage of African American women enlisted in the U.S. Army is much smaller than their proportion in the U.S. population.
    d. People of color and poor people from all racial ethnic groups may enlist in the military because of the more limited options available to them in society at large.

TRUE FALSE QUESTIONS

1. Political sociology is the same as political science.
    True or False

2. Power is a social relationship that involves both leaders and followers.
    True or False

3. Charismatic authority tends to be temporary and relatively unstable.
    True or False

4. Globally, today everyone is born, live, and dies under the auspices of a nation-state.
    True or False

5. In a representative democracy, elected representatives are expected to keep the "big picture" in mind, and they do not necessarily need to convey the concerns of those they represent in all situations.
   True or False

6. Functionalists suggest that divergent viewpoints lead to a system of political pluralism in which the government functions as an arbiter between competing interests and viewpoints.
   True or False

7. Over the past two decades, special interest groups have become more involved in multiple-issue politics because so many political issues are intertwined with other concerns.
   True or False

8. Sociologist G. William Domhoff believes that the ruling class wields sufficient power to constrain political processes in the United States.
   True or False

9. Structural Marxists content that that state is a passive instrument of the capitalist class.
   True or False

10. Children do not typically identify with the political party of their parents until they reach college-age.
    True or False

11. People in the upper classes tend to vote based on a philosophy of *noblesse oblige.*
    True or False

12. The United States has one of the highest percentages of voter turnout of all Western nations.
    True or False

13. The U.S. governmental bureaucracy has been able to perpetuate itself and expand because many of its employees have highly specialized knowledge and skills and cannot be replaced easily by "outsiders."
    True or False

14. Pork barrel projects are a recent political practice in the United States.
    True or False

15. According to symbolic interactionists, militarism may be related to the social construction of masculinity in societies.
    True or False

FILL IN THE BLANK QUESTIONS

1. Some social analysts refer to the government as the _____ , which possesses a legitimate monopoly over the use of force.

2. The main types of political systems are _____ , _____ , _____ , and _____ .

3. _____ is the ability of persons or groups to achieve their goals, despite opposition of others.

4. Power legitimized by law or written rules and regulations is _____ .

5. According to C. Wright Mills, the _____ is comprised of political, economic, and military elite.

6. The mutual interdependence of the military establishment and private military contractors is known as the _____ .

7. The three types of political terrorism are: _____ , _____ , and _____ .

8. The organized, armed conflict between nations is known as _____ .

9. According to Sociologist _____ , the U.S.A. actually has a ruling class who wield power to constrain political processes.

10. The two worst terrorist attacks that ever occurred in the U.S.A. were in the years _____ and _____ .

SHORT ANSWER/ESSAY QUESTIONS

1. What is the role of the individual in politics, considering such issues as political socialization, political action, lobbying activities, voter apathy and political elites?

2. What is the importance of political parties? What do they do? Are they good for democracies? Why? Why not?

3. What are the major political systems around the world?

4. What are the three ideal types of authority? In what ways are some more effective than others in achieving certain goals?

5. How do the pluralists and the elite models explain power in the Unites States? Which do you think best represents the U.S.A political system? Why?

STUDENT CLASS PROJECTS AND ACTIVITIES

1. The text notes the low rate of voter participation in our country. You are to attempt to discover some explanations for this condition. You are to conduct an informal survey of a cross section of 20 people of different ages, ethnicity, social class, race, and sex. On your survey forms, you must include the basic background information of your respondents (name, race, sex, address, age ethnicity, occupation, or student status). Obtain responses from the following questions: (1) When was the last time you voted? Why? (2) Did you vote for the President in the last election? (3) Do you usually vote in all elections? Why? Why not? (4)Do you actually vote along political party lines, such as for the Democrats or Republicans? If so, which party? Why? (5) Do other members of your family vote? (6) Do you know at least one elected official? Who? (7) Do you support the present position of the President of the United States on most issues? Explain. Formulate any other question you may want to ask. Provide a conclusion, an analysis, and an evaluation of the data in the writing up of this project. Submit your paper at the appropriate time.

2. Conduct an informal survey of 10 male and 10 female students on campus. Provide the necessary biographical background of your respondents, such as name, address, age, sex, and college classification. The survey is called "What If Women Ran America?" Ask and record all responses to the following questions: If women ran America: (1) Would child care be more available and maternity leave (with pay) guaranteed? Explain. (2) Would government be more attentive to the needy? Explain. (3) Would abortion be legal? Explain. (4) Would there be greater equality for working women? Explain. (5) Would there be greater sexual tolerance? Explain. (6) Would there be stricter gun control? Explain. (7) Would they be tougher on crime? Explain. (8) Would America be a better place? Explain. Summarize the response and provide an evaluation of this project.

INTERNET ACTIVITIES

1. *The Center for Democracy and Technology* tracks the impact of new information technologies on the constitutional rights and liberties of Americans. www.cdt.org/

2. Sociologists are frequently interested in surveys and opinion polls to determine how members of a society feel about a particular issue. One organization that is well known for conducting such research is the *Gallup* organization. Search the site for polling data related to this chapter. www.gallup.com

3. In addition to the Gallup organization, the *Roper Center for Public Opinion Research*. Investigate the Public Opinion Matters section of the web site to find data and articles on several topics that bear relevance to this chapter. www.ropercenter.uconn.edu/

4. Most of the major political parties now have an online presence. After visiting these sites, what are the major similarities or differences among the political parties?

   a. The *Democratic Party* can be found at http://democrats.org/

   b. The *Republican National Committee* can be found at http://rnc.org/

   c. The *Libertarian Party* can be found at www.lp.org/

   d. The *Socialist Party* is located at http://sp-usa.org/

5. As discussed in the text, lobbying groups are a powerful force in **politics** in the United States. Each of these organizations provides information about their legislative concerns and activities. For instance, the NRA keeps track of bills and proposed laws that might impact gun ownership. Overall, how do the agendas of these organizations compare? Some of the best-known lobbying groups are:

   a. The *National Rifle Association* (NRA) www.nra.org/

   b. The *American Association of Retired Persons* (AARP) www.aarp.org/

   c. The *National Education Association* (NEA) www.nea.org/

6. *The Center for Responsive Politics* maintains an interesting site with valuable information on both PACs (political action committees) and lobbyist groups. For instance, they maintain an online lobbyist report called "Influence Inc," which includes background on an issue, analysis of industry spending, and provides a relevant database. They also profile every political action committee registered in the Federal Election Commission. www.opensecrets.org/about/index.asp

INFOTRAC EXERCISES

1. Search for articles and news stories about **voter apathy**. The United Sates has a low voting turnout. Investigate research on this phenomenon.

2. Opponents of the **death penalty** contend that it is cruel and unusual punishment, and that our legal system makes mistakes and wrongfully executes innocent people. Research this issue to find out how often this happens, and what states are doing about it.

3. Hundreds of **interest groups** seek to influence the outcome of elections and specific legislation. Investigate the range of interest groups, or focus on one group in particular.

4. **Campaign reform** is an important current issue, as the amount of money candidates can raise dictates the quality of their campaign, or even if they will be able to run at all. Look at news stories about this issue. See if you can collect information to present a pro and con class discussion.

5. The media attention given to recent school shootings have left many feeling that we should have some type of **gun control**; the NRA opposes this. Investigate this issue.

6. There are an enormous number of articles under the topic **terrorism** on InfoTrac. Assign various subsections to your class with the goal of constructing a comprehensive understanding of terrorism and war. Plan to make an oral presentations, create posters, make a mural, or a write brief essay.

Solutions

MULTIPLE CHOICE QUESTIONS

1. B p. 456

2. C p. 456

3. C p. 459

4. D p. 459

5. A p. 459

6. B p. 459

7. C p. 460

8. A p. 461

9. C p. 463

10. B pp. 464

11. A p. 465

12. C p. 466

13. C p. 467

14. D p. 468

15. A p. 470

16. D p. 473

17. B p. 473

18. C p. 477

19. A p. 480

20. D p. 481

TRUE FALSE QUESTIONS

1. F p. 436 p. 457

2. T p. 458 p. 437

3. T p. 459 p. 438

4. T p. 460 p. 440

5. F p. 442 p. 464

6. T p. 465 p. 443

7. F p. 444 p. 466

8. T pp. 468 pp. 446-447

9. F p. 447 p. 470

10. F p. 450 p. 473

11. T p. 473 p. 452

12. F p. 452 p. 474

13. T p. 477 p. 454

14. F p. 458 p. 479

15. T p. 480 p. 458

FILL IN THE BLANK QUESTIONS

1. state

2. monarchy, authoriarian systems, totalitarian systems, democratic system

3. Power

4. rational-legal authority

5. power elite

6. military-industrial complex

7. revolutionary, state-sponsored, repressive terrorism

8. war

9. William Domhoff

10. 1995, 2001

Chapter 15

FAMILIES AND INTIMATE RELATIONSHIPS

BRIEF CHAPTER OUTLINE

Families in Global Perspective

- Family Structure and Characteristics
- Marriage Patterns
- Patterns of Descent and Inheritance
- Patterns of Power and Authority in Families
- Residential Patterns

Theoretical Perspectives on Families

- Functionalist Perspectives
- Conflict and Feminist Perspectives
- Symbolic Interactionist Perspectives
- Postmodernists Perspectives

Developing Intimate Relationships and Establishing Families

- Love and Intimacy
- Cohabitation and Domestic Partnerships
- Marriage
- Housework and Child-care Responsibilities

Child-Related Family Issues and Parenting

- Deciding to Have Children
- Adoption
- Teenage Pregnancies
- Single-parent Households
- Two-parent Households

Transitions and Problems in Families

- Family Violence
- Children in Foster Care
- Divorce

- Remarriage

Diversity in Families

- Diversity Among Singles

- African American Families

- Latina/o Families

- Asian American Families

- Native American Families

- Biracial Families

Family Issues in the Future

CHAPTER SUMMARY

Families are relationships in which people live together with commitment, form an economic unit and care for any young, and consider their identity to be significantly attached to the group. While the **family of orientation** is the family into which a person is born and in which early socialization usually takes place, the **family of procreation** is the family a person forms by having or adopting children. Sociologists investigate marriage patterns (such as **monogamy** and **polygamy**), descent and inheritance patterns (such as **patrilineal**, **matrilineal**, and **bilateral** descent), familial power and authority (such as **patriarchal**, **matriarchal**, and **egalitarian** families), residential patterns (such as **patrilocal**, **matrilocal**, and **neolocal** residence, and in group or out group marriage patterns (i.e. **endogamy** and **exogamy**). Functionalists emphasize that families fulfill important societal functions, including sexual regulation, socialization of children, economic and psychological support, and the provision of social status. By contrast, conflict and feminist perspectives view the family as a source of social inequality and focus primarily on the problems inherent in relationships of dominance and subordination. Symbolic Interactionists focus on family communication patterns and subjective meanings that members assign to everyday events. Postmodern perspectives view the family as *permeable* – one that is subject to modification or change. The nuclear family, therefore, is one of many family forms. Families have changed dramatically in the United States where there have been significant increases in cohabitation, domestic partnerships, dual earner marriages, single parent families, and rates of divorce and remarriage. Housework and child-care responsibilities remain key issues for the family. Violence in the family is more common than violence among groups of people. Problems in the family contribute to the large numbers of children who are in *foster care*, where adults other than a child's own parents or biological relatives serve as caregivers. Divorce has contributed to greater diversity in family relationships, including stepfamilies or blended families and the complex binuclear family. Most people who divorce get remarried. While some never married singles choose to remain single, others do so out of necessity. Support systems and extended family networks are important in African American, Latina/o, Asian American, and Native American families; however, factors such as age and class may reduce such family ties. Biracial families have greatly increased; today skin color and place of birth are not reliable indicators of a person's identity and origin. In the future, people's perceptions of family will continue to change, as will the major issues facing the family.

LEARNING OBJECTIVES

After reading Chapter 15, you should be able to:

1. Explain why it has become increasingly difficult to develop a concise definition of family.

2. Describe kinship ties and distinguish between families of orientation and families of procreation.

3. Compare and contrast extended and nuclear families.

4. Describe the different forms of marriage found across cultures.

5. Discuss the system of descent and inheritance, and explain why such systems are important in societies.

6. Distinguish between patriarchal, matriarchal, and egalitarian families.

7. Explain the differences in residential patterns and note why most people practice endogamy.

8. Describe functionalist, conflict and feminist, and symbolic interactionist perspectives on families.

9. Explain the postmodernist perspectives of the family.

10. Describe how U.S. families have changed over the past two decades.

11. Describe cohabitation and domestic partnerships and note key social and legal issues associated with each.

12. Describe the major problems faced in dual-earner marriages, and note why the double shift most often is a problem for women.

13. Discuss the major issues associated with adoption, teenage pregnancies, single-parent households, two-parent households, family violence, and children in foster care.

14. Explain the major causes and consequences of divorce and remarriage in the United States.

15. Describe the diversity found in contemporary U.S. families.

KEY TERMS
(defined at page number shown and in glossary)

bilateral descent 495

cohabitation 503

domestic partnerships 494

dual earner marriages 505

egalitarian families 495

endogamy 496

exogamy 496

extended family 492

family 490

family of orientation 491

family of procreation 492

homogamy 496

kinship 491

marriage 493

matriarchal family 495

matrilineal descent 495

matrilocal residence 496

monogamy 493

neolocal residence 496

nuclear family 493

patriarchal family 495

patrilineal descent 494

patrilocal residence 496

polyandry 494

polygamy 493

polygyny 493

second shift 504

sociology of family 497

KEY PEOPLE
(identified at page number shown)

Peter Berger and Hansfried Kellner 500

Jessie Bernard 500

Francesca Cancian 503

Andrew Cherlin 514

Emile Durkheim 497

David Elkind 500

Becky Friedan 492

Donna Haraway 491

Arlie Hochschild 505

Alfred C. Kinsey 503

Charlene Maill 507

Margaret Mead 503

Sara McLanahan and Karen Booth 509

Talcott Parsons 497

Brian Robinson 508

Alice Rossi 510

Lillian Rubin 518

Lenore Walker 500

Jane Riblett Wilkie 499

Norma Williams 516

CHAPTER OUTLINE

I.   FAMILIES IN GLOBAL PERSPECTIVE

    A.   **Families** are relationships in which people live together with commitment, form an economic unit and care for any young, and consider their identity to be significantly attached to the group.

    B.   Family Structure and Characteristics

        1.   In preindustrial societies, the primary social organization is through **kinship** -- a social network of people based on common ancestry, marriage, or adoption.

        2.   In industrialized societies, other social institutions fulfill some functions previously taken care of by kinship ties; families are responsible primarily for regulating

sexual activity, socializing children, and providing affection and companionship for family members.

3.   Many of us will be members of two types of families: **a family of orientation** -- the family into which we are born or adopted and in which early socialization usually takes place, and a **family of procreation** -- the family we form by having or adopting children.

4.   Extended and nuclear families

a.   An **extended family** is a family unit composed of relatives (such as grandparents, uncles, and aunts) in addition to parents and children who live in the same household.

b.   A **nuclear family** is a family composed of one or two parents and their dependent children, all of whom live apart from other relatives.

C.   Marriage Patterns

1.   **Marriage** is a legally recognized and/or socially approved arrangement between two or more individuals that carries certain rights and obligations and usually involves sexual activity.

2.   In the United States, **monogamy** -- a marriage between two partners, usually a woman and a man -- is the only form of marriage sanctioned by law.

3.   **Polygamy** is the concurrent marriage of a person of one sex with two or more members of the opposite sex.

a.   The most prevalent form of this marriage pattern is **polygyny** -- the concurrent marriage of one man with two or more women.

b.   **Polyandry** -- the marriage of one woman with two or more men -- is very rare.

D.   Patterns of Descent and Inheritance

1.   In preindustrial societies, the most common pattern of unilineal descent is **patrilineal descent** -- tracing descent through the father's side of the family -- whereby a legitimate son inherits his father's property and sometimes his position upon the father's death.

2.   **Matrilineal descent** traces descent through the mother's side of the family; however, inheritance of property and position usually is traced from the maternal uncle (mother's brother) to his nephew (mother's son).

3.   In industrial societies such as the United States, kinship usually is traced through both parents; **bilateral descent** is a system of tracing descent through both the mother's and father's sides of the family.

E.   Patterns of Power and Authority in Families:

1.   **Patriarchal family**: a family structure in which authority is held by the eldest male (usually the father), who acts as head of household and holds power over the women and children.

2.   **Matriarchal family**: a family structure in which authority is held by the eldest female (usually the mother), who acts as head of household.

3.   **Egalitarian family**: a family structure in which both partners share power and authority equally.

F.   Residential Patterns:

1. **Patrilocal residence**: the custom of a married couple living in the same household (or community) with the husband's family.

2. **Matrilocal residence**: the custom of a married couple living in the same household (or community) with the wife's parents.

3. In industrialized nations, most couples hope to live in a **neolocal residence**: the custom of a married couple living in their own residence apart from both the husband's and the wife's parents.

G. Endogamy and Exogamy:

1. **Endogamy** is the practice of marrying within one's own group. In the U.S. people practice endogamy.

2. **Exogamy** is the practice of marrying outside one's own social group or category. The family, the church, and the state are the most important sources of positive or negative sanction for practicing exogamy.

3. Most people engage in **homogamy** -- the pattern of individuals marrying those who have similar characteristics, such as race/ethnicity, religious background, age, education, or social class.

II. THEORETICAL PERSPECTIVES ON FAMILIES

A. The **sociology of family** is the subdiscipline of sociology that attempts to describe and explain patterns of family life and variations in family structure.

B. Functionalist Perspectives

1. The family is important in maintaining the stability of society and the well being of individuals.

2. According to Emile Durkheim, both marriage and society involve a mental and moral fusion of individuals; division of labor contributes to greater efficiency in all areas of life.

3. Talcott Parsons further defined the division of labor in families: the husband/father fulfills the instrumental role (meeting the family's economic needs, making important decisions, and providing leadership) while the wife/mother fulfills the expressive role (doing housework, caring for children, and meeting the emotional needs of family members).

4. Four key functions of families in advanced industrial societies are:

    a. sexual regulation
    b. socialization
    c. economic and psychological support for members
    d. provision of social status and reputation.

C. Conflict and Feminist Perspectives

1. Families are a primary source of inequality.

2. According to some conflict theorists, families in capitalist economies are similar to workers in a factory: women are dominated at home by men the same way workers are dominated by capitalists in factories; reproduction of children and care for family members at home reinforce the subordination of women through unpaid (and devalued) labor.

3. Some feminist perspectives focus on patriarchy rather than class because men's domination over women existed long before private ownership of property; contemporary subordination is rooted in men's control over women's labor power.

4. Conflict and feminist perspectives on families focus primarily on the problems inherent in relationships of dominance and subordination.

D. Symbolic Interactionist Perspectives

1. Interactionists examine the roles of husbands, wives, and children as they act out their own parts and react to the actions of others.

2. According to Peter Berger and Hansfried Kellner, interaction between marital partners contributes to a shared reality: newlyweds bring separate identities to a marriage but gradually construct a shared reality as a couple.

3. According to Jessie Bernard, women and men experience marriage differently: there is "his" marriage and "her" marriage.

E. Postmodern Perspectives

1. In the information age, the postmodern family is *permeable* --capable of being diffused or invaded in such a way that an entity's original purpose is modified or changed.

   a. The nuclear family is only one of many family forms.

   b. Maternal love is transformed into shared parenting.

   c. The individual values autonomy of the individual more than the family unit.

2. Urbanity is another characteristic of the postmodern family.

   a. The boundaries between the workplace and the home become more open and flexible.

   b. New communications technologies integrate and control labor.

3. Some paint a bleak future for families in the age of the "integrated circuit."

   a. There is a growing "digital divide" and a type of "cyber class warfare."

   b. Many families are left out of Internet access.

III. DEVELOPING INTIMATE RELATIONSHIPS AND ESTABLISHING FAMILIES

A. Love and Intimacy

1. Although the ideal culture emphasizes romantic love, men and women may not share the same perceptions about love: women tend to express their feelings verbally, while men tend to express their love through nonverbal actions.

2. Scholars suggest that love and intimacy are closely intertwined.

   a. Perspectives about sexual activities vary according to culture and time period.

   b. Kinsey's research provided a model for research on human sexuality for over forty years; today the national

B. Cohabitation and Domestic Partnerships

1. **Cohabitation** refers to a couple who live together without being legally married.

2. Characteristics of persons most likely to cohabit are as follows: under age 45, have been married before, or are older individuals who do not want to lose financial benefits (such as retirement benefits) that are contingent upon not marrying.

3. Many lesbian and gay couples cohabit because they cannot enter into a legally recognized marriage; some have sought recognition of **domestic partnerships** -- household partnerships in which an unmarried couple lives together in a committed sexually intimate relationship and is granted the same benefits as those accorded to married heterosexual couples.

C. Marriage

1. Couples marry for reasons such as being "in love," desiring companionship and sex, wanting to have children, feeling social pressure, attempting to escape from their parents' home, or believing they will have greater resources if they get married.

2. Communication and support are crucial to the success of marriages; problems that cause the most concern are lack of emotional intimacy, poor communication, and lack of companionship.

D. Housework and Child-care Responsibilities

1. Over 50% of all U.S. marriages are **dual-earner marriages** -- marriages in which both spouses are in the labor force. Over half of all employed women hold full-time, year-round jobs.

2. Many married women also have a **second shift** -- the domestic work that employed women perform at home after they complete their workday on the job; this amounts to an extra month of work for women each year.

3. In families where the wife's earnings are essential to family finances, more husbands have attempted to chare some of the household and child-care responsibilities.

    a. Women and men perform different household tasks.

    b. Recurring tasks tend to be more the women's responsibilities while men are more likely to do periodic tasks.

IV. CHILD-RELATED FAMILY ISSUES AND PARENTING

A. Deciding to have children

1. Couples deciding not to have children may consider themselves "child free," while those who do not produce children through no choice of their own may consider themselves "childless."

    a. Advances in birth control techniques now make it possible to determine choice of parenthood, number of children, and the spacing of their births.

    b. Some couples experience *involuntary infertility*, a leading cause is sexually transmitted diseases.

    c. Women who are involuntarily childless engage in "information management" to combat the social stigma associated with childlessness.

B. Adoption

1. *Adoption* is a legal process through which rights and duties of parenting are transferred from a child's biological and/or legal parents to new legal parents.

2. About 6.4 million women become pregnant each year in the United States; of that number about 44% of pregnancies are intended while 56% are unintended.

C.   Teen pregnancies have decreased over the past three decades; however, they are viewed as a crisis because an increase has occurred in the number of births among unmarried teenagers and the rates have not declined as rapidly as for older married women.

D.   Recently, single- or one-parent households have increased significantly due to divorce and to births outside marriage.

E.   Two-parent households

   1.   Parenthood in the United States is idealized, especially for women.

   2.   Children in two-parent families are not guaranteed a happy childhood.

V.   TRANSITIONS IN FAMILIES AND PROBLEMS IN FAMILIES

A.   Family Violence

   1.   Violence between men and women in the home is often referred to as *spouse abuse* or domestic violence.

   2.   Physical violence is more common among family members than any other group of people.

   3.   A common pattern of *nonintervention* results in slow or little assistance from individuals or law enforcement officials.

B.   Divorce

   1.   Divorce is the legal process of dissolving a marriage that allows former spouses to remarry if they so choose. Most divorces are based on "*irreconcilable differences*" (there has been a breakdown of the marital relationship for which neither partner is specifically blamed).

   2.   Under *no-fault divorce laws*, proof of the blame is generally no longer necessary.

   3.   Recent studies have shown that 43 percent of first marriages end in separation or divorce within fifteen years; one in three first marriages ends within ten years, where one in five ends within five years.

   4.   Causes of Divorce

      a.   At the macrolevel, societal factors contributing to higher rates of divorce include changes in social institutions such as religion and law.

      b.   At the microlevel, characteristics that appear to contribute to divorce are:

         i.   Marriage at an early age;

         ii.   A short acquaintanceship before marriage;

         iii.   Disapproval of the marriage by relatives and friends;

         iv.   Limited economic resources;

         v.   Having a high-school education or less;

         vi.   Parents who are divorced or have unhappy marriages;

         vii.   Parents who are divorced or have unhappy marriages;

   5.   Consequences of Divorce

      a.   An estimated 60 percent of divorcing couples have one or more children.

      b.   By age 16, about one in every three white and two in every three African American children will experience divorce within their families. Some children experience more than one divorce during their childhood because one or both of their parents may remarry and subsequently divorce again.

    c.   Divorce changes relationships for other relatives, especially grandparents.

C.   Remarriage

1.   Most people who divorce get remarried: more than 40% of all marriages take place between previously married brides and/or grooms, and about half of all persons who divorce before age 35 will remarry within three years.

2.   Most divorced people remarry others who have been divorced. At all ages, a greater proportion of men than women remarry and often relatively soon after divorce. Among women, those who divorce at younger ages are more likely to remarry than are those who are older; women with a college degree and without children are less likely to remarry.

3.   As a result of divorce and remarriage some people become part of *blended families*.

VI.   DIVERSITY IN FAMILIES

A.   Diversity among Singles

1.   Some never married singles choose to remain single because of opportunities for a career (especially for women), the availability of sexual partners without marriage, a belief that the single lifestyle is full of excitement, and a desire to be self sufficient and have the freedom to change and experiment.

2.   Other never married singles remain single out of necessity; they cannot afford to marry and set up their own household.

3.   Among persons age 15 and over, over 43.5% of African Americans have never married, as compared with almost 33.2% of Latinas/os, 33.1% of Asian and Pacific Islander Americans, and 24.5% of whites. Among women age 20 and over, the difference is even more pronounced.

B.   African American Families

1.   A higher proportion of African Americans than whites lives in extended family households that may provide emotional and financial support not otherwise available.

2.   Among middle and upper-middle class African American families, nuclear families are more prevalent than extended family ties.

C.   Latina/o Families

1.   Family support systems found in many Latina/o families -- "*la familia*" -- cover a wide array of relatives including parents, aunts, uncles, cousins, brothers and sisters, and their children.

2.   Some sociologists question the extent that *familialism* exists across social classes. Norma Williams found that extended family networks are disappearing, especially among advantaged urban Latinos/as.

D.   Asian American Families

1.   While many Asian Americans live in nuclear families, others (especially those residing in Chinatowns) have extended family networks. Some are referred to as semi-extended families because other relatives live in close proximity but not necessarily in the same household.

     2.   Extended family networks of some Vietnamese Americans are limited because family members died in the war in Vietnam, and others did not migrate to the United States.

  E.   Native American Families

     1.   Family ties remain strong among many Native Americans, who have always been known for their strong family ties.

     2.   Extended family patterns are common among lower income Native Americans living on reservations; most others live in nuclear families.

  F.   Biracial Families

     1.   Since the 1970's, there has been a 300 percent increase in marriages between people of different races; when these couples produce offspring, their children are considered to be biracial.

     2.   Interracial marriage was illegal in sixteen states until 1967.

     3.   At the beginning of the twenty-first century, skin color and place of birth have ceased to be reliable indicators of a person's identity or origin; the term *interracial marriage* has taken on a much broader interpretation.

VII. FAMILY ISSUES IN THE FUTURE

  A.   Some people believe that the family as we know it is doomed; others believe that a return to traditional family values will save this social institution and create greater stability in society.

  B.   Sociologist **Lillian Rubin** suggests that clinging to a traditional image of families is hypocritical in light of our society's failure to support them. Some laws have the effect of hurting children whose families do not meet the traditional model. For example, cutting down on government programs which provide food and medical care for pregnant women and infants will result in seriously ill children rather than model families.

  C.   People's perceptions about what constitutes a family will continue to change in the next century: the family may become those persons on whom one can depend for emotional support, who are available in crises and emergencies, or who provide continuing affections, concern, and companionship.

PRACTICE TESTS

MULTIPLE CHOICE QUESTIONS

Select the response that best answers the question or completes the statement:

1. According to the text, traditional definitions of the family:

  a.   are still highly applicable to today's families.

  b.   include all persons in a relationship who wish to consider themselves a family.

  c.   need to be expanded to provide a more encompassing perspective on what constitutes a family.

  d.   are indistinguishable from contemporary definitions of the family.

2. A social network of people based on common ancestry, marriage, or adoption is known as:

   a. kinship.

   b. a family.

   c. a clan.

   d. subculture.

3. The family of procreation is defined as "the family _____."

   a. into which a person is born.

   b. in which people receive their early socialization.

   c. that is composed of relatives in addition to parents and children who live in the same household.

   d. a person forms by having or adopting children.

4. Families that include grandparents, uncles, aunts, or other relatives who live in close proximity to the parents and children are known as a(n):

   a. clan.

   b. extended family.

   c. nuclear family.

   d. family of procreation.

5. _____ is the concurrent marriage of one man with two or more women, while _____ is the concurrent marriage of one woman with two or more men.

   a. Monogamy - polygamy

   b. Patriarchy - matriarchy

   c. Polygyny - polyandry

   d. Polyandry - polygyny

6. The most prevalent pattern of power and authority in families is:

   a. matriarchy.

   b. monarchy.

   c. oligarchy.

   d. patriarchy.

7. All of the following statements are correct regarding power and authority in families, **except**:

   a. Recently, there has been a trend toward more egalitarian family relationships in a number of countries.

   b. Some degree of economic independency makes it possible for women to delay marriage.

   c. The egalitarian family places a heavier burden on women around the globe than does patriarchal.

   d. Scholars have found no historical evidence to indicate that true matriarchies ever existed.

8. The custom of a married couple living in their own residence apart from both the husband's and the wife's parents is known as:

    a. isolated residence.

    b. neolocal residence.

    c. neutral local residence.

    d. exogamous residence.

9. When a person marries someone who comes from the same social class, racial-ethnic group, and religious affiliation, sociologists refer to this marital pattern as:

    a. endogamy.

    b. exogamy.

    c. inbreeding.

    d. intraclass reproduction.

10. In the United States, _____ was a key figure in developing a functionalist model of the family.

    a. C. Wright Mills

    b. Talcott Parsons

    c. Charles H. Cooley

    d. Peter Berger

11. According to functionalists, all of the following are key functions of families, **except**:

    a. provision of social status.

    b. economic and psychological support.

    c. maintenance of workers so that they can function effectively in the workplace.

    d. sexual regulation and socialization of children.

12. According to _____ theorists, interaction between marital partners contributes to a shared reality.

    a. feminist

    b. conflict

    c. functionalist

    d. symbolic interactionist

13. According to Lenore Walker, females are socialized to be _____ while males are socialized to be _____.

    a. jealous; possessive.

    b. passive; aggressive.

    c. dominant in the home; dependent in the work force.

    d. passive; communicative.

14. At what point in history did people in the United States come to view home and work as separate spheres?

    a. during colonial times.

    —b. during the Industrial Revolution.

    c. at the end of World War II.

    d. in the 1980s when more middle class, white women entered the paid workforce.

15. Which of the following statements regarding cohabitation is true?

    a. Attitudes about cohabitation have not changed very much in the past two decades.

    b. The Bureau of the Census recently developed a more inclusive definition of cohabitation.

    c. People most likely to cohabit are those who are under age 30 and who have not been married before.

    —d. In the United States, many lesbian and gay couples cohabit because they cannot enter into a legally recognized marital relationship.

16. Sociologist _____ coined the term "second shift" to refer to the domestic work that employed women perform at home after they complete their workday on the job.

    —a. Arlie Hochschild

    b. Talcott Parsons

    c. Kath Weston

    d. Francesca Cancian

17. Recent studies of teen pregnancy have concluded that:

    a. teenage pregnancies are increasing rapidly in the United States.

    b. teenage mothers often are as skilled at parenting as older mothers.

    —c. there has been an increase in teenage pregnancies among unmarried teenagers.

    d. the media no longer focuses on "the problem" of teenage pregnancies.

18. According to sociologist Alice Rossi, men secure their status as adults by _____; women secure their status as adults by _____.

    a. fathering - mothering.

    b. their employment - their employment.

    c. their sports abilities - their housekeeping skills.

    — d. their employment - maternity.

19. All of the following are cited in the text as primary social characteristics of those most likely to get divorced, **except**:

    — a. marriage at a later age and being set in one's ways.

    b. a short acquaintanceship before marriage.

    c. disapproval of marriage by relatives and friends.

    d. parents who are divorced or have unhappy marriages.

20. In discussing diversity in families, the text points out that:

    a.   a higher percentage of whites live in extended family households than do African Americans.

— b.   there is no such thing as "the" African American, Latina/o, Asian American, or Native American family.

    c.   working-class African American women often are encouraged by their families to choose marriage over education.

    d.   extended family patterns are no longer common among lower income Native Americans living on reservations.

TRUE FALSE QUESTIONS

1. The standard sociological definition of "family" is still in use today.
   True or False

2. In industrialized societies, other social institutions fulfill some of the functions previously taken care of by the kinship network.
   True or False

3. In the United States, the only legally sanctioned form of marriage is monogamy.
   True or False

4. Today, there are no known societies that practice polyandry.
   True or False

5. In industrial societies, kinship is usually traced through patrilineal descent.
   True or False

6. Functionalists suggest that the erosion of family values may occur when religion becomes less important in everyday life.
   True or False

7. According to Parsons, the husband/father fulfills the expressive role in the family.
   True or False

8. According to some feminist scholars, hostility and violence against women and children may be attributed to patriarchal attitudes, economic hardship, and rigid gender roles in society.
   True or False

9. Postmodernists perspectives describe the post-modern family as permeable.
   True or False

10. A domestic partnership is a household partnership in which an unmarried couple lives together in a committed, sexually intimate relationship that is granted the same rights and benefits as those accorded to married heterosexual couples.
    True or False

11. Over 50 percent of all marriages in the United States are dual-earner marriages.
    True or False

12. According to research many U.S. women spend up to one-third of their life attempting to control their reproductivity.
    True or False

13. Women who are involuntarily childless are often thought of as "selfish."
    True or False

14. An estimate 60 percent of divorcing couples have one or more children.
    True or False

15. Interracial marriage was illegal in sixteen states until 1950 when the Supreme Court overturned miscegenation.
    True or False

FILL IN THE BALNK QUESTIONS

1. The family of _____ is the one into which a person is born.

2. The most prevalent form of polygamy is _____ .

3. A system of tracing decent through the mother's side is known as _____ decent.

4. The practice of marrying those with similar characteristics is known as _____ and is somewhat similar to the practice of _____ .

5. For over forty years, the eminent _____ was considered to be the definite researcher on human sexuality.

6. Margaret Mead suggested that the _____ marriage pattern would best prepare couples for commitment and parenthood.

7. Household partnerships wherein an unmarried couple lives together in a committed sexually intimate relationship and is granted the same benefits as those accorded to married heterosexual couples are defined as _____ .

8. According to sociologist Arlie Hoschild, the _____ is the domestic work that employed women perform at home after they complete their work day on the job.

9. Over 50 percent of all marriages in the United States are _____ .

10. The _____ nanny is the best paid and most prestigious home caregiver.

SHORT ANSWER/ESSAY QUESTIONS

1. How do sociologists define family?

2. What are the functionalists, symbolic interactionists, conflict, feminists, and postmodernists perspectives on families?

3. What are some of the problems of the family in the United States today? What would you recommend as some solutions to these problems?

4. How could the family be described s both a "haven in a heartless world" and a "cradle of violence"?

5. What are some of the causes and consequences of divorce?

STUDENT CLASS PROJECTS AND ACTIVITIES

1. Select and then research a topic of unconventional reproduction, such as IN VITRO fertilization, (also known as test-tube fertilization), artificial insemination, or surrogacy. After selecting the topic, (1) trace the history of the development of that specific type of reproduction; (2) provide a description and definition of the reproduction procedure; (3) describe the widespread use of the procedure; and (4) discuss any complications, moral, legal, or medical that have surfaced related to the practice. Additionally, (5) examine and report any court cases that relate to your specific topic that have surfaced. In the writing of your paper, ensure that you provide a conclusion and a personal evaluation of this specific project.

2. Write a paper on the American family in the century ahead. Provide at least four bibliographic sources, (such as the text, other books, periodicals, newspaper articles, etc.). The paper could center on the topic: "The American Family in the Twenty-First Century." Issues to be included are the following: (1) what type of family form will be dominant; has the nuclear family disappeared? (2) as families change, has the type of community changed as well? (3) what is the status of commuter marriage? (4) describe the dating practice: will the dating game be a "dangerous sport" because of the health risk? (5) what about life-expectancy? Has the life span increased? (6) what about "variations of the theme family"? Are there a variety of new categories, such as gay and lesbian couples with and without children, single women having babies by donor insemination, etc.? (7) what about diet? (8) what type of child care is available; (9) what is the size of the family; (10) who is taking care of aged relatives; (11) describe the place of residence. Include any other information that pertains to this topic. In the writing of this project, follow any other specific guidelines and submit your paper at the appropriate time.

3. This is a short assignment that should typed. Be sure and submit your paper to your instructor on the due date. This paper should be a minimum of five pages. Instructions: construct a "sociological" family tree of your relatives of at least three generations (your grandparents, parents, aunts, uncles, and your own generation). Record names, dates, and information as you gather this information. Examine your genealogy for some of the following norms of marriage: (1) who married, who did not; (2) who did your relatives marry; (3) age at marriage; (4) did the norms of homogamy operate; (5) did they marry "up" or "down"; (6) number of children in the marriage; (7) number of divorces, if any; and (8) their religion. You may need to interview several family members, perhaps, to get the correct information for the above. Record all information carefully. After recording the information, examine how closely your family's marital choices follow the patterns of the typical American explained in the text and why variations might have occurred in your family tree. In your paper, include your reactions to your research on your family.

INTERNET ACTIVITIES

1. This family education page contains gateways to a number of sites with information relative to a study of the family and children. Surf these sites

and write up a critique or summary about the information each contains.
www.familyeducation.com/home/

2. This "family.com" site is a resource center for busy families. Can you guess who the primary user of this site might be? Imagine yourself as a working parent. What kinds of information on this site could you use? What information would not be useful? http://family.go.com/

3. The Economic and Legal Benefits of Marriage - search the site and present a debate on the pros and cons of **cohabitation**. www.religioustolerance.org/mar_bene.htm

4. Here you will find resources related to domestic violence. Contact one or more references and report back to class on the value of the resource. www.silcom.com/~paladin/madv/astrid.html

5. Use these sites to produce a report on the state of children both here in the United States and globally. Describe the ways that the welfare of children is directly connected to the state of families.

   a. www.unicef.org/sowc96/contents.htm?477,233

   b. www.futureofchildren.org/

   c. www.researchforum.org/

INFOTRAC EXERCISES

1. Investigate **domestic partnerships** (legal relationships between gay/lesbian couples that grant them some of the same rights as married couples) to distinguish them from marriage.

2. An increasing number of children are raised in **single parent households**; most of these are female headed. What are the social and social psychological consequences of being without a father?

3. Search for the term, **domestic violence**, and learn about measures being taken to combat this social problem. See report on African-American resources reported in Ebony magazine.

4. Search the category **polygamy**. Compare research about cross-cultural marriage practices. Apply the functionalist perspective to these kinds of practices.

5. Divide up the subdivisions on **teenage pregnancy** among class members. Construct a collective report on this phenomenon using a contribution from each class member.

6. Search for the keywords **dual career families**. Most of your students will probably fall into this category. Have students search through these reports and compose a list of good advice that they might put to use in their own future.

7. The number of reported incidents of **child abuse** in this country is very high. Analyze the incidence and types of child abuse, as well as risk factors.

8. Assess the incidence of and reasons for **international adoptions**. From which countries are American parents most likely to adopt and why?

9. Assess the social consequences of **cohabitation**, especially from a global perspective.

Solutions

MULTIPLE CHOICE QUESTIONS

1. C p. 490

2. A p. 491

3. D p. 492

4. B p. 492

5. C p. 493-494

6. D p. 495

7. C p. 495

8. B p. 497

9. A p. 497

10. B p. 497

11. C p. 498

12. D p. 500

13. B p. 500

14. B p. 503

15. D p. 504

16. A p. 504

17. C p. 508

18. D p. 510

19. A p. 512-513

20. B p. 516

TRUE FALSE QUESTIONS

1. F p. 490

2. T p. 491

3. T p. 493

4. F p. 494

5. F p. 495

6. T p. 499

7. F p. 498

8. T p. 499-500

9. T p. 501

10. T p. 504

11. T p. 504

12. F p. 506

13. T p. 507

14. T p. 513

15. F p. 518

FILL IN THE BALNK QUESTIONS

1. orientation

2. polygyny

3. matrilineal

4. homogamy, endogamy

5. Alfred Kinsey

6. two-step

7. domestic relationships

8. second shift

9. dual earner marriages

10. "six-figure"

Chapter 16

EDUCATION

BRIEF CHAPTER OUTLINE

An Overview of Education

Education in Historical-Global Perspective

- Informal Education in Preliterate Societies
- Formal Education in Preindustrial, Industrial Societies, and Postindustrial Societies.
- Contemporary Education in Other Nations

Sociological Perspectives on Education

- Functionalist Perspectives
- Conflict Perspectives
- Symbolic Interactionist Perspectives
- Postmodernist Perspectives

Inequality Among Elementary and Secondary Schools

- Inequality in Public vs. Private Schools
- Unequal Funding of Public Schools
- Inequality within Public School Systems
- Racial Segregation and Resegregation of Schools

Problems Within Elementary and Secondary Schools

- School Discipline and Teaching Styles
- Bullying, Teasing, and Sexual Harassment
- School Violence
- Dropping Out

Problems in — Colleges and Universities

Racial and Ethnic Differences in Enrollment
Academic Standards and Functional Illiteracy
The Soaring Cost of a College Degree
Racial and Ethnic Differences in Enrollment
The Lack of Faculty Diversity
The Debate over Affirmative Action

Future Issues and Trends in Education

The Debate over Bilingual Education

CHAPTER SUMMARY

Education is one of the most significant social institutions in the United States and other high-income nations; however, there is a lack of consensus regarding the effect of social factors upon individuals' access to and differential rewards of academic achievement. **Education** is the social institution responsible for the systematic transmission of knowledge, skills, and cultural values within a formally organized structure. People in preliterate societies acquire knowledge and skills through **informal education**; in preindustrial and industrial societies, people acquire specific knowledge, skills, and thinking processes through **formal education**. **Mass education** refers to providing free public schooling for wide segments of a nation's population. In addition to teaching the basics, U.S. schools today also teach a myriad of topics ranging from computer skills to AIDS prevention. In examining contemporary education in other nations, education in Japan and in Bosnia, are contrasted; Japan's system is centralized; in Bosnia, many schools identify and educate their students by their ethnic background. Functionalists have suggested that education performs a number of essential functions for society; however, conflict theorists emphasize that education perpetuates class, racial ethnic, and gender inequalities. Symbolic Interactionists point out that education may become a *self-fulfilling prophecy* for students who perform up -- or down -- to the expectations held for them by teachers. Postmodernists highlight the permeability of both lower and higher education today, with urbanity, autonomy, and consumption, as major characteristics. The U. S. public schools today are a microcosm of many of the problems facing the country: inequality in public vs. private schools, unequal funding of public schools, inequality within public school systems, and racial and ethnic segregation and resegregation. Problems within elementary and secondary schools include school discipline and teaching styles, bullying, teasing, and sexual harassment, school violence, and students dropping out. Problems in higher education include: the soaring cost of a college degree, racial and ethnic differences in enrollment, lack of faculty diversity, and the debate over affirmative action. Much has been written about the issues facing education in the United States and other nations. Some social analysts believe that academic standards are not high enough in U.S. schools. Suggestions for reducing both illiteracy and **functional literacy** have focused on school reforms. As the U.S. becomes more racially, ethnically, and culturally diverse, the issue of *bilingual education* becomes even more critical. In Lau v. Nichols the court affirmed the responsibility of the states and local districts for providing education for minority-language students. Another recent concern in education has been how to provide better educational opportunities for student with disabilities. The debate continues over school vouchers, which give parents the choice of what school their child will attend. As compared to the voucher system, the charter school movement creates public schools that operate under a charter contracts negotiated by the school's organizers and a sponsor. Another alternative educational program is home schooling, which is chosen by some parents who hope to avoid the problems of public schools while providing a quality education for their children. In 2001, Congress passed the "No Child Left Behind Act." intended to challenge the state's public school systems to meet certain education goals. In the United States, education in the future must accommodate the increasing diversity of the U. S. population at all levels of education.

LEARNING OBJECTIVES

After reading Chapter 16, you should be able to:

1. Describe the type of education found in preliterate societies.

2. Trace the history of education in preindustrial and industrial societies to the present.

3. Compare and contrast contemporary education in other nations using Japan and Bosnia as the models.

4. Describe the functionalist perspective on education and note the societal importance of manifest and latent functions fulfilled by this social institution.

5. Describe conflict perspectives on education and note how they differ from a functionalist perspective.

6. Discuss symbolic interactionist perspectives on education, and describe the significance of the self-fulfilling prophecy and labeling on educational achievement.

7. Explain postmodernist perspectives in lower and higher education.

8. Explain the four major types of inequality among elementary and secondary schools

9. List and discuss some major problems in U. S. elementary and secondary education.

10. Describe four recent problems in U. S. higher education and discuss possible solutions to these problems.

11. Trace the history of the debate over affirmative action in higher education, citing the two U. S. Supreme Court 2003 decisions and the influence of those decisions.

12. Explain the purpose and provisions of the "No Child Left Behind Act" report.

13. Describe some of the leading discipline problems in today's public schools.

14. List and discuss four alternative approaches for improving education.

KEY TERMS

(defined at page number shown and in glossary)

credentialism 535
cultural capital 533
cultural transmission 524
education 525
formal education 525

functional illiteracy 550
hidden curriculum 534
informal education 524
mass education 525
tracking 533

KEY PEOPLE

(identified at page number shown)

CHAPTER OUTLINE

I.   AN OVERVIEW OF EDUCATION:

    A.   Education is a powerful and influential institution that imparts values, beliefs, and knowledge considered essential to the social reproduction of individual personalities and entire cultures.

    B.   Education is a socializing institution: early socialization primarily takes place in families and friendship networks; later socialization occurs in more formalized organizations created for the purposes of educating people.

II. EDUCATION IN HISTORICAL-GLOBAL PERSPECTIVE

    A.   **Education** is the social institution responsible for the systematic transmission of knowledge, skills, and cultural values within a formally organized structure.

    B.   **Informal education:** learning that occurs in a spontaneous, unplanned way- is found in preliterate societies.

    C.   **Formal education:** learning that takes place within an academic setting such as a school, which has a planned instructional process and teachers who convey specific knowledge, skills, and thinking process to students- is found in preindustrial and industrial societies.

    D.   Early Formal Education

        1.   Earliest formal education probably occurred in ancient Greece and Rome where philosophers taught elite males to become thinkers and orators.

        2.   Between the fall of the Roman Empire and the beginning of the Middle Ages, only the sons of wealthy lords received formal education; other children were trained through apprenticeships in merchant and crafts guilds.

        3.   During the Middle Ages, the first colleges and universities were developed under the auspices of the church and the concept of human depravity was introduced into the curriculum.

        4.   During the Renaissance, education shifted from a focus on human depravity to the importance of developing well-rounded and liberally educated people.

        5.   As societies industrialize, the need for formal education for the masses increases. **Mass education** refers to providing free, public schooling under the leadership of Horace Mann.

        6.   In addition to teaching the basics, U.S. schools teach a myriad of topics and perform many tasks that previously were performed by other social institutions.

7. Controversy exists over whose values should be taught.

E. Contemporary Education in Other Nations

1. In Japan, when the country began to industrialize during the Meiji Period (1868-1912), public education became mandatory for children.

   a. An educational system and national educational goals were set up.

   b. Education was linked with economic and national development;conformity and nationalism was emphasized.

   c. Today toddlers are sent to cram schools (*jukus*) to ensure enrollment in good pre-schools.

   d. Middle school academic achievement determines the high school; to enter colleges and universities, students must score well on a variety of college entrance exams prepared by each college or university.

   e. At the college and university level, there is an absence of female students and professors.

2. In Bosnia, in spite of the peace agreement among the Muslims, Eastern Orthodox Serbs, and Roman Catholic Croats, animosities remain.

   a. Each group has taken control over how its children are educated; in certain classes, students are segregated into ethnically distinct classrooms.

   b. Students are taught different versions of history, language, and art depending upon their ethnic identity.

   c. Schools with integrated classrooms have increase in conflicts among the different ethnic groups.

III. SOCIOLOGICAL PERSPECTIVES ON EDUCATION

A. Functionalists view education as one of the most important components of society.

1. Education serves five major **manifest functions** -- open, stated, and intended goals or consequences of activities within an organization or institution:

   a. Socialization

   b. Transmission of culture

   c. Social control

   d. Social placement

   e. Change and innovation.

2. Education has at least three **latent functions** -- hidden, unstated, and sometimes unintended consequences of activities within an organization or institution:

   a. Restricting some activities

   b. Matchmaking and production of social networks

   c. Creation of a generation gap.

B. According to conflict theorists, schools perpetuate class, race-ethnic, and gender inequalities as some groups seek to maintain their privileged position at the expense of others.

1. Cultural Capital and Class Reproduction: education is a vehicle for reproducing existing class relationships.

     a.   According to Pierre Bourdieu, children have less chance of academic success when they lack **cultural capital** -- social assets that include values, beliefs, attitudes, and competencies in language and culture.

     b.   Children from middle and upper income families are endowed with more cultural capital than children from working class and poverty level families.

2.   Tracking and Social Inequality:

     a.   Class reproduction also occurs through standardized tests, ability grouping, and **tracking** -- the assignment of students to specific courses and educational programs based on their test scores, previous grades, or both.

3.   Social Class and The Hidden Curriculum:

     a.   The **hidden curriculum** is the transmission of cultural values and attitudes, such as conformity and obedience to authority, through implied demands found in rules, routines, and regulations of schools.

     b.   Lower class students may be disqualified from higher education and the credentials needed in a society that emphasizes **credentialism** -- a process of social selection in which class advantage and social status are linked to the possession of academic qualification.

     c.   Credentialism is closely related to *meritocracy* -- a social system in which status is assumed to be acquired through individual ability and effort.

4.   Gender Bias in Schools

     a.   Studies show that gender bias pervades the overall academic environment and cuts across lines of race and class.

     b.   Teachers tend to encourage boys to be the problem solvers; through reading materials, classroom activities, and treatment by teachers and peers, female students learn that they are less important than male students.

     c.   Some analysts suggest that girls receive subtle cues from adults that lead them to attribute success to their intelligence and ability. Conversely, girls attribute failure to lack of ability, while boys attribute failure to lack of effort.

5.   Ethnicity, Language and Hidden Curriculum

     a.   English as a second language instructors frequently find that they not only teach children English, but social skills as well.

     b.   The children are exposed to a wide range of beliefs, values, attitudes and behavior expectations that are not directly related to their subject matter.

     c.   Conflict theorists argue that inequality is structurally produced and reproduced by formal and informal socialization processes in schools and other educational settings.

C.   Symbolic Interactionist Perspectives on Education

1.   Labeling and the Self-Fulfilling Prophecy

     a.   For some students, schooling may become a self-fulfilling prophecy -- an unsubstantiated belief or prediction that results in behavior which makes the originally false belief come true.

2.   Using Labeling Theory to Examine the IQ Debate

        a.   The experiment of Rosenthal and Jacobson demonstrated the effect of teacher expectation upon the resultant IQ scores.

        b.   If a teacher (as a result of stereotypes based on the relationship between IQ and race) believes that some students of color are less capable of learning, that teacher (sometimes without even realizing it) may treat them as if they were incapable of learning.

    3.   Education and Labeling

        a.   IQ testing has resulted in labeling of students (e.g., African American and Mexican American children have been placed in special education classes on the basis of IQ scores when they could not understand the tests).

        b.   A *self-fulfilling prophecy* also can result from labeling students as gifted. When some students are labeled as better than others, they may achieve at a higher level because of the label, or they may face discrimination from others (e.g., Asian Americans as super intelligent).

D.   Postmodern Perspectives

    1.   Postmodernists often highlight differences and inequality in society; therefore education is characterized by its permeability.

    2.   Urbanity is reflected in multicultural and anti-bias curricular introduced in early childhood education.

    3.   Autonomy is evidenced in policies such as voucher systems.

    4.   In higher education, the permeability is exemplified by "educational consumption," the offering of "high-tech" or "wired" campuses, virtual classrooms, and student centers offering extravagant activities and services.

    5.   According to Ritzer, "McUniversity" can be thought of as a means of educational consumption that allows students to consumer educational services and eventually obtain "goods" such as degrees and credentials.

IV.   INEQUALITIES AMONG ELEMENTARY AND SECONDARY SCHOOLS

A.   Inequality in Public vs. Private Schools

    1.   Almost 90 percent of U. S. elementary and secondary students are educated in public schools; about 9.5 percent of all students are educated in low-tuition private schools, primarily Catholic; 1.5 percent of all students attend high-tuition private school.

    2.   Private schools are perceived as better than public schools, but according to some social analysts, there is little to substantiate this claim.

B.   Unequal Funding of Public Schools

    1.   Most educational funds are derived from local property taxes and state legislative appropriations.

    2.   Children living in affluent suburbs often attend relatively new schools and have access to the latest equipment which students in central city schools and poverty-ridden rural areas lack.

C.   Inequality within Public School Systems

1. Using the New York City public schools as a case study, the research shows that schools are stratified into higher-, middle-, and lower-tiered schools.

2. Higher-tier schools are highly specialized; admission is limited based upon competitive entrance examination; dropout rates are low. A large number of graduates attend prestigious universities.

3. Middle-tier schools, located in fairly well-integrated neighborhoods are often referred to as "ed op"(educational option) schools; they offer training for specific careers; some serve as *magnet schools*, offering a specialized curriculum and enrolling high-achieving students from other neighborhoods.

4. Lower-tier high schools are very large, overcrowded, and located in highly segregated, deteriorating, and violent neighborhoods. Students have the highest dropout rate, the lowest graduate rates, the worst scores on standardized tests, the poorest attendance patterns, and the worst statistics on assaults and possession of weapons.

D. Racial Segregation and Resegregation of Schools

1. In many areas of the U.S. schools remain segregated or have become resegregated after earlier attempts at integration failed.

    a. Four decades after the 1954 U.S. Supreme Courtt ruled in Brown v. The Board of Education of Topeka, Kansas that segregated schools were unconstitutional, racial segregation remains.

    b. Racial segregation is increasing in many school districts and efforts to bring about desegregation or integration have failed in many school districts.

2. Racially segregated schools often have low retention rates, students with below-grade level reading skills, high teacher-student ratios, less qualified teachers, and low teacher expectations.

    a. Even in supposedly integrated schools, tracking and ability grouping may produce resegregation at the classroom level.

    b. African-American and white achievement differences increase with every year of schooling; thus, schools may reinforce, rather than eliminate the disadvantages of race and class.

V. PROBLEMS WITHIN ELEMENTARY AND SECONDARY SCHOOLS

A. School Discipline and Teaching Styles

1. Leading discipline problems include violence, drug abuse, suicide, robbery, assault, and other forms of aggressive behavior.

2. Most states now prohibit the use of corporal punishment and some school districts prohibit various forms of disciplinary actions.

3. Teaching and disciplinary styles may differ across racial and ethnic lines; some argue that color should be noticed.

4. Jean Anyon suggests that structural inequalities need to be addressed in order to achieve educational reform.

B. Bulling, Teasing, and Sexual harassment

1. According to research on behalf of the AAUW, 83 percent of girls and 79 percent of boys report experiencing harassment.

2. Seventy-six percent of students have experienced nonphysical harassment while 58 percent have experienced physical harassment.

3. Harassed girls report being negatively affected by harassment more often then do boys.

4. Substantial numbers of students fear that they will be sexually harassed or hurt in school; for those who are constantly picked on , ridiculed, or harassed, school becomes sheer torture.

C. School Violence

1. In U. S. schools, there is an increase in violence and in the number of students who bring guns, knives, and other weapons on school premises.

2. Many students must learn in an academic environment that is similar to a maximum security prison.

3. John Devine argues that violence in schools will not end until guns in the US. are eliminated.

D. Dropping Out

1. Dropout rates vary by race/ethnic, class and regional differences.

2. Explanations for the group having highest rate of dropouts (Hispanics, or Latinos/as) vary:

   a. Labeled as troublemakers, they actually become "dropouts."

   b. They view school as a waste of time.

   c. They may be skeptical about the value of school

3. From the research of Romo and Falbo, the most common reasons given for dropping out included: lack of interest in school, serious personal problems, serious family problems, poor grades, and alcohol and/or drug problems.

4. The same research found that a growing number of students are taking the GED (General Equivalent Diploma) exam rather than graduating from high school, which puts many in dead-end situations.

VI. PROBLEMS IN COLLEGES AND UNIVERSITIES

A. The Soaring Cost of a College Degree

1. The cost of attending private and public institutions has increased dramatically over the past decade; higher than the overall rate of inflation.

2. This high cost of a college education reproduces the existing class system: students who lack money may be denied access to higher education, and those who are able to attend college tend to receive different types of education based on their ability to pay.

B. Racial and Ethnic Differences in Enrollment

1. Latina/o college enrollment increased from about 3.5 percent to 6.0 percent between 1976 and 2000, accounting for 8.9 percent of all college students, but 13.4 percent of the total U.S. population.

2. African American enrollment increased somewhat between 1970 and 2000, and remained steady at about 11 percent through the 1990s; gender differences are

evident: women accounted for more than 63 percent of all African American College students in 1999.

3. Native Americans remained at about 00.9 percent of enrollment from the 1970s to the 2000s; however, two-year community colleges — known as tribal colleges — on reservations have experienced an increase in Native American student enrollment.

4. At the doctorate degree level, only 18 percent of the doctorates awarded in 1999-2000 were to minority-group members; African Americans earned 6.6 percent; Asian Americans earned 7.1 percent; Latino/as 2.8 percent and Native Americans 0.5 percent.

C. Lack of Faculty Diversity

1. African Americans, Latinas/os, Asian Americans, and other people of color accounted for only about ten percent of all faculty members.

2. Minority faculty members are less likely to be full professors with tenure.

3. Women are underrepresented at the level of full professor and over represented at the assistant professor and instructor levels.

4. Minority faculty members are more likely than their white counterparts to be employed at two-year colleges; for example, 36 percent of Native American faculty members are employed at tribal colleges located on the reservations. Likewise, 39 percent of Latino/a faculty members are at two-year colleges; only 23 percent of white (non -Latina/o) faculty members are employed at two-year institutions.

5. The lack of Native Americans and Latinos/as as college students, especially in Ph.D. programs perpetuates the problem of diversity among faculty members; Asian American scholars are the exception to this problem: they are more likely to have a terminal degree in their field and to be employed at a research university.

D. The Debate over Affirmative Action

1. In 2003, the Supreme Court ruled in *Grutter v. Bollinger* (involving admissions policies of the University of Michigan's law school) and in *Gratz v. Bollinger* (involving the undergraduate admissions policies of the same university) that race can be a factor for universities in shaping their admissions programs, but only within carefully defined limits.

2. The debate over affirmative action continues; there are more questions on how to achieve greater representation of all racial and ethnic groups, gender and nationality among students, faculty, and administrators.

VII. FUTURE ISSUES AND TRENDS IN EDUCATION

A. Academic Standards and Functional Illiteracy

1. Some social analysts cite the rate of **functional illiteracy**, which is the inability to read and/or write at the skill level necessary for carrying out everyday tasks.

2. Estimates are that 56 percent of adult Latinas/os are functionally illiterate in English, compared with 44 percent of adult African Americans and 16 percent of adult (non-Latino/a) whites.

3. Most suggestions for reducing both illiteracy and functional illiteracy focus on school reforms such as: more testing of students and teachers, increasing the

requirements for high school graduation, and increasing the number of school days per year.

4. Illiteracy is a global problem as well as a national one; low rates of literacy for women in lower income nations reflect how different nations view education and gender.

B. The Debate over Bilingual Education

1. The issue of bilingual education is not a new one.

 a. During the late nineteenth and early twentieth centuries, children of U. S. immigrants often received classroom instruction from a teacher who spoke the children's native language.

 b. During World War I, members of white ethnic groups, in a demonstration of loyalty to the U. S., advocated that their children should be taught in English.

 c. Little bilingual education was offered until after World War II when a large influx of Mexican and Asian immigrants arrived in the United States, and schools enrolled large numbers of students who did not speak English.

 d. Congress mandated in 1968 that public schools must provide non-English speaking students with *bilingual education* - instruction in both a non-English language and in English.

 e. The U. S. Supreme Court decision, *Lau v Nichols* (1974) affirmed the responsibility of the states and local districts for providing appropriate education for minority-language students.

 f. Critics of TBE (transitional bilingual education) program believe that TBE programs are less effective than classes that are conducted primarily in English.

 g. Supporters of TBE believe that these programs are effective in helping children build competency both in their native language and in English.

C. Equalizing Opportunities for Students with Disabilities

1. *Disability* is regarded as any physical and/or mental condition that limits students' access to, or full involvement, in school life.

2. The Americans with Disabilities Act of 1990 requires schools and government agencies to make their facilities, services, activities, and programs accessible to people with disabilities.

3. The Individuals with Disabilities Education Act (IDEA) mandates that students with disabilities receive free and appropriate education.

 a. Many schools have attempted to *mainstream* children with disabilities by *inclusion programs* under which the special education curriculum is integrated with the regular education program, on *an individualized education plan* that provides annual education goals for each child.

4. Many schools have attempted to *mainstream* children with disabilities by *inclusion programs* under which the special education curriculum is integrated with the regular education program, on an *individualized* education plan that provides annual education goals for each child

D. School Vouchers give parents the choice of a school for the child.

1. Public funds are provided to students to pay for their choice of school, which can be public or private schools.

2. Research findings of a voucher program in Cleveland, Ohio found that parents with children in a voucher school were more satisfied with the voucher system than were the parents having their children in public schools.

E. Charter Schools and For Profit Schools

1. These types of schools operate under a charter contract negotiated by the schools' organizers and a sponsor who oversees the provisions of the contract.

2. Charter schools are said to be less bureaucratic and more responsive to the student's needs than public schools in large school districts.

3. Critics argue that these schools take money away from conventional public schools.

4. Proponents argue that charter schools provide a large number of minority students a higher quality education than they would in public schools.

5. The "contracting out" hiring for-profit companies are a more recent approach; companies are contracted to operate public schools. Nation-wide, most of the contracting is done by three private companies; about the privatization of education, which they believe undermines the public schools system.

F. Home Schooling is a choice by parents who seek to avoid the problems of public school while providing a quality education for their children.

1. Home-schoolers are more likely than other students to live with two or more siblings in a two-parent family, with only one parent working outside the home.

2. Typically, these parents are better educated, on average, than other parents, but their income is about the same. Researchers have found that boys and girls are equally likely to be home-schooled.

3. Proponents believe that their children are receiving a better education at home for various reasons; critics question the knowledge and competence of the typical parent to educate their own children at home.

G. Concluding Thoughts

1. The education needed for the future is different from that of the past.

2. Creating a system that encompasses vast cultural differences, but yet respects and preserves those differences and presents a challenge.

3. President George W. Bush signed into law the "No Child Left Behind Act of 2001," which requires that schools must be accountable for students' learning and sets forth steps for producing an accountable education system.

4. Will these changes make a difference; how critical are other pressing social problems, such as harassment, guns and violence in the schools?

5. Ultimately, the institution of education must be maintained and enhanced in various ways yet all of the varieties of programs have their critics and their supporters.

6. In the United States, education in the future must accommodate the increasing diversity of the U.S. population at all levels of education.

PRACTICE TESTS

MULTIPLE CHOICE QUESTIONS

Select the response that best answers the question or completes the statement:

1. _____ is the social institution responsible for the systematic transmission of knowledge, skills, and cultural values within a formally organized structure.
   a. Religion
   b. Mass media
   c. The government
   d. Education

2. The process by which children become acquainted with the value and knowledge of a society is called:
   a. a latent function of education.
   b. cultural transmission.
   c. cultural diffusion.
   d. formal education.

3. Preliteratel societies:
   a. have no written language.
   b. have a formal educational system.
   c. have an informal educational system.
   d. have a mass educational system.

4. The core curriculum consists of all the following courses **except**:
   a. mathematics.
   b. English.
   c. music education.
   d. social sciences.

5. According to the text, all of the following statements regarding contemporary U.S. education are true, except:
   a. U.S. schools are teaching a more limited number of topics so that they can focus on the "basics."
   b. U.S. schools are attempting to meet the needs of post industrial society.
   c. Controversy exists over what should be taught.
   d. Many educators believe that their job description now encompasses numerous tasks that previously were performed by other social institutions.

6. According to sociologist _____, education is crucial for promoting solidarity and stability in society.
   a. Emile Durkheim
   b. Pierre Bourdieu
   c. Amitai Etzion
   d. Max Weber

7. Which of the following is a manifest function of education?

    a. Creation of a generation gap.

    b. Restricting some activities.

    c. Matchmaking and production of social networks.

    d. Social control.

8. _____ functions are hidden, unstated, and sometimes unintended consequences of activities within an organization or institution.

    a. Manifest

    b. Dormant

    c. Latent

    d. Covert

9. Sociologist _____ has suggested that students come to school with differing amounts of cultural capital.

    a. Emile Durkheim

    b. Pierre Bourdieu

    c. Jeannie Oakes

    d. Max Weber

10. The assignment of students to specific courses and educational programs based on their test scores, previous grades, or both is known as:

    a. tracking.

    b. the hidden curriculum.

    c. equitable assessment.

    d. class reproduction.

11. According to the _____ perspective, the hidden curriculum affects working class and poverty level students more than it does students from middle and upper income families.

    a. functionalist

    b. conflict

    c. symbolic-interactionist

    d. feminist

12. The _____ focus on the classroom communication patterns and educational practices, such as labeling, that affect students' self-concept and aspirations.

    a. conflict theorists

    b. functionalists

    c. interactionists

    d. credentialists

13. A teacher who believes (as a result of stereotypes based on the relationship between IQ and race) that some students of color are less capable of learning and treats them accordingly may contribute to:

    a. a self-fulfilling prophecy.

    b. the labeling process.

    c. tracking.

    d. the hidden curriculum.

14. About _____ of the U.S. elementary and secondary students are educated in public schools.

    a. 54 percent

    b. 65 percent

    c. 80 percent

    d. 90 percent

15. HEAD START programs are funded by:

    a. the federal government.

    b. state legislative appropriations.

    c. local property taxes.

    d. special revenue programs such as, a state lottery.

16. In public schools in the 1940s, some of the leading discipline problems included:

    a. getting out of place in line.

    b. not putting paper in the trash can.

    c. talking without permission

    d. all of the above were a part of discipline problems.

17. The National Literacy Act of 1991 defines _____ as an individual's ability to read, write, and speak English and compute and solve problems at levels of proficiency necessary to function on the job and in society.

    a. functional illiteracy

    b. minimum literacy

    c. literacy

    d. functional literacy

18. In _____, the Supreme Court affirmed the responsibility of the states and local districts for providing appropriate education for minority-language students.

    a. *Brown v. Board of Education*

    b. *Lau v. Nichols*

    c. *Hopwood v. State of Texas*

    d. *Bakke v. The University of California at Davis*

19. According to some analysts, in entering college, _____ more likely enroll in clerical classes, while _____ are more likely to enroll in computer program courses.

    a. Boys; girls

    b. Teachers; principals

    c. Girls; boys

    d. Japanese students; African American students

20. Which of the following statements regarding higher education is true?

    a. The enrollment of low-income students has increased since the 1980s.

    b. There has been an increase in scholarship funds over the past decade.

    c. College students are stratified according to their ability to pay.

    d. Latinos/as earned more college doctorates than African Americans in the past two decades.

TRUE FALSE QUESTIONS

1. During the Middle Ages, the first colleges and universities were developed under the auspices of the government.
   True or False

2. *Jukus* are cram schools available only to middle and high school Japanese students.
   True or False

3. In public schools in Bosnia, class content is taught on a highly-structured centralized government approach.
   True or False

4. Manifest functions in education include teaching specific subjects, such as science, history, and reading.
   True or False

5. Meritocracy is the process of social selection in which class advantage and social status are linked to the possession of academic qualifications.
   True or False

6. Labeling students as "gifted" can result in a self-fulfilling prophecy.
   True or False

7. The issue of IQ and race/ethnicity originated with the highly controversial book by Herrnstein and Murray.
   True or False

8. Labeling and self-fulfilling prophecy are unique to U.S. schools.
   True or False

9. According to the postmodernists, higher education is not affected by the "McUniversity" phenomenon.
   True or False

10. Japan has the most decentralized system of public education on the modern industrialized countries.
    True or False

11. Most public educational funds come from the federal government.
    True or False

12. In the New York City school system, any student can attend the higher-tier high schools provided that she/he is a legal resident of the city.
    True or False

13. Most states now prohibit the use of corporal punishment of students in their public schools.
    True or False

14. Boys seldom report harassment from their classmates.
    True or False

15. One major problem of the voucher system is that poor children cannot transfer out of their neighborhood inner-city, lower-tier public school.
    True or False

FILL IN THE BLANK QUESTIONS

1. _____ refers to providing free public schooling for wide segments of a nation's population.

2. Intended goals or consequences of education such as socialization, transmission of culture, social control, social placement, and change and innovation are _____ functions.

3. _____ is the assignment of students to specific courses and educational programs based on their test scores, previous grades, or both.

4. About _____ percent of people between the ages of fourteen and twenty-four have left school before earning a high school diploma.

5. According to _____ , certain racial-ethnic groups differ in average IQ and are likely to differ in "intelligence genes" as well.

6. _____ offer specialized curriculum that focuses on areas such as science, music, or art, and enroll high-achieving students from other neighborhoods.

7. Education scholar _____ emphasized that violence in schools will not end until guns are eliminated from U.S. society.

8. Minority-groups members accounted for about _____ percent of the doctorates awarded in 1999-2000.

9. Some analysts believe that _____ has fulfilled its purpose and is no longer necessary, other analyst believe that the playing field remains uneven for many white women and people of color.

10. _____ means that children with disabilities work with a wide variety of people; over the course of a day, children may interact with their regular education teacher, the special education teacher, a speech therapist, an occupational therapist, a physical therapist, and a resource teacher, depending on the child's individual needs.

SHORT ANSWER/ESSAY QUESTIONS

1. Is education a vehicle for decreasing social inequality or is it that education reproduces existing class relationships? How might computer technology influence schools?

2. Compare and contrast the U.S. public schools with those of other countries?

3. What are the major problems in public schools today? In higher education?

4. What do you think are the most significant changes in education over the past twenty years? What changes would you predict for the future?

5. Based upon the postmodernist perspectives on education, what educational services and goods will students in both early childhood and higher education consume in the future? What will be the major attractions in the future educational setting?

STUDENT CLASS PROJECTS AND ACTIVITIES

1. In an October 1997 issue of *Time* magazine provides a special report on "How to save our schools." *Time* provides an analysis of America's best schools and not-so-good schools. Read the report and respond to the following questions: (1) What are some of the criteria that make for a good school? (2) Do inner-city schools support the voucher system of education? (3) What standards do many of the states advocate? (4) How should "Johnny" learn to read? Is the method of phonics the best program? Or is it the "whole-language" method of learning to read the better method? (5) Critique the "success" stories of three schools in three different places. Where are the schools? Why are they considered to be successful?

2. In the same issue, *Time* examines a major issue, "Where does the money go?" This article tracks the flow of cash through a single large urban district. Read the article and answer the following questions: (1) Do some urban schools fail to because they don't have the money to do better? (2) What is meant by the "dance of the lemons?" (3) What are some of the advantages/disadvantages of educational localism? (4) How can "bad" schools be fixed? (5) What are the roles of the federal government and external governmental control? (6) Critique the article.

3. Research the topic of public education in several high-income countries, such as France, Japan, New Zealand, the Netherlands, Sweden, England, Norway, Canada, or Germany. In the writing up of your paper include the following information: (1) a description of their educational system; (2) a description of their specific or unique feature; (3) a description of their curriculum; (4) a description of some of the strengths and weaknesses of their program; (5) a critique of their programs: which do you think work well? Which do not? (6) any other information that will enhance our understanding of their education; (7) provide a bibliography of your references; (8) turn your paper in to your instructor at the appropriate time.

263

INTERNET ACTIVIITES

1. The *National Education Association* (NEA) is currently the largest teachers' organization in the United States. Its purpose is to advance the interests of the teaching profession, push for teaching reform, and press for quality education in the United States. When you visit their site, see if you can analyze their core concerns. www.nea.org

2. The NEA also addresses the issue of low performing schools and what can be done to increase their performance. Analyze this plan using your Sociological Imagination and then brainstorm to create a list of obstacles that might prevent this plan from happening. www.nea.org/priorityschools/priority.html

3. The *American Federation of Teachers* (affiliated with the labor union the AFL-CIO) is one of the largest teachers' unions in the United States. Like the NEA, the AFT tries to represent teacher interests and further the quality of education. The AFT, like the NEA, sponsors research and reports on education. Explore and discover the current concerns of this teachers group. www.aft.org/index.html

4. The NCES is the *National Center for Education Statistics*. This organization is the primary federal entity that collects and analyzes educational data for the United States and other countries. This site gives you fast facts topics like the transition from high school to college, and educational statistics, e.g., earnings of college graduates. www.ed.gov/NCES/index.html

5. To look at information on home schooling, you may wish to visit the following sites. These kinds of sites provide information about the home school movement and provide resources for homeschoolers.

    a. http://homeschooling.about.com/mbody.htm

    b. www.home-school.com

    c. www.hslda.org/splash/default.asp

INFOTRAC EXERCISES

1. More and more states are turning to **standardized tests** to assess proficiency as a measure of school accountability and to determine whether students should pass to the next grade. What are some the costs and benefits of this approach?

2. **Home schooling** has become increasingly popular. What kinds of research questions are sociologists and educators asking? Compose a list of five research questions from articles listed on InfoTrac.

3. In the aftermath of Columbine and other school shootings, parents, students, and teachers are increasingly fearful of **school violence**. Investigate this issue with respect to its incidence and social policy implications.

4. Many states allow parents vouchers that permit them to send their child to a school outside their district. Investigate the **school voucher** system and see if you can learn what are the costs and benefits.

5. **Charter schools** operate in accordance with a "bottom line" that is specified by their charter. In exchange for meeting their educational goals, they are exempt from meeting traditional state rules and restrictions. Research the trend towards charter schools. What makes one school succeed and another fail?

6. There is currently an explosion of **on-line education** at the college level. On line courses offer convenience to the student, but at the same time, do not offer the same type of classroom interaction, even if the professor and students interact in a "chat room." Assess this trend and its significance for American education.

Solutions

MULTIPLE CHOICE QUESTIONS

1. D p. 524

2. B p. 524

3. C p. 524

4. C p. 526

5. A p. 526

6. A p. 529

7. D p. 530

8. C p. 530

9. B p. 532

10. A p. 533

11. B p. 534

12. C p. 536

13. A p. 537

14. D p. 539

15. A p. 539

16. D p. 543

17. C p. 550

18. B p. 551

19. C p. 535

20. C p. 546

TRUE FALSE QUESTIONS

1. F p. 525

2. F p. 527

3. F p. 528

4. T p. 530

5. F p. 535

6. T p. 536

7. F p. 537

8. F p. 538

9. F p. 538

10. F p. 539

11. F p. 539

12. F p. 540

13. T p. 543

14. F p. 546

15. F p. 554

FILL IN THE BLANK QUESTIONS

1. Mass education

2. manifest

3. Tracking

4. 10

5. Hernstein and Murray

6. Magnet schools

7. John Devine

8. 18

9. affirmative action

10. Inclusion

Chapter 17

RELIGION

BRIEF CHAPTER OUTLINE

The Sociological Study of Religion

- Religion and the Meaning of Life
- Religion and Scientific Explanations

Sociological Perspectives on Religion

- Functionalist Perspectives on Religion
- Conflict Perspectives on Religion
- Symbolic Interactionist Perspectives on Religion

World Religions

- Hinduism
- Buddhism
- Confucianism
- Judaism
- Islam
- Christianity

Types of Religious Organization

- Ecclesia
- The Church Sect Typology
- Cults

Trends in Religion in the United States

- Religion and Social Inequality
- Race and Class in Central-City and Suburban Churches
- Secularization and the Rise of Religious Fundamentalism

Religion in the Future

CHAPTER SUMMARY

Religion is one of the most significant social institutions in society. It can be a highly controversial topic; one group's deeply-held or cherished religious practices may be a source of irritation to another; it is a source of both stability and conflict not only in the United States but throughout the world. **Religion** is a system of beliefs, symbols, and rituals, based on some sacred or supernatural realm that guides human behavior, gives meaning to life, and unites believers into a moral community. Although religion seeks to answer important questions such as why we exist, why people suffer and die, and what happens when we die, increases in scientific knowledge have contributed to **secularization** -- the process by which religious beliefs, practices, and institutions lose their significance in sectors of society and culture. According to functionalists, religion provides meaning and purpose to life, promotes social cohesion and a sense of belonging, and provides social control and support for the government. The conflict perspective suggests that religion can have negative consequences: the capitalist class uses religion as a tool of domination to mislead workers about their true interests and retard social change. However, Max Weber believed that religion could be a catalyst for social change. Symbolic interactionists examine the meanings that people give to religion and the meanings they attach to religious symbols in their everyday life. Religions vary around the world. *Hinduism*, one of the world's oldest religion, is complex and diverse, comprising numerous varieties of beliefs and practices. *Buddhism* first emerged in India about 2500 years ago. It is based on the teachings of Buddha, who perceived that life is suffering and pain; the answer to world problems is achieved through mediation which leads to personal transformation and a spiritual existence. *Confucianism*, based upon the teachings of Confucius was the official religion of China until the Communist takeover and establishment of the People's Republic of China. Order in human relationships and a strict code of moral conduct are some of the basic concepts. Despite centuries of religious hatred and discrimination, *Judaism* persists as one of the world's most influential religions. The three key components of Judaism are: God (the deity), Torah (God's teachings), and Israel (the community or holy nation). *Islam* is based on the teachings of Muhammad, a prophet, not a deity; followers must adhere to the five Pillars of Islam. Almost one-third of the world's population is *Christian*, the dominant world religion today. The Christian deity is a sacred Trinity comprised of God the Father, Jesus the Son, and the Holy Spirit. Contemporary religious organizations may be categorized as **ecclesia**, **churches**, **denominations**, **sects**, and **cults**. Religion in the United States is diverse; pluralism and religious freedom are among the cultural values most widely espoused. Social science research continues to identify significant patterns between social class and religious denominations. With the increase of **secularization**, there has been a resurgence of religious **fundamentalism**. Maintaining an appropriate balance between religion and other aspects of social life will be an important challenge for the United States and other nations of the world in the future.

LEARNING OBJECTIVES

After reading Chapter 17, you should be able to:

1. Discuss the relationship between religion and the meaning of life.

2. Define and discuss the four main categories of religions.

3. Describe the functionalist perspective on religion and discuss its major functions in societies.

4. Compare and contrast civil religion with other forms of religion.

5. Describe conflict perspectives on religion and distinguish between the approaches of Karl Marx and Max Weber.

6. Describe symbolic interactionist perspectives on religion and explain how religion may be viewed differently by women and men.

7. List the six major world religions and state their basic beliefs.

8. Distinguish between the different types of religious organizations and note why a religious group may move from one category to another over time.

9. Describe the relationship between religion and social inequality.

10. Discuss the effects of race and class on central city and suburban churches in the United States.

11. Explain the relationship between the growth of secularization and the rise of religious fundamentalism.

12. Describe the future of religion in the United States and in other nations of the world.

KEY TERMS

(defined at page number shown and in glossary)

animism 564
church 582
civil religion 568
cult 583
denomination 582
ecclesia 582
faith 563
fundamentalism 586
liberation theology 586
monotheism 565

nontheism 565
polytheism 565
religion 564
rituals 562
sacred 564
sect 583
secularization 566
simple supernaturalism 564
theism 565

KEY PEOPLE

(identified at page number shown)

Nancy Ammerman 585
Robert Bellah 569
Peter Berger 563
Randall Collins 571
Emile Durkheim 564
Clifford Geertz 564

Lester Kurtz 562
Karl Marx 570
Meredith B. McGuire 569
Wade Clark Roof 567
Max Weber 571

CHAPTER OUTLINE

I.   THE SOCIOLOGICAL STUDY OF RELIGION

    A.   Religion and the Meaning of Life

        1.   **Religion** is a system of beliefs, symbols, and rituals, based on some sacred or supernatural realm, that guides human behavior, gives meaning to life, and unites believers into a community.

        2.   Religion seeks to answer important questions such as why we exist, why people suffer and die, and what happens when we die.

            a.   According to Peter Berger, religion is a sacred canopy, a sheltering fabric hanging over people providing security and answers to questions of life.

            b.   This sacred canopy requires **faith**, unquestioning belief that does not require proof or scientific evidence.

        3.   Sacred and Profane

            a.   According to Emile Durkheim, **sacred** refers to those aspects of life that are extraordinary or supernatural; those things that are set apart as "holy."

            b.   Those things people do not set apart as sacred are referred to as **profane** -- the everyday, secular or "worldly," aspects of life.

        4.   In addition to beliefs, religion also is comprised of symbols and **rituals** -- symbolic actions that represent religious meanings -- that range from songs and prayers to offerings and sacrifices.

        5.   Religions have been classified into four main categories based on their dominant belief:

            a.   **Simple supernaturalism** is the belief that supernatural forces affect people's lives either positively or negatively.

            b.   **Animism** is the belief that plants, animals, or other elements of the natural world are endowed with spirits or life forces having an impact on events in society.

            c.   **Theism** is a belief in one or more god or gods.

                i.   **Monotheism** is a belief in a single, supreme being or god who is responsible for significant events such as the creation of the world. Examples include: Christianity and Judaism.

                ii.   **Polytheism** is a belief in more than one god. Examples include Hinduism, Buddhism, and Shinto.

            d.   **Nontheistic religion** is based on a belief in divine spiritual forces such as sacred principles of thought and conduct , rather than a God or gods.

    B.   Religion and Scientific Explanation

        1.   During the Industrial Revolution, rapid growth in scientific and technological knowledge gave rise to the idea that science ultimately would answer questions that previously had been in the realm of religion.

        2.   Many scholars believed that scientific knowledge would result in **secularization** -- the process by which religious beliefs, practices, and institutions lose their significance in sectors of society and culture -- but others point out a resurgence

of religious beliefs and an unprecedented development of alternative religions in recent years.

II. SOCIOLOGICAL PERSPECTIVES ON RELIGION

    A. Functionalist Perspectives on Religion

        1. According to Emile Durkheim, all religions share in common three elements: (a) beliefs held by adherents; (b) practices (rituals) engaged in collectively by believers; and (c) a moral community which results from the groups shared beliefs and practices pertaining to the sacred.

        2. Religion has three important functions in any society:

            a. providing meaning and purpose to life

            b. promoting social cohesion and a sense of belonging

            c. providing social control and support for the government.

        3. The informal relationship between religion and the state is referred to as **civil religion**, the set of beliefs, rituals, and symbols that make sacred the values of the society and place the nation in the context of the ultimate system of meaning.

    B. Conflict Perspectives on Religion

        1. According to Karl Marx, the capitalist class uses religious ideology as a tool of domination to mislead the workers about their true interests; thus, religion is the "opiate of the people."

        2. By contrast, Max Weber argued that religion could be a catalyst to produce social change.

            a. In *The Protestant Ethic and the Spirit of Capitalism*, Weber linked the teachings of John Calvin with the rise of capitalism.

            b. John Calvin emphasized the doctrine of *predestination* -- the belief that all people are divided into two groups -- the saved and the damned -- and only God knows who will go to heaven (the elect) and who will go to hell, even before they are born.

            c. Because people cannot know whether they will be saved, they look for signs that they are among the elect. As a result, people work hard, save their money and do not spend it on worldly frivolity; instead, they reinvest it in their land, equipment, and labor.

            d. As people worked ever harder to prove their religious piety, structural conditions in Europe led to the industrial revolution, free markets, and the commercialization of the economy, which worked hand in hand with Calvinist religious teachings.

    C. Symbolic Interactionist Perspectives on Religion

        1. For many people, religion serves as a reference group to help them define themselves. Religious symbols, for example, have a meaning to large bodies of people (e.g., the Star of David for Jews; the crescent moon and star for Muslims; and the cross for Christians).

        2. *Her* Religion and *His* Religion: all people do not interpret religion in the same way. Women and men may belong to the same religions, but their individual religion will not necessarily be a carbon copy of the group's entire system of beliefs.

3.   Religious symbolism and language typically create a social definition of the roles of men and women.

III.   World Religions

A.   Hinduism

1.   Hinduism is one of the world's oldest current religions originating in Pakistan between 3,500 and 4,500 years ago.

2.   Hinduism does not have a specific founder or worship of a single god; it is considered by many to be polytheistic.

3.   Because this religion does not have a sacred book inspired by a god or gods; is not based on the teachings of any one person, some religion scholars refer to it as an *ethical religion*-a system of beliefs that calls upon adherents to follow an ideal way of life, which is achieved by adhering to the duties of one's caste.

4.   Individuals pass through cycles of life, death, and rebirth until the soul earns liberation; the soul's acquisition of each new body is tied to the law of *karma*; the ultimate goal is to enter the state of *nirvana*-becoming liberated from the world by uniting the individual soul with the universal soul.

5.   Of the more than 700 million Hindus, 95 percent reside in India; over 80 percent of India's population is Hindu.

B.   Buddhism

1.   Buddhism first emerged in India about 2500 years ago, but expanded into other nations in various forms.

2.   The founder, Siddhartha Gautama, spent his life teaching others how to obtain Enlightenment and how to reach nirvana.

3.   The Four Noble Truths, and the Eightfold Path to Nirvana are incorporated in some form in the three major branches of Buddhism today.

4.   Today, Buddhism is one of the fastest-growing Eastern religions in the United States.

C.   Confucianism

1.   Confucianism-which means the "family of scholars"-existed before its eventual leader, Confucius was born; he emerged as a teacher about the same time that the Buddha became a significant figure in India.

2.   Important teachings are: order in human relationships, a strict code of moral conduct, respect for others, benevolence and reciprocity. Humans are by nature good and learn from good role models.

3.   Confucius established the social hierarchy of Five Constant Relationships: ruler-subject, husband-wife, elder brother-younger brother, elder friend-junior friend, and father-son.

4.   Confucianism was the official religion of China until the Communist takeover and the establishment of the People's Republic of China.

D.   Judaism

1.   About 18 million Jews reside in about 134 countries; the majority reside in the U.S. or in Israel.

2. Jewish belief is monotheism; a single God, called Yahweh, made a covenant with his chosen people following a critical element in Judaism: the Exodus from Egypt in the 13th Century.

3. Believers of Judaism find the source of their beliefs in the Ten Commandments, and in the moral, ceremonial, and cultural laws contained in four books of the Torah: Exodus, Leviticus, Numbers and Deuteronomy. The Torah, also called the Pentateuch, is the sacred book of contemporary Judaism.

4. Jews worship in synagogues on the Sabbath, which is observed from sunset Friday to sunset Saturday. They celebrate a set of holidays that are distinct from U. S. dominant cultural religious celebrations, and believe that one day the Messiah will come to earth ushering in an age of peace and justice for all.

5. Throughout their history, Jews have been the object of prejudice and discrimination; the Holocaust that took place in Nazi Germany between 1933 and 1945 took the lives of six million Jews.

6. The three branches of Judaism-Orthodox, Reformed, and Conservative provide for a variety of cultural practices and teachings.

E. Islam

1. Islam, whose followers are known as Muslims, is based on the life and teachings of Muhammad, who was born about 570 C.E. in the city of Mecca, located today in Saudi Arabia.

2. Followers must adhere to the five Pillars of Islam.

3. Allah is the one God of Islam; the Qur'an is their holy book and was revealed to the Prophet Muhammad through the Angel Garbriel at the command of God.

4. A core belief is the idea of *jihad*, meaning struggle; the Greater Jihad is the internal struggle against sin; the Lesser Jihad is the external struggle that takes place in the world, including violence and war. The term jihad is typically associated with religious fundamentalism.

5. Some social analysts believe that Islamic fundamentalism is uniquely linked to the armed struggles of some groups.

6. Because of a high recent wave of migration and a relatively high rate of conversion, Islam is one of the fastest growing religions in the United States.

F. Christianity

1. As does Judaism and Islam, Christianity follows the Abrahamic tradition; although Jews and Christians share some common scriptures in what Christians call the "Old Testament," they interpret them differently.

    a. God offers to Christians a new covenant, to the followers of Jesus Christ.

    b. The central themes in the teachings of Jesus are the Kingdom of God and standards of personal conduct.

    c. Central teachings of Christianity are: the death and then the resurrection of Jesus—establishing that He is the son of God—and the ascension of Jesus into heaven forty days after His resurrection with an eventual "second coming" marking the end of the world as it is now known.

2. The Christian deity is a sacred Trinity comprised of God the Father, Jesus the Son, and the Holy Spirit.

3. Almost one-third of the world's population refer to themselves as Christian; it is the world's dominant religion.

IV. TYPES OF RELIGIOUS ORGANIZATION

A. Some countries have an official or state religion known as an **ecclesia** -- a religious organization that is so integrated into the dominant culture that it claims as its membership all members of a society. Examples include: the Anglican Church (the official Church of England), the Lutheran Church in Sweden and Denmark, the Catholic Church in Italy and Spain, and Islam in Iran and Pakistan.

B. The Church Sect Typology.

1. A church is a large, bureaucratically organized religious organization that tends to seek accommodation with the larger society in order to maintain some degree of control over it.

2. Mid way between the church and the sect is a **denomination** -- a large organized religion characterized by accommodation to society but frequently lacking in ability or intention to dominant society.

3. A **sect** is a relatively small religious group that has broken away from another religious organization to renew what it views as the original version of the faith.

C. A **cult** is a religious group with practices and teachings outside the dominant cultural and religious traditions of a society

1. Some major religions (including Judaism, Islam, and Christianity) and some denominations (such as the Mormons) started as cults.

2. Cult leadership is based on charismatic characteristics of the individual, including an unusual ability to form attachments with others.

3. Over time, some cults undergo transformation into sects or denominations.

V. TRENDS IN RELIGION IN THE UNITED STATES

A. Religion and Social Inequality

1. Religion in the United Sates is diverse; pluralism and religious freedom are among the cultural values.

2. Social scientists identify patterns between social class and religious denominations.

   a. Denominations with affluent members and high social status are the mainline liberal churches; the earliest members were immigrants from Britain, who helped establish the U. S. government and capitalist economy.

   b. Denominations that adhere to conservative religious beliefs are often in the middle to lower socioeconomic status and tend to discourage women from working outside the home.

B. Race and Class in Central-City and Suburban Churches

1. As more middle and upper-income individuals and families moved to the suburbs, some churches relocated to the suburbs.

2. The former building site is often replaced by a minority congregation, working class, and older members living on fixed income, or recent immigrant groups.

C.   Secularization and the Rise of Religious Fundamentalism

1.   *Secularization* - the decline in the significance of the sacred in daily life- has occurred, causing an increase of religious fundamentalism among some groups.

2.   **Fundamentalism** is a traditional religious doctrine that is conservative, typically opposed to modernity, and rejects worldly pleasures in favor or other worldly spirituality.

a.   In the United States it originally appealed to people from low-income, rural, southern backgrounds.

b.   The "new" fundamentalist movement has a wider appeal to people from all socioeconomic levels, geographical areas, and occupations.

c.   Some political leaders vow to bring the Christian religion "back" into schools and public life.

VI.   RELIGION IN THE FUTURE

A.   New religious forms are being created, while traditional forms of religious life are experiencing dramatic revitalization; liberation theology is one example.

1.   **Liberation theology** is the Christian movement that advocates freedom from political subjugation within a traditional perspective and advocates the need for social transformation to benefit the poor and powerless.

2.   Some feminist movements have turned to pagan religions and witchcraft to counter the patriarchal structure and content of the world's religions.

a.   The *Goddess movement* acknowledges the legitimacy of female power and encompasses a variety of counterculture beliefs based on paganism and feminism.

3.   In other nations, the rise of religious nationalism has led to the blending of strongly held religious and political beliefs; it is strong in the Middle East, where Islamic nationalism has spread, strongly affecting women and children.

4.   In the U. S., the influence of religion will be evident in ongoing battles over school prayer, abortion, gay rights, and women's issues.

B.   On some fronts, religion may unify people; on others it may contribute to confrontations among individuals and groups.

C.   Maintaining an appropriate balance between religion and other aspects of social life will be an important challenge in the future—the debate continues over what religion it is and what it should do.

PRACTICE TESTS

MULTIPLE CHOICE QUESTIONS

Select the response that best answers the question or completes the statement:

1. The famous court case that dealt with the teaching of evolution in the public school classroom was:

   a. the Scopes trial.

   b. *Brown v. Board of Education*.

   c. *Plessey v. Ferguson*.

   d. the Hopwood trial.

2. _____ study specific religious doctrines or belief systems, including answers to questions such as the nature of God or the gods, and the relationships between the sacred and human beings.

   a. Priests

   b. Prophets

   c. Theologians

   d. Millennialists

3. Sociologist _____ referred to religion as a sacred canopy.

   a. Emile Durkheim

   b. Clifford Geertz

   c. Peter Berger

   d. Robert Bellah

4. According to Emile Durkheim, _____ refers to those aspects of life that are extraordinary or supernatural.

   a. religion

   b. sacred

   c. profane

   d. superhuman

5. The belief that spirits or life forces inhabit virtually everything in the natural world is called:

   a. polytheism.

   b. animism.

   c. theism.

   d. monotheistic religion.

6. Three of the major world religions -- Christianity, Judaism, and Islam -- are characterized as:

   a. simple supernaturalism.

   b. animism.

   c. polytheism.

   d. monotheism.

7. Which of the following is not one of the elements Durkheim believed to be common to all religions:

   a. a liberating theology.

   b. a system of beliefs.

   c. a moral community.

   d. practices or rituals.

8. According to the functionalist perspective, religion offers meaning for the human experience by:

   a. providing an explanation for events that create a profound sense of loss on both an individual and a group basis.

   b. offering people a reference group to help them define themselves.

   c. reinforcing existing social arrangements, especially the stratification system.

   d. encouraging the process of secularization.

9. Celebrations on Memorial Day and the Fourth of July are examples of:

   a. .religious tolerance.

   b. civil religion.

   c. patriotic ethnocentrism.

   d. separation of church and state.

10. According to _____, the capitalist class uses religious ideology as a tool of domination.

    a. Emile Durkheim

    b. C. Wright Mills

    c. Karl Marx

    d. Max Weber

11. In regard to religion, Max Weber asserted that:

    a. church and state should be separated.

    b. religion could be a catalyst to produce social change.

    c. religion retards social change.

    d. the religious teachings of the Catholic church were directly related to the rise of capitalism.

12. "Her religion" and "his religion" have been examined from a(n) _____ perspective.

    a. functionalist

    b. neo Marxist

    c. conflict

    d. interactionist

13. The ideas of dharma, karma, and nirvana are associated with:

    a. animism.

    b. Buddhism.

    c. Confucianism.

    d. Hinduism.

14. The "Four Noble Truths" and the practice of the "eight-fold path" are today recognized as teachings of:
    a. Hinduism.
    b. Buddhism.
    c. Confucianism.
    d. Islam.

15. All of the following are one of the "Five Constant Relationships of Confucianism" except:
    a. mother-daughter.
    b. father-son.
    c. husband-wife.
    d. elder brother-younger brother.

16. Which one of the following is not associated with Judaism?
    a. People are responsible for making ethical choices.
    b. The Messiah will come to earth one day.
    c. God rested on the seventh after God had created the world.
    d. The messiah has already come to earth.

17. Which of the following is not associated with Islam?
    a. Muslim.
    b. the Qur'an.
    c. The Greater Jihad.
    d. Five Noble Truths.

18. The Anglican church in England and the Lutheran church in Sweden are examples of a(n):
    a. church
    b. sect.
    c. denomination.
    d. ecclesia.

19. In a _____, membership is largely based on birth, and children of members typically are baptized as infants.
    a. church
    b. sect
    c. denomination
    d. cult

20. According to the text, religious nationalism -- the blending of strongly held religious and political beliefs -- is especially strong today in:
    a. the United States.
    b. Middle Eastern nations.
    c. Japan.
    d. Brazil.

TRUE FALSE QUESTIONS

1. According to Peter Berger, the sacred canopy is the institution of the family.
   True or False

2. Across cultures and in different eras, a wide variety of things have been considered sacred.
   True or False

3. Secularization is the process by which religious beliefs, practices, and institutions lose their significance in sectors of society and culture.
   True or False

4. Marx used the phrase, the "opiate of the masses" to refer to the organized activity of religious people seeking a change in society.
   True or False

5. Karl Marx wrote *The Protestant Ethic and the Spirit of Capitalism* to explain how religion may be used by the powerful to oppress the powerless.
   True or False

6. Ninety-five percent of all Hindus in the world today reside in Pakistan.
   True or False

7. The Dalai Lama is associated with Hinduism.
   True or False

8. Today, Confucianism is the official religion of the People's Republic of China.
   True or False

9. Because it has fewer adherents worldwide than some other major religions, the influence of Judaism is weak in Western culture today.
   True or False

10. In the United States, today, Muslims outnumber Presbyterians and Episcopalians.
    True or False

11. More people in the world today refer to themselves as Christians than any other religion.
    True or False

12. Even though Christianity spread outward from Europe to other cultures, it changed very little, utilizing one highly integrated body of integrated religious beliefs.
    True or False

13. Denominations tend to be more tolerant and less likely than churches to expel or excommunicate members.
    True or False

14. "New" fundamentalists have encouraged secular humanism in U.S. schools.
    True or False

15. Liberation theology initially emerged in Latin America.
    True or False

FILL IN THE BLANK QUESTIONS

1. Those things that are considered secular or "worldly" are referred to as _____ .

2. _____ is the belief that supernatural forces affect people's lives either positively or negatively.

3. The belief in one or more gods is known as _____ .

4. The process by which religious beliefs lose their significance in sectors of society is known as _____ .

5. According to anthropologist _____ , religion is a set of cultural symbols that establishes powerful motivation.

6. According to _____ , religion is the opiate of the masses.

7. Max Weber wrote that classical book, _____ , religion could be a catalyst to produce social change.

8. In the United States today, one of the fastest growing eastern religions is _____ .

9. According to table 17.3 the largest Christian denomination in the United States is the _____ .

10. The informal relationship between religion and the state is referred to as _____ , the set of beliefs, rituals, and symbols that make sacred the values of the society and place the nation in the context of the ultimate system of meaning.

SHORT ANSWER/ESSAY QUESTIONS

1. What are some of the central beliefs of the six largest world religions?

2. What is religion and how do three major sociological perspectives — functionalist, conflict, and symbolic interactionists — differ in their perspectives on religion.

3. What are some of the relationships among race, class gender, and religion?

4. What does it mean by civil religion? In what ways are people affected in their everyday lives by civil religion?

5. What are some of the current trends and changes in worldwide religion? Do you think there will be a continuing tendency toward secularization, or toward fundamentalism? Will religion continue as a major social institution?

STUDENT CLASS PROJECTS AND ACTIVITIES

1. Compare and contrast the religious books of law of at least two different religions. The Torah, the Qur'an, or the New Testament are some suggestions. Answer the following questions: (1) What are some similarities of the two books? (2) What are some unique differences? (3) How do they treat the issue of gender, and gender roles? (4) What are the expectations of a believer dealing with a non-believer? (5) What are some of the ethical laws, such as: (a) how do the believers relate to the poor, or the rich; (b) how do the believers relate to those who have disobeyed the rules? (c) What are the expected rites and rituals of the believer; (d) What are the "sacreds" (as defined by Durkheim) of the religion; (6) What are the major beliefs; and (7) What happens to believers after their death? Provide bibliographical information in preparing your paper. Summarize your findings and provide a personal evaluation of this project. Submit your paper to your instructor at the appropriate time, following any instructions given to you.

2. Research a particular cult found in the United States or elsewhere. You should, in this research project, provide in your paper: (1) a definition of the cult; (2) the purpose of the cult; (3) a general description of the cult which should include: (a) its origin; (b) its membership and method of acquiring members; (4) the nature of its group life, including advantages and disadvantages of membership in the cult. After providing this basic information, include a two-page paper on a day in the life of the cult. Pretend to be a member and take the membership point of view in the writing up of a "day in the life of this cult." This day could be a very special day, such as your wedding day, or a typical school, work, or ceremonial day. Submit your papers to your instructor on the appropriate date, following any additional instructions you have been given.

3. Conduct an informal survey of any twenty people in order to obtain their opinion of the ordination of women in our society. You must provide this basic information about your respondents: (1) their name, age, and address; (2) if possible, their religious affiliation (if any); (3) their gender. Provide responses to the following questions: (1) Do you support the entry of women into the seminary schools? Why? Why not? (2) Do you support the ordination of women? Why? Why not? (3) Should women be allowed to serve as full-time professional clergy or rabbi or cantor? Why? Why not? (4) What do you think should be the primary role of women in the church? (5) What do you think should be the role of women who are clergy (pastor, rabbi, cantor, priest)? (6) Do you support the decision of the Anglican Church of England to ordain women? (7) Do you support the position of the Roman Catholic Church to not allow women to become priests? Why? Why not? (8) Do you have other statements you would like to make regarding the issue of women and the church? Summarize your findings and provide a conclusion statement per each respondent. Include any raw data that you have collected. Submit your paper to your instructor at the appropriate time.

INTERNET ACTIVITIES

1. Peggy Wehmeyer, a reporter for abcnews.com contends that the Internet is having much the same effect on transforming religion as printing the Bible did. Explore a comparative religious community that provides information on the major world religions, information on morality and culture, family and prayer circles. www.beliefnet.com

2. To illustrate the extent to which the Internet is shaping religious experience, go to this site and explore the uniquely American interplay between religion and entertainment. www.hollywoodjesus.com/

3. The American Atheists frequently asked questions (FAQ's) about prayer in public school web page. Use information from this site for in class discussions about the interconnections between religion and education. www.atheists.org/schoolhouse/faqs.prayer.html

4. Explore information on the Islamic faith, news, and social organizations. www.islamworld.net/www.islam.org

5. Compare and contrast Internet sites of insiders and outsiders on the subject of Islam and Terrorism.
   a. www.submission.org/terrorism.html
   b. www.islam101.com/terror/
   c. www.islam-guide.com/ch3-11.htm
   d. http://groups.colgate.edu/aarislam/response.htm
   e. http://answering-islam.org/Terrorism/

INFOTRAC EXERCISES

1. The Southern Baptist Convention, the largest Protestant denomination in the U.S., is deeply divided over many issues. One issue is that of the status of women serving in the ministry. Research the issue of the role of **women in religious life**.

2. To what extent can you find evidence of how religious Americans are? Use the keyword **religiosity** (the sociological concept for religious belief and behavior).

3. Many churches and religious groups explicitly condemn **homosexuality**. Frame the debate among the various major world religions. Where do the various religious groups stand on this issue?

4. Fundamentalist religious organizations continue to grow, while other religious organizations have experienced declining memberships. Research **religious fundamentalism** and why it appeals to new adherents.

5. Many Islamic groups advocate a "holy war" against westernization. What does this term really mean to them? Does a holy war necessarily mean resorting to terrorist tactics? Look up the words: **jihad**, **holy war**, **religious conflict** and **terrorism**. Don't limit your search to stories from the Middle East and Islam. Investigate the religious war that has been going on in Northern Ireland for decades. Look up articles on Bosnia-Herzegovina as well.

6. The issue of prayer in schools continues to be important as some groups contend that **school prayer** would improve the moral fiber of children, while others contend that it violates the premise of separation of church and state.

Solutions

MULTIPLE CHOICE QUESTIONS

1. A p. 561

2. C p. 563

3. C p. 563

4. B p. 564

5. B p. 564

6. D p. 565

7. A p. 566

8. A p. 567

9. B p. 569

10. C p. 570

11. B p. 571

12. D p. 572

13. D p. 573-574

14. B p. 575

15. A p. 576

16. D p. 579

17. D p. 579

18. A p. 582

19. A p. 583

20. B p. 587

TRUE FALSE QUESTIONS

1. F p. 563

2. T p. 564

3. T p. 566

4. F p. 570

5. F p. 571

6. F p. 574

7. F p. 575

8. F p. 576

9. F p. 576

10. T p. 579

11. T p. 581

12. F p. 582

13. T p. 583

14. F p. 586

15. T p. 586

FILL IN THE BLANK QUESTIONS

1. profane

2. Simple supernaturalism

3. theism

4. secularization

5. Clifford Geertz

6. Karl Marx

7.

8. Buddhism

9. Roman Catholic Church

10. civil religion

Chapter 18

HEALTH, HEALTH CARE, AND DISABILITY

BRIEF CHAPTER OUTLINE

Health in Global Perspective

Health in the United States

- Social Epidemiology
- Lifestyle Factors

Health Care in the United States

- The Rise of Scientific Medicine and Professionalism
- Medicine Today
- Paying for Medical Care in the United States
- Paying for Medical Care in Other Nations
- Social Implications of Advanced Medical Technology
- Holistic Medicine and Alternative Medicine

Sociological Perspectives on Health and Medicine

- A Functionalist Perspective on Health: The Sick Role
- A Conflict Perspective: Inequalities in Health and Health Care
- A Symbolic Interactionist Perspective: The Social Construction of Illness
- A Postmodernist Perspective: The Clinical Gaze

Mental Illness

- Treatment of Mental Illness
- Race, Class, Gender, and Mental Disorders

Disability

- Sociological Perspectives on Disability
- Social Inequalities Based on Disability

Health Care in the Future

CHAPTER SUMMARY

Although many people may think of health as simply being the absence of disease, the World Health Organization defines **health** as a state of complete physical, mental and social well-being. **Health care** is any activity intended to improve health. The **infant mortality rate**, the number of deaths of infants under one year of age per 1,000 live births in a given year, and **life expectancy**, the estimate of the average lifetime of people born in a specific year, are two indicators of the well-being of people in a society. A vital part of health care is **medicine**, an institutionalized system for the scientific diagnosis, treatment, and prevention of illness. In analyzing health from a global perspective, we find that health and health care expenditures vary widely among nations. **Social epidemiology** is the study of the causes and distribution of health, disease, and impairment throughout a population. Social factors such as age, sex, race/ethnicity, social class, lifestyle choices, and drug use and abuse affect the health and longevity of people in a given area. Sexual activity, usually associated with good physical and mental health, may involve health-related hazards, such as transmission of sexually transmitted diseases. The fee-for-service method continues in the United States, which is expensive; few restrictions are placed on medical fees. The United States and the Union of South Africa are the only high-income nations without some form of universal health coverage for all citizens. Private health insurance, public health insurance—consisting of Medicare and Medicaid—health maintenance organizations, and managed care compromise the major approaches for paying for U.S. health care. Advances in high-tech medicine is becoming a major part of overall health care; however, many people are turning to holistic medicine -- is an approach to health care that focuses on prevention of illness and disease and is aimed at treating the whole person-body and mind-rather than just the part or parts in which symptoms occur. Many practitioners of **alternative medicine**-healing practices inconsistent with dominant medical practice- take a holistic approach. According to a **functionalist** approach, if a society is to function as a stable system, people must be healthy in order to contribute to their society. People who assume the **sick role** are unable to fulfill their necessary social roles, contributing to an inability to fulfill their functions. Unequal access to good health and health care is a major issue of concern to **conflict** theorists. The **medical-industrial complex**-that which encompasses both local physicians and hospitals as well as global health-related industries-produces and sells medicine as a commodity; people below the poverty level and those just above it have great difficulty gaining access to medical care. **Symbolic Interactionists**, in explaining the social construction of illness, focus on the meaning that social actors give their illness or disease and how that meaning affects their self-concept and their relationships with others. According to a postmodernist approach, doctors have gained power through the clinical gaze, and gained prestige through the classification of disease. **Mental illness**, a condition in which a person has a severe **mental disorder** requiring extensive treatment, differs from a mental disorder, a condition that makes it difficult or impossible for a person to cope with everyday life. **Disability**, a physical or health condition that stigmatizes or causes discrimination, is often defined in terms of work from a business perspective, or in terms of organically based impairments from a medical professional perspective. Health care in the future is critically affected by health care technologies; however, health in the future will somewhat be up to each of us- how we safeguard ourselves against illness, and how we help others who are victims of diseases and disabilities.

LEARNING OBJECTIVES

After reading chapter 18, you should be able to:

1. Define health, health care and disability and explain the importance of these issues for individuals the whole of society.

2. Compare health in a global perspective to health in the United States.

3. Define social epidemiology and its role in society.

4. Compare and contrast how age, sex, race/ethnicity and social class affect health and mortality.

5. Explain how lifestyle choices affect health, disease, and impairment.

6. Describe the rise of scientific medicine in the United States.

7. Explain four methods of paying for health care and controlling health care costs in the United States.

8. List and discuss three major social implications of advanced medical technology.

9. Compare and contrast holistic medicine and alternative medicine with traditional, or orthodox medical treatment.

10. Distinguish between health care in the United States to that of other countries.

11. Describe functionalist, conflict, symbolic interactionist, and postmodernist perspectives on health and medicine.

12. Define and explain mental illness and mental disorder and explain the treatment of each in the United States.

13. Describe the relationships of race, class, gender and mental disorders.

14. Explain the sociological perspectives on disability.

15. Discuss inequalities related to disability and describe the impact of stereotypes, prejudice, and discrimination on persons with disabilities.

KEY TERMS

(defined at page number shown and in glossary)

acute diseases 596
chronic diseases 596
deinstitutionalization 615
demedicalization 613
disability 617
drug 597
health 592
health care 592
health maintenance organization (HMO) 604
holistic medicine 608

infant mortality rate 592
life expectancy 592
managed care 604
medical-industrial complex 611
medicalization 612
medicine 592
sick role 609
social epidemiology 594
socialized medicine 607
universal health care 606

KEY PEOPLE
(identified at page number shown)

Ronald Angel 620
Joe R. Feagin and Melvin Sikes 616
Deborah Findlay and Leslie Miller 612
Abraham Flexner 601
Michel Foucault 613
Eliot Freidson 619

Erving Goffman 616
Talcott Parsons 619
Thomas Pettigrew 616
Paul Starr 604
Ingrid Waldron 596
Gregory Weiss and Lynne E. Lonnquist 604

CHAPTER OUTLINE

I. HEALTH IN GLOBAL PERSPECTIVE

    A.   The World Health Organization defines **health** as a state of complete physical, mental and social well-being.

    B.   Medical sociology, as a subdiscipline, is the study of health, healing, and illness.

    C.   **Health care** is any activity intended to improve health.

    D.   Some measures of health and well-being are:

        1.   The **infant mortality rate**, the number of deaths of infants under one year of age per 1,000 live births in a given year

        2.   **Life expectancy**, the estimate of the average lifetime of a people born in a specific year.

        3.   **Medicine**, an institutionalized system for the scientific diagnosis, treatment, and prevention of illness; it is a vital part of health care.

    E.   Health care and health care expenditures vary widely among nations; the WHO reports that babies born in low-income countries will not live as long compared with children in high-income countries. Almost 14 percent of all children born in low-income countries die before they reach their first birthday.

II. HEALTH IN THE UNITED STATES

    A.   **Social epidemiology**, the study of the causes and distribution of health, disease, and impairment throughout a population, provides some explanations of health and disease.

    B.   Social epidemiologists investigate disease agents, the environment, and the human host as sources of illness.

    C.   Younger people are more likely to have **acute diseases**, illnesses that strike suddenly and cause dramatic incapacitation and sometimes death, while older people are more likely to have **chronic diseases**, illnesses that are long-term and develop gradually or are present from birth.

    D.   Today, women on average now live longer than men; at birth, females have lower mortality rates both in the prenatal stage and during the first month of life.

    E.   Some research points out that social class is a greater determinant of health than race/ethnicity; however, illness is also related to a person's occupation.

    F.   Three (of many) **lifestyle factors** relate to health:

1. **Drugs**, any substances-other than food and water- that, when taken into the body, alter its functioning in some way, affect health in many ways.
    a. Long-term heavy use of **alcohol** can damage the brain and other parts of the body, cause nutritional deficiencies, cardiovascular problems, and alcoholic cirrhosis.
    b. **Nicotine** (tobacco) is a toxic, dependency producing psychoactive drug that is more addictive than heroin; smoking tobacco is linked to cancer and other serious diseases. Environmental tobacco smoke-- the smoke in the air that nonsmokers inhale from other people's tobacco smoking is hazardous for nonsmokers.
    c. The use of **illegal drugs**, like cocaine and marijuana, affects the lifestyle and the health of individuals.
2. Sexual activity may involve health-related hazards such as transmission of certain **sexually transmitted diseases**.
    a. The most prevalent STDs are HIV/AIDS, gonorrhea, syphilis, and genital herpes. All of these affect the health of individuals; however, the most serious of these is AIDS.
    b. On a global basis, the number people infected with HIV or AIDS is increasing; ten percent of all new cases worldwide are children; nearly two-thirds of all people with HIV/AIDS live in sub-Saharan Africa; 14 percent live in south and southeast Asia.
    c. HIV is transmitted through unprotected sexual intercourse with an infected partner, sharing a hypodermic needle with someone who is infected, by exposure to contaminated blood or blood products, and by an infected woman passing the virus on to a child during pregnancy, childbirth, or breast feeding.
3. Staying healthy: diet and exercise
    a. Lifestyle choices can include positive actions such as maintaining a healthy diet and good exercise program.
    b. Both of these have contributed to a significant decrease in heart disease and some cancers.

III. HEALTH CARE IN THE UNITED STATES
    A. The rise of scientific medicine resulted from several significant discoveries during the nineteenth century in areas such as bacteriology and anesthesiology; at the same time advocates of reform in medical education were promoting scientific medicine.
        1. The **Flexner Report**, complied by Abraham Flexner, included a model of medical education; those medical schools that did not fit the "model" were closed. Only two of the African American medical schools survived; and only one of the medical schools for women survived.
        2. With professionalization resulting from the Flexner Report, licensed medical doctors gained control over the entire medical establishment; this continues today-and may continue into the future.
    B. Medicine Today
        1. In the U.S.A., patients are billed individually for each service they receive.

      a.   This includes treatment by doctors, laboratory work, hospital visits, other health related expenses, and prescriptions.

      b.   This payment is expensive; few restrictions are placed on the fees that doctors, hospitals, and medical providers can charge.

      c.   This method, representing the "true spirit" of capitalism, has led to advances in medicine.

      d.   However, this fee-for-service medicine results in its inequality of distribution.

C.   Paying for medical care in the United States

    1.   Private health insurance expansion in the United States led to escalated costs.

      a.   Third party providers pay large portions of doctor and hospital bills for insured patients.

      b.   Private health insurance plans are organized like other large-scale for-profit corporations.

    2.   Public health insurance is subsidized by federal and state taxes; the U.S.A, has two nationwide public health insurance programs: Medicare, for those 65 or older who are eligible; and Medicaid, a jointly funded federated-state program to make health care more available to the poor. Both programs are in financial difficulty today.

    3.   **Health Maintenance Organizations (HMOs)** were created to provide workers with health coverage by keeping costs down.

      a.   **HMOs** provide, for a set monthly fee, total care with an emphasis on prevention to avoid costly treatment later.

      b.   Supporters applaud the emphasis on preventative care.

      c.   Critics charge that some HMOs require their physicians to withhold vital information and medical treatment from their patients in order to reduce potential large sums of money for medical procedures or hospitalization.

    4.   **Managed care**, any system of cost containment that closely monitors and controls health care providers' decisions about medical procedures, diagnostic tests, and other services that should be provided to patients.

      a.   Patients choose a primary-care physician from a list of participating doctors.

      b.   Doctors must get approval before they perform any procedures or admit a patient to a hospital; if they fail to obtain advance approval, the insurance company has the right to refuse to pay for the treatment or the hospital stay.

    5.   The **uninsured and the underinsured** comprise one-third of all U. S. citizens.

      a.   Children comprise a large amount not covered by insurance.

      b.   The working poor constitutes a large portion; they earn too little to afford health insurance, too much to qualify for Medicaid, and their employers do not provide health insurance.

D.   Paying for Medical Care in Other Nations

    1.   Canada has a **universal health care system**, a health care system in which all citizens receive medical services paid for by tax revenues; in Canada these revenues are supplemented by insurance premiums paid by all taxpaying citizens. It does not

constitute what is referred to as **socialized medicine**, a health care system in which the government owns the medical care facilities and employs the physicians; the physicians are not government employees.

2. Great Britain, in l946, passed the National Health Service Act, which provided for all health care services to be available at no charge to the entire population. The government sets health care policies, raises funds and controls the medical care budget, owns health care facilities, and directly employs physicians and other health personnel.

3. China adopted innovative strategies after the Civil War in order to improve the health of its populace; physician extenders, known as *street doctors* in urban areas and *barefoot doctors* in rural areas, had little formal training and worked under the supervision of trained physicians. Today, medical training is more rigorous; all doctors receive training in both Western and traditional Chinese medicine. Doctors who work in hospitals receive a salary; all other doctors are on a fee-for-service basis. The cost of health care generally remains low, but the cost of hospital care has risen. Chinese who can afford it purchase health care insurance to cover the rising cost of hospitalization. The health of its citizens is only slightly below that of most industrialized nations.

E. Social implications of advanced medical technology include:
1. The new technologies create options for people and society, but options that alter human relationships.
2. The new technologies increase the cost of medical care (such as the computerized axial tomography, CT of CAT scanner).
3. The new technologies raise provocative questions about the very nature of life, such as duplicating mammals from adult DNA.

F. **Holistic** medicine and alternative medicine provide variations from traditional (or orthodox) medical treatment.
1. **Holistic medicine** focuses on prevention of illness and disease and aims at treating the whole person-body and mind, rather than just the part or parts in which symptoms occur.
2. Alternative medicine involve healing practices inconsistent with dominant medical practice which take a holistic approach; many people today are utilizing this in addition to or in lieu of traditional medicine.

IV. SOCIOLOGICAL PERSPECTIVES ON HEALTH AND MEDICINE
A. A functionalists perspective on health: the **sick role**
1. According to Talcott Parson, the sick role is the set of patterned expectations that define the norms and values appropriate for individuals who are sick and for those who interact with them.
2. The sick role has four characteristics:
a. A person's sickness is not deliberate;
b. A sick person is exempted from responsibilities;
c. A sick person must want to get well;
d. A sick person must seek competent help from a medical profession.

3.   Illness is dysfunctional for individuals and the larger society; sick people are unable to fulfill their necessary social roles; it is important for the society to maintain social control over people who enter the sick role.

B.   A conflict perspective: inequalities in health and health care

1.   Conflict theorists emphasize the political, economic, and social forces that affect health and the health care delivery system.

2.   Medicine is a commodity that is produced and sold by the **medical-industrial complex**, that which encompasses both local physicians and hospitals as well as global health-related industries such as insurance companies and pharmaceutical and medical supply companies that deliver health care today.

3.   Medical care is linked to people's ability to pay and their position within the class structure; the affluent or those who have good medical insurance most likely receive care; the medically indigent, those who cannot qualify for Medicaid, but do not earn enough cannot afford private medical care.

4.   Physicians hold a legal monopoly over medicine; they can charge inflated fees; clinics, pharmacies, laboratories, hospitals, insurance companies, and many other corporations derive excessive profits from the existing system of payment in medicine.

C.   A symbolic interactionist perspective: the social construction of illness

1.   Symbolic interactionists focus on the meaning that actors give their illness or disease and how this will affect their self-concept and their relationship with others.

2.   In addition to the objective criteria for determining medical conditions, the subjective component is very important; the term **medicalization** refers to the process whereby nonmedical problems become defined and treated as illness or disorders.

3.   Medicalization may occur on three levels: (a) the conceptual level; (b) the institutional level; and (c) the interactional level. Medicalization is typically the result of a lengthy promotional campaign, often culminating in legislation or other social policy changes that institutionalize a medical treatment of a new "disease."

4.   **Demedicalization** refers to a problem that no longer retains its medical definition; an example is the work of women's health advocates seeking to redefine menopause as natural a process rather than as an illness or psychological disorder.

5.   Symbolic interactionists provide new insights on how illness may be socially constructed, and not strictly determined by medical criteria.

D.   A postmodernist perspective: the clinical gaze

1.   According to Michel Foucault, the formation of clinical medicine led to the power that doctors gained over other medical personnel and everyday people.

2.   Doctors gain power through the *clinical gaze*, which they use to gather information.

a.   As doctors "diagnose", they become experts.

b.   As a definition network of disease classification, new rules and new tests developed, the dominance of doctor's wisdom became enhanced.

3.   Foucault's analysis is not limited to doctors who treat bodily illness, but also psychiatrists and the treatment of insanities.

V.   MENTAL ILLNESS

   A.   **Mental illness**, a condition in which a person has a severe mental disorder requiring extensive treatment, differs from a **mental disorder**, a condition that makes it difficult or impossible for a person to cope with everyday life.

   B.   According to the National Comorbidity Survey, nearly 50 percent of respondents between the ages of 15 and 54 years had been diagnosed with a mental disorder sometime in their lives.

   C.   Treatment of mental illness

      1.   Substance-related disorders are the leading cause of hospitalization for men between the ages of 15 and 44 and the second leading cause for women in that age group.

      2.   The introduction of new psychoactive drugs to treat mental disorders and the **deinstitutionalization** movement have created dramatic changes in how people with mental disorders are treated; deinstitutionalization refers to the practice of rapidly discharging patients from mental hospitals into the community.

      3.   **Deinsitutionalization** is now viewed as a problem by many social scientists; in the l960s, it was believed that many state mental patients had been deprived of their civil rights, housed in what Goffman called a *total institution*; they were released, many having no place to go, except to reside on the streets and became part of the homeless population.

      4.   Involuntary commitment, used as a social control mechanism to keep mentally ill people off the streets, does little to treat underlying medical and social conditions that contribute to mental disorders.

   D.   Race, Class, Gender, and Mental Disorders

      1.   Most studies examining race/ethnicity and mental disorders have compared African Americans and white Americans and have uncovered no significant differences in diagnosable mental illness.

      2.   In a qualitative study about the effects of racism, Feagin and Sikes concluded that repeated personal encounters with racial hostility deeply affect the psychological well-being of most African Americans, regardless of their level of education or social class.

      3.   According to Pettigrew, racism in all it forms constitutes a mentally unhealthy situation, wherein people do not achieve their full potential.

      4.   Researchers agree that social class has a significant impact on mental disorders; as social class increases, rates of mental disorders decrease.

      5.   The rate of diagnosable depression is about twice as high for women as for men; this gender difference typically emerges in puberty and increases in adulthood as women and men enter and live out their unequal adult statuses.

VI.   DISABILITY

   A.   **Disability**, a physical or health condition that stigmatizes or causes discrimination, is often defined in terms of work form a business perspective, or in terms of organically based impairments from a medical professional perspective.

B.   An estimated 48 million persons in the U.S. have one or more physical or mental disabilities, and the number is increasing as medical advances make it possible for those who would have died from an accident or illness to survive, but with an impairment, and as life expectancies increases. Environment, lifestyle, and working conditions may contribute to disability.

C.   Many disability right advocates argue that persons with a disability are kept out of the mainstream of society, being denied equal opportunities in education by being consigned to special education classes or schools.

D.   Sociological Perspectives on Disability

    1.   Functionalist Talcott Parsons focused on how people who are disabled fill the sick role. This is a *medical model* of disability; people with disabilities become chronic patients.

    2.   Symbolic interactions examine how people are labeled as a result of disability; Eliot Freidson determined that the particular label results from (1) the person's degree of responsibility for the impairment, (2) the apparent seriousness of the condition, and (3) the perceived legitimacy of the condition.

    3.   From a conflict perspective, persons with disabilities are a subordinate group in conflict with persons in positions of power in the government, the health care industry, and the rehabilitation business. When people with disabilities are defined as a social problem and public funds are spent to purchase goods and services for them, rehabilitation becomes big business.

E.   Social inequalities based on disability include prejudice and discrimination.

    1.   Stereotypes of persons with a disability fall into two categories: (1) deformed individuals who also may be horrible deviants; or (2) persons who are to be pitied. Even positive stereotypes become harmful to people with a disability, those that excel despite the impairment. Disability rights advocates note that such stereotypes do not reflect the daily struggle of most people with disabilities.

    2.   Employment, poverty, and disability are related; people may become economically disadvantaged as a result of chronic illness or disability; on the other hand, poor people are less likely to be educated and more likely to be malnourished and have inadequate access to health care.

    3.   Disability has a stronger negative effect on women's labor participation than it does on men's.

    4.   The cost of "mainstreaming" persons with disabilities closely relates to current expenditures that provide greater access to education and jobs.

VII.   HEALTH CARE IN THE FUTURE

    A.   In the future, advanced health care technologies for high income countries will provide more accurate and quicker diagnosis, effective treatment techniques, and increased life expectancy; however new ethical concerns; the inability of the poor of the world, (including the U.S.) to have access to health care, the growth of managed-care companies in the U.S. making decisions formerly reserved for physicians and hospital personnel and ethical concerns of technological advances all indicate a change in the future of health and medicine.

B. Ultimately, healthcare in the future will somewhat be up to each of us-what measures we take to safeguard ourselves against illness and disorders, and how we help others who are victims of diseases and disabilities.

PRACTICE TESTS

MULTIPLE CHOICE QUESTIONS

Select the response that best answers the question or completes the sentence:

1. The World Health Organization (WHO) defines health as the:

   a. absence of disease.

   b. complete physical, mental, and social well-being.

   c. body in a state of equilibrium, with all parts in balance.

   d. absences of sickness, viruses, and pains.

2. _____ refers to the positive sense of complete well being; while _____ refers to an interference with health.

   a. Healing; disease

   b. Health; healing

   c. Health; illness

   d. Health care; disease

3. Health care in the United States:

   a. is positively linked to money spent on health care and people's physically, mental, and social well-being.

   b. equates positively with longevity.

   c. is more expensive, but more productive for individuals.

   d. is any activity intended to improve health.

4. _____ is an institutionalized system for the scientific diagnosis, treatment, and prevention of illness.

   a. The medical-industrial complex

   b. Universal health care

   c. Medicine

   d. Disease

5. The World Health Organization reports that about _____ babies born in low-income countries during 1998 died during the _____

   a. five million; first year of life.

   b. five million; first month of life.

   c. one million; first year of life.

   d. one million; first month of life.

6. Social epidemiologists are people who study the causes and distribution of:
   a. health, disease, and impairment in a population.
   b. epidemics that occur throughout a population.
   c. mental illness and behavior disorders in a population.
   d. the role of degenerative diseases in a population.

7. _____ are illnesses that strike suddenly, cause dramatic incapacitation, and sometimes death.
   a. Chronic diseases.
   b. Disabilities.
   c. Epidemics.
   d. Acute diseases.

8. _____ live longer than _____, but have higher rates of _____ illness.
   a. Men; women; chronic
   b. Women; men; acute
   c. Women; men; chronic
   d. Men; women; acute

9. _____ is a toxic, dependency producing drug that is more addictive than _____.
   a. Heroin; nicotine
   b. Nicotine; heroin
   c. Nicotine; marijuana
   d. Marijuana; alcohol

10. Until the 1960s, _____ and _____ were the principal STDs in this country.
    a. genital herpes; syphilis
    b. gonorrhea; genital herpes
    c. gonorrhea; syphilis
    d. genital herpes; HIV/AIDS

11. Nearly 70 percent of all people with HIV/AIDS live in:
    a. sub-Saharan Africa.
    b. South Asia.
    c. Southeast Asia.
    d. the United States.

12. The Flexner Report stated in 1910 that:
    a. new medical schools should be developed for women.
    b. more medical schools should be developed for African Americans.
    c. new medical schools should be developed in rural areas.
    d. most existing medical schools were inadequate for teaching.

13. Throughout most of the twentieth century, medical care in the United States was paid for:
    a. by HMOs.
    b. on a fee-for-service basis.
    c. by third party providers.
    d. managed care.

14. _____ is a jointly funded federal-state local health care program for the poor.
    a. Medicare
    b. Medical
    c. Medicaid
    d. Managed care

15. The only high-income nations without some form of universal health coverage for all its citizens are:
    a. the United States and the Union of South Africa.
    b. Canada and the United States.
    c. Japan and the United States.
    d. Great Britain and the United States.

16. Individuals who had little medical formal training in China who worked in rural communities, emphasizing health and health care and treating illness and disease are known as:
    a. barefoot doctors.
    b. Red Guard doctors.
    c. street doctors.
    d. communist herb doctors.

17. An approach to health care that treats the whole person rather than just symptoms that occur is known as _____:
    a. mainstream medicine
    b. managed care.
    c. holistic medicine.
    d. medicalization.

18. People in the sick role are expected to:
    a. be responsible for their condition.
    b. desire to get well.
    c. continue their normal roles and obligations.
    d. ignored competent medical assistance.

19. The practice of rapidly discharging patients from mental hospitals into the community is referred to as _____.
    a. reinstitutionalization.
    b. demedicalization.
    c. deconstruction.
    d. deinstitutionalization.

20. In contemporary industrial societies, disability often can be attributed to:

    a. epidemics related to poor sanitation and overcrowding.

    b. urban density and poverty.

    c. environment, lifestyle, and working conditions.

    d. employment in high stress jobs in the primary tier of the labor market.

TRUE-FALSE QUESTIONS

1. Sociologist Ingrid Waldron believes that life expectancy is linked to gender roles and gender socialization.
   True or False

2. Class is generally more of a factor for health problems than race or ethnicity.
   True or False

3. Therapeutic use of drugs occurs when a person takes a drug for a specific purpose, such as reducing fever or a cough.
   True or False

4. Cocaine is the most extensively used illegal drug in the United States.
   True or False

5. HIV can be transmitted by an infected woman breast feeding her child.
   True or False

6. As a result of the Flexner report, medical schools for African Americans and women were expanded.
   True or False

7. According to Paul Starr, third-party health insurance providers are the main reason for medical inflation.
   True or False

8. Managed care allows doctors more individual freedom in choosing the medical treatment for their patients.
   True or False

9. The Canadian health care system is an example of socialized medicine.
   True or False

10. According to conflict theorists, physicians hold a legal monopoly over medicine.
    True or False

11. The subjective component of medicalization and demedicalization reflects the major concern of the interactionist perspective of health.
    True or False

12. According to Foucault, doctors gain power through the "clinical gaze."
    True or False

13. According to researchers, the prevalence of mental disorders in the U.S.A. is much less than most analysts had previously believed.
    True or False

14. Less than 15 percent of persons with a disability today were born with it.
    True or False

15. On average, male workers with a severe disability make 50% of what their co-workers without disabilities earn.
    True or False

FILL IN THE BLANK QUESTIONS

1. The state of complete physical, mental, and social well-being is defined as _____ .

2. The average lifetime of people born in a specific year is known as the _____ .

3. The _____ report changed the practice of medical education in the U.S.A.

4. A _____ is one wherein all citizens receive medical services paid for by tax revenues.

5. The _____ is the set of patterned expectations that defines the norms and values appropriate for individuals who are sick and for those who interact with them.

6. _____ is an approach to health care that focuses on prevention of illness and disease and is aimed at treating the whole person.

7. The _____ perspective focuses on the meaning that social actors give their disease or illness.

8. The _____ perspective on health and illness that the myth of the wise doctor was supported by the development of disease classification systems and new tests.

9. The research of _____ suggested that about 15 percent of whites have such high levels of racial prejudice that they tend to exhibit symptoms of serious mental illness.

10. A _____ is a physical of mental health condition that stigmatizes or causes discrimination.

SHORT ANSWER/ESSAY QUESTIONS

1. What is it meant by health, health care, and disability and why are these important concerns for both individual and entire societies?

2. How is health care paid for in the United States? In some other countries? Which system do you think is better for people in a society? Explain your response.

3. What is holistic medicine and how does it differ from traditional health care? What is it meant by alternative health care?

4.   What is meant by disability and what are three theoretical perspectives on disabilities?

5.   What are some of the major issues and concerns of health care in the future?

STUDENT CLASS PROJECTS AND ACTIVITIES

1.   Collect at least 10 articles dealing with current issues of health and health care found in the text, such as alcoholism, concerns about diet and exercise, AIDS, current causes of death, the American health care system, the profession of medicine (including doctors, nurses, hospitals), health insurance, prepaid health care, managed health care, and health care in other countries. The articles can come from newspapers, professional journals, magazines, etc. You are to: (1) collect the articles; (2) write a summary explaining the message of each article; (3) write a personal reaction to each article; (4) provide a conclusion and personal evaluation of the project, and (5) provide a bibliographic reference for each article selected. Submit the articles at the appropriate time.

2.   Investigate a health care system found in another modern industrial country that has a reputation of having a fairly good, reliable health care delivery system. Some suggestions are: Great Britain, Canada, Germany, Sweden, Norway, and Japan. You are to describe in your paper: (1) the specific type(s) of health care system; (2) who receives the health care; (3) how the program is funded; (4) if personal choice is allowed--even for the higher income; (5) who the professionals are in the system; (6) their training; (7) how serious illness or disease is treated; (8) any other information pertinent to this research. In the writing of your paper, include a bibliography, a summary, a conclusion, and a personal evaluation of this project. Submit your paper to your instructor at the appropriate time.

3.   The May/June 2002 issue of *AARP*, listed the 50 top hospitals in the United States, as cited by *Consumer's Checkbooks*, a nonprofit consumer education organization. This article summarizes the major findings of the publication, *Consumer's Checkbook's Guide to Hospitals*, which rates more than 4,500 hospitals nationwide. Read this article and summarize the major criteria and the major findings of the report. Are there any surprises? What constitutes the accreditation score, the physician's rating, and special offerings/programs/research of the top-ranked hospitals? List the top 25 hospitals in the nation. Next, discuss the top-ranked hospital, noting the explanations for its ranking. Write up your research following any specific directions provided by your instructor.

4.   According to an article in *Time* magazine,(November 8, 1999) what are the ten causes of death and disabilities in the 1990's? What are the projections for the top ten causes of death and disability in the year 2020? Select one of these causes of the year 2020 and research that specific cause. Why is it a projected cause of death or disability? Why is it listed as a top ten projected cause of death or disability? What should be done to diminish the devastating effects of that cause? Submit your paper following any directions provided by your instructor.

INTERNET ACTIVITIES

1. The *National Institute of Health* is one of eight agencies that are part of the Department of Health and Human Services; in turn, it consists of over twenty-five agencies such as the National Institute of Allergy and Infectious Diseases, the National Institute on Alcohol Abuse and Alcoholism, and the National Institute of Drug Abuse. www.nih.gov

2. To explore one of the major medical and **health** research institutions in the U.S., visit the web site for the *Centers for Disease Control* and read about the CDC, its facilities, mission, people, budget, data and statistics. The CDC collects data on a wide range of topics, including cancer rates, AIDS rates, violence, and rare illnesses (e.g., Ebola and Hanta viruses). www.cdc.gov

3. **Health** problems in other countries are often linked to poor sanitation and hygiene. To learn more about these kinds of diseases, including the guinea worm, which causes internal injuries and permanent, disfiguring scarring, visit the web site for the *World Health Organization*. Be sure to note some of the differences between the kinds of diseases the CDC focuses on compared to the World Health Organization. www.who.int/home-page/

4. The *Department of Health and Human Services* is a federal agency that provides information on numerous government programs, including Medicare and Medicaid, and the State Children's Health Insurance Program, as well as medical fraud. www.os.dhhs.gov

5. The *National Institute of Mental Health* (also belongs to the NIH), provides information on mental illness, child and adolescent violence, and rural mental health. www.nimh.nih.gov/home.cfm

INFOTRAC EXERCISES

1. Search for articles (both professional and news) related to **Health Maintenance Organizations**. How effective are **HMO**s? Are they more interested in cutting costs than in providing quality health care?

2. How pervasive is **Medicare** fraud or **medical fraud** in general? How does this impact our society? Search for news articles that expose these kinds of problems. What are the social issues involved?

3. A general search using the topic **disability** will allow you to get a sense of how this condition touches on a broad range of social life.

4. After searching for periodical references for **holistic medicine** examine the range of journals that this term appears in. Talk about the different "backdoors" that these nontraditional methods often have to take.

Solutions

MULTIPLE CHOICE QUESTIONS

1. B p. 592

2. C p. 592

3. D p. 592

4. C p. 592

5. B p. 592

6. A p. 594

7. D p. 596

8. C p. 597

9. B p. 598

10. C p. 599

11. A p. 600

12. D p. 601

13. B p. 602

14. C p. 604

15. A p. 604

16. A p. 607

17. C p. 609

18. B p. 610

19. D p. 615

20. C p. 618

TRUE-FALSE QUESTIONS

1. T p. 596

2. T p. 597

3. T p. 597

4. F p. 598

5. T p. 600

6. F p. 601

7. T p. 604

8. F p. 604

9. F p. 607

10. T p. 611

11. T p. 613

12. F p. 613

13. F p. 614

14. T p. 617

15. T p. 620

FILL IN THE BLANK QUESTIONS

1. health

2. life expectancy

3. Flexner

4. universal health care system

5. sick role

6. Holistic medicine

7. symbolic interaction

8. postmodern

9. Thomas Pettigrew

10. disability

Chapter 19

POPULATION AND URBANIZATION

BRIEF CHAPTER OUTLINE

Demography: The Study of Population

- Fertility

- Mortality

- Migration

- Population Composition

Population Growth in Global Context

- The Malthusian Perspective

- The Marxist Perspective

- The Neo Malthusian Perspective

- Demographic Transition Theory

- Other Perspectives on Population Change

A Brief Glimpse at International Migration Theories

Urbanization in Global Perspective

- Emergence and Evolution of the City

- Preindustrial Cities

- Industrial Cities

- Postindustrial Cities

Perspectives on Urbanization and the Growth of Cities

- Functionalist Perspectives: Ecological Models

- Conflict Perspectives: Political Economy Models

- Symbolic Interactionist Perspectives: The Experience of City Life

Problems in Global Cities

Urban Problems in the United States

- Divided Interests: Cities, Suburbs, and Beyond

- The Continual Fiscal Crisis of the Cities

Rural Community Issues in the United States

Population and Urbanization in the Future

CHAPTER SUMMARY

Demography is the study of the size, composition, and distribution of the population. Population growth is the result of **fertility** (births), **mortality** (deaths), and **migration**. The **population composition** — the biological and social characteristics of a population is affected by changes in fertility, mortality, and migration. One measure of population composition is **sex ratio** — the number of males for every hundred females in a given population. For demographics, sex and age are significant characteristics; they are key indicators of fertility and mortality rates. Over two hundred years ago, Thomas Malthus warned that overpopulation would result in major global problems such as poverty and starvation. According the Marxist perspective, overpopulation occurs because of capitalists' demands for a surplus of workers to suppress wages and heighten workers' productivity. More recently, neo-Malthusians have re-emphasized the dangers of our population, depicting earth as a dying planet with too many people, too little food, compounded by environmental degradation. **Demographic transition** is the process by which some societies have moved from high birth and death rates to relatively low birth and death rates as a result of technological development. Other perspectives on population change include rational choice theory, the epidemiological transition, economic development, and the process of "westernization." In explaining international migration theories, the neoclassical economics approach, the new household's economics of migration approach, conflict and world systems theory, all add to our knowledge of the way people migrate. *Urban sociology* is the study of social relationships and political and economic structures in the city. Cities are a relatively recent innovation when compared to the length of human existence. Because of their limited size, preindustrial cities tend to provide a sense of community and a feeling of belonging. The Industrial Revolution changed the size and nature of the city; people began to live close to the factories and to one another, which led to overcrowding and poor sanitation. In postindustrial cities, some people live and work in suburbs or outlying edge cities. Functionalist perspectives (ecological models) of urban growth include the *concentric zone model*, the *sector model*, and the *multiple nuclei model*. According to the political economy models of conflict theorists, urban growth is influenced by capital investment decisions, power and resource inequality, class and class conflict, and government subsidy programs. Feminist theorists suggest that cities have *gender regimes*; women's lives are affected by both public and private patriarchy. Symbolic interactionists focus on the positive and negative aspects of peoples' experiences in the urban settings. Rapid population growth in many global cities is producing a wide variety of urban problems including overcrowding, environmental pollution and disappearance of farmland as well as creating a limit in the availability of basic public services. Urbanization, suburbanization, **gentrification**, and the growth of edge cities have had a dramatic impact on the U.S. population. Many central cities continue to experience fiscal crises that have resulted in cuts in services, lack of maintenance of the infrastructure, as well as loss of resources because of terrorist attacks.. Many cities and large urban areas have created a "disabling" environment for many people; access is critical in order for persons with a disability to become productive members of the community. Some of the traditional issues of the rural community include financial and emotional, proliferation of superstores, and increase in tourism. Rapid global population growth is inevitable in the future. The urban population will triple as increasing numbers of people in lesser developed and developing nations migrate from rural areas to megacities that contain a high percentage of a region's population.

LEARNING OBJECTIVES

After reading Chapter 19, you should be able to:

1. Describe the study of demography and define the basic demographic concepts.

2. Explain the Malthusian perspective on population growth.

3. Discuss the Marxist perspective on population growth and compare it with the Malthusian perspective.

4. Describe the neo Malthusian perspective on population growth and note the significance of zero population growth to this approach.

5. Discuss demographic transition theory and explain why this theory may not apply to population growth in all societies.

6. Trace the historical development of cities and identify the major characteristics of preindustrial, industrial, and postindustrial cities.

7. Discuss functionalist perspectives on urbanization and outline the major ecological models of urban growth.

8. Compare and contrast conflict and functionalist perspectives on urban growth.

9. Describe global patterns of urbanization in core, peripheral, and semiperipheral nations.

10. Explain symbolic interactionist perspectives on urban life and note the key assumptions of the major urban theorists.

11. Discuss the major problems facing urban and rural areas in the United States today.

12. Explain the issues of the continual fiscal crises of the cities.

KEY TERMS

(defined at page number shown and in glossary)

crude birth rate 629
crude death rate 630
demographic transition 638
demography 628
fertility 628
gentrification 643
invasion 642

migration 632
mortality 630
population composition 633
population pyramid 633
sex ratio 633
succession 642
zero population growth 636

KEY PEOPLE
(identified at page number shown)

CHAPTER OUTLINE

I. DEMOGRAPHY: THE STUDY OF POPULATION

   A. **Demography** is a subfield of sociology that examines population size, composition, and distribution.

   B. **Fertility** is the actual level of childbearing for an individual or a population.

      1. The **crude birth rate** is the number of live births per 1,000 people in a population in a given year.

      2. In most areas of the world, women are having fewer children; women who have six or more children tend to live in agricultural regions where children's labor is essential to the family's economic survival and child mortality rates are very high.

   C. A decline in **mortality** -- the incidence of death in a population -- has been the primary cause of world population growth in recent years.

      1. The **crude death rate** is the number of deaths per 1,000 people in a population in a given year.

      2. The **infant mortality rate** is the number of deaths of infants under 1 year of age per 1,000 live births in a given year.

   D. **Migration** is the movement of people from one geographic area to another for the purpose of changing residency.

      1. While **immigration** is the movement of people into a geographic area to take up residency, **emigration** is the movement of people out of a geographic area to take up residency elsewhere.

      2. The **crude net migration rate** is the net number of migrants (total in migrants minus total out migrants) per 1,000 people in a population in a given year.

   E. **Population composition** is the biological and social characteristics of a population, including age, sex, race, marital status, education, occupation, and income.

      1. The **sex ratio** is the number of males for every hundred females in a given population; a sex ratio of 100 indicates an equal number of males and females.

      2. A **population pyramid** is a graphic representation of the distribution of a population by sex and age.

II. POPULATION GROWTH IN GLOBAL CONTEXT

A. The Malthusian Perspective

1. According to **Thomas Robert Malthus**, the population (if left unchecked) would exceed the available food supply; population would increase in a geometric progression (2, 4, 8, 16 . . .) while the food supply would increase only by an arithmetic progression (1, 2, 3, 4 . . .).

2. This situation could end population growth and perhaps the entire population unless positive checks (such as famines, disease and wars) or preventive checks (such as sexual abstinence and postponement of marriage) intervened.

B. The Marxist Perspective

1. According to Karl Marx and Friedrich Engels, food supply does not have to be threatened by overpopulation; through technology, food for a growing population can be produced.

2. Overpopulation occurs because capitalists want a surplus of workers (an industrial reserve army) to suppress wages and force employees to be more productive.

3. Overpopulation will lead to the eventual destruction of capitalism; when workers become dissatisfied, they will develop class consciousness because of shared oppression.

C. The Neo Malthusian Perspective

1. Neo Malthusians (or "New Malthusians") reemphasized the dangers of overpopulation and suggested that an exponential growth pattern is occurring.

2. Overpopulation and rapid population growth result in global environmental problems, and people should be encouraging **zero population growth** -- the point at which no population increase occurs from year to year because the number of births plus immigrants is equal to the number of deaths plus emigrants.

D. Demographic Transition Theory

1. **Demographic transition** is the process by which some societies have moved from high birth and death rates to relatively low birth and death rates as a result of technological development.

2. Demographic transition is linked to four stages of economic development:

    a. Stage 1: Preindustrial Societies -- little population growth occurs, high birth rates are offset by high death rates.

    b. Stage 2: Early Industrialization -- significant population growth occurs, birth rates are relatively high while death rates decline.

    c. Stage 3: Advanced Industrialization and Urbanization -- very little population growth occurs, both birth rates and death rates are low.

    d. Stage 4: Postindustrialization -- birth rates continue to decline as more women are employed full-time and raising children becomes more costly; population growth occurs slowly, if at all, due to a decrease in the birth rate and a stable death rate.

    e. Other perspectives on population change.

        i. Other perspectives on population change include rational choice theory, the epidemiological transition, economic development and the process of "westernization."

ii. Critics suggest that demographic transition theory may not accurately explain population growth in all societies; this theory best explains growth in Western societies.

III. A BRIEF GLIMPSE AT INTERNATIONAL MIGRATION THEORIES

A. In explaining international migration theories, the neoclassical economics approach, the new households economics of migration approach, conflict and world systems theory, all add to our knowledge of the way people migrate

B. Network theory, push or pull factors, and institutional theory provide further explanation of global migrations.

IV. URBANIZATION IN GLOBAL PERSPECTIVE

A. *Urban sociology* is a subfield of sociology that examines social relationships and political and economic structures in the city.

B. Emergence and Evolution of the City

1. Cities are a relatively recent innovation as compared with the length of human existence. According to Gideon Sjoberg, three preconditions must be present in order for a city to develop:

   a. A favorable physical environment

   b. An advanced technology that could produce a social surplus

   c. A well-developed political system to provide social stability to the economic system.

2. Sjoberg places the first cities in the Mesopotamian region or areas immediately adjacent to it at about 3500 B.C.E; however, not all scholars agree on this point.

C. Preindustrial Cities

1. The largest preindustrial city was Rome.

2. Preindustrial cities were limited in size because of crowded housing conditions, lack of adequate sewage facilities, limited food supplies, and lack of transportation to reach the city.

3. Many preindustrial cities had a sense of community -- a set of social relationships operating within given spatial boundaries that provide people with a sense of identity and a feeling of belonging.

D. Industrial Cities

1. The nature of the city changed as factories arose and new forms of transportation and agricultural production made it easier to leave the countryside and move to the city.

2. Between 1700 and 1900 the population of many European cities mushroomed; London increased to about 6.5 million.

3. New York City became the first U.S. *metropolis* -- one or more central cities and their surrounding suburbs that dominate the economic and cultural life of a region.

4. The countries of Japan and Russia industrialized later and the pattern of urbanization began to move quickly.

E. Postindustrial Cities

1. Since the 1950s, postindustrial cities have emerged as the U.S. economy has gradually shifted from secondary (manufacturing) to tertiary (service and information processing) production.

2. Postindustrial cities are dominated by "light" industry, such as computer software manufacturing, information processing services, educational complexes, medical centers, retail trade centers, and shopping malls.

V. PERSPECTIVES ON URBANIZATION AND THE GROWTH OF CITIES

   A. Functionalist Perspectives: Ecological Models

      1. **Robert Park** based his analysis of the city on human ecology -- the study of the relationship between people and their physical environment -- and found that economic competition produces certain regularities in land use patterns and population distributions.

      2. Concentric zone model

         a. Based on Park's ideas, **Ernest W. Burgess** developed a model that views the city as a series of circular zones, each characterized by a different type of land use, that developed from a central core: (1) the central business district and cultural center; (2) the zone of transition -- houses where wealthy families previously lived that have now been subdivided and rented to persons with low incomes; (3) working class residences and shops, and ethnic enclaves; (4) homes for affluent families, single family residences of white collar workers, and shopping centers; and (5) a ring of small cities and towns comprised of estates owned by the wealthy and houses of commuters who work in the city.

         b. Two important ecological processes occur: **invasion** is the process by which a new category of people or type of land use arrives in an area previously occupied by another group or land use, and **succession** is the process by which a new category of people or type of land use gradually predominates in an area formerly dominated by another group or activity.

         c. **Gentrification** is the process by which members of the middle and upper middle classes, especially whites, move into the central city area and renovate existing properties.

      3. Sector Model

         a. **Homer Hoyt**'s sector model emphasizes the significance of terrain and the importance of transportation routes in the layout of cities.

         b. Residences of a particular type and value tend to grow outward from the center of the city in wedge shaped sectors with the more expensive residential neighborhoods located along the higher ground near lakes and rivers, or along certain streets that stretch from the downtown area.

         c. Industrial areas are located along river valleys and railroad lines; middle class residences exist on either side of wealthier neighborhoods; lower class residential areas border the central business area and the industrial areas.

      4. Multiple Nuclei Model

         a. According to **Chauncey Harris** and **Edward Ullman**, cities have numerous centers of development; as cities grow, they annex outlying townships.

       b.   In addition to the central business district, other nuclei develop around activities such as an educational institution or a medical complex; residential neighborhoods may exist close to or far away from these nuclei.

    5.   Contemporary Urban Ecology.

       a.   Amos Hawley viewed urban areas as complex social systems in which growth patterns are based on advances in transportation and communication.

       b.   Social area analysis examines urban populations in terms of economic status, family status, and ethnic classification.

B.   Conflict Perspectives: Political Economy Models

    1.   According to Marx, cities are arenas in which the intertwined processes of class conflict and capital accumulation take place; class consciousness is more likely to occur in cities where workers are concentrated.

    2.   Three major themes are found in political economy models:

       a.   Patterns of urban growth and decline are affected by: (1) economic factors such as capitalist investments; and (2) political factors, including governmental protection of private property and promotion of the interests of business elites and large corporations.

       b.   Urban space has both an exchange value and a use value: (1) exchange value refers to the profits industrialists, developers, and bankers make from buying, selling, and developing land and buildings; (2) use value is the utility of space, land, and buildings for family life and neighborhood life.

       c.   Structure and agency are both important in understanding how urban development takes place: (1) structure refers to institutions such as state bureaucracies and capital investment circuits that are involved in the urban development process; and (2) agency refers to human actors who participate in land use decisions, including developers, business elites, and activists protesting development.

    3.   According to political economy models, urban growth is influenced by capital investment decisions, power and resource inequality, class and class conflict, and government subsidy programs.

    4.   Gender Regimes in Cities

       a.   According to feminist perspectives, urbanization reflects the workings of the political economy and patriarchy.

       b.   Different cities have different gender regimes -- prevailing ideologies of how women and men should think, feel, and act; how access to positions and control of resources should be managed; and how women and men should relate to each other.

       c.   Gender intersects with class and race as a form of oppression, especially for lower income women of color who live in central cities.

C.   Symbolic Interactionist Perspectives: The Experience of City Life

    1.   Simmel's View of City Life

       a.   According to **Georg Simmel**, urban life is highly stimulating; it shapes people's thoughts and actions.

b.   However, many urban residents avoid emotional involvement with each other and try to ignore events taking place around them.

c.   City life is not completely negative; urban living can be liberating -- people have opportunities for individualism and autonomy.

2.   Urbanism as a Way of Life

a.   **Louis Wirth** suggested that urbanism is a "way of life." Urbanism refers to the distinctive social and psychological patterns of city life.

b.   Size, density, and heterogeneity result in an elaborate division of labor and in spatial segregation of people by race/ethnicity, class, religion, and/or lifestyle; a sense of community is replaced by the "mass society" -- a large scale, highly institutionalized society in which individuality is supplanted by mass media, faceless bureaucrats, and corporate interests.

3.   Gans's Urban Villagers

a.   According to **Herbert Gans**, not everyone experiences the city in the same way; some people develop strong loyalties and a sense of community within central city areas that outsiders may view negatively.

b.   Five major categories of urban dwellers are: (1) cosmopolites -- students, artists, writers, musicians, entertainers, and professionals who choose to live in the city because they want to be close to its cultural facilities; (2) unmarried people and childless couples who live in the city because they want to be close to work and entertainment; (3) ethnic villagers who live in ethnically segregated neighborhoods; (4) the deprived -- individuals who are very poor and see few future prospects; and (5) the trapped -- those who cannot escape the city, including downwardly mobile persons, older persons, and persons with addictions.

4.   Gender and City Life

a.   According to **Elizabeth Wilson**, some men view the city as sexual space in which women, based on their sexual desirability and accessibility, are categorized as prostitutes, lesbians, temptresses, or virtuous women in need of protection.

b.   More affluent, dominant group women are more likely to be viewed as virtuous women in need of protection while others are placed in less desirable categories.

5.   Cities and Persons with a Disability

a.   Many cities and urban areas create a "disabling" environment for many people.

b.   **Harlan Hahn** suggests that historical patterns in the dynamics of capitalism contributed to discrimination against persons with disabilities, and this legacy remains today.

VI.   PROBLEMS IN GLOBAL CITIES

A.   Natural increases in population account for two-thirds of new urban growth, and rural-to-urban migration accounts for the remainder.

B. Rapid global population growth in Latin American and other regions is producing a wide variety of urban problems, including overcrowding, environmental pollution and the disappearance of farmland.

C. Most cities in Africa, South America, and the Caribbean are in peripheral nations.

D. Cities in semiperipheral nations—such as India, Iran, and Mexico are confronted with unprecedented population growth.

VII. URBAN PROBLEMS IN THE UNITED STATES

A. Divided Interests: Cities, Suburbs, and Beyond

1. Since World War II, the U.S. population has shifted dramatically as many people have moved to the suburbs.

2. Suburbanites rely on urban centers for employment and some services but pay property taxes to suburban governments and school districts; some affluent suburbs have state of the art school districts and infrastructure while central city services and school districts lack funds.

3. Race, Class, and Suburbs

   a. The intertwining impact of race and class is visible in the division between central cities and suburbs.

   b. Most suburbs are predominantly white; many upper middle and upper class suburbs remain virtually all white; people of color who live in suburbs often are resegregated.

4. Beyond the Suburbs

   a. Edge cities initially develop as residential areas beyond central cities and suburbs; then retail establishments and office parks move into the area and create an unincorporated edge city.

   b. Corporations move to edge cities because of cheaper land and lower utility rates and property taxes.

5. Likewise, Sunbelt cities grew in the 1970s, as millions moved from the north and northeastern states to southern and western states where there were more jobs and higher wages, lower taxes, pork barrel programs funded by federal money that created jobs and encouraged industry, and the presence of high technology industries.

B. The Continual Fiscal Crisis of the Cities

1. During the 1980s, many cities experienced fiscal crises as federal and state aid was drastically cut; many services had to be cut or taxes raised at the same time that the tax base was shrinking due to suburban flight.

2. The past fiscal crises of the largest U.S.A. cities have been intensified by terrorists' attacks.

3. About the beginning of the twenty-first century, the nation's economy slumped; the situation worsened by the terrorists' attack of 9-11-01; tourism fell creating loss of tax revenues and other problems.

VIII. RURAL COMMUNITY ISSUES IN THE UNITED STATES

    A.   About 25 percent of the U.S. population resides in rural areas, identified as communities of 2,500 or less by the U.S. Census Bureau.

        1.   This definition was established in the 1920s.

        2.   Rural communities today are more diverse; recently more people from large urban areas and suburbs have moved into rural areas.

        3.   These recent immigrants to rural areas do not face some traditional problems experienced by long-term rural residents.

    B.   Individuals in rural areas whose livelihood is farming or other agricultural endeavors have experienced several difficulties.

        1.   Crop failures

        2.   Loss of small businesses

        3.   Problems of divorce, alcoholism, and abuse

        4.   Loss of farm

        5.   Limited economic opportunities

        6.   Limited health care

    C.   Other influencing factors

        1.   Proliferation of superstores—putting local small businesses out of business.

        2.   Increase in tourism.

    D.   Some commonalities of U.S. rural with rural in other countries are health, nutrition, concerns about educational opportunities for children, among other things.

IX. POPULATION AND URBANIZATION IN THE FUTURE

    A.   Rapid global population growth is inevitable: although death rates have declined in many developing nations, there has not been a corresponding decrease in birth rates.

    B.   In the future, many people will live in a *megalopolis* -- a continuous concentration of two or more cities and their suburbs that form an interconnected urban area.

    C.   At the macrolevel, we may be able to do little about population and urbanization; at the microlevel, we may be able to exercise some degree of control over our communities and our own lives.

PRACTICE TESTS

MULTIPLE CHOICE QUESTIONS

Select the response that best answers the question or completes the statement:

1.   Demography is a subfield of sociology that examines:

    a.   population size.

    b.   population composition.

    c.   population distribution.

    d.   all of the above.

2.   _____ is the actual level of childbearing for an individual or a population, while _____ is the potential number of children that could be born if every woman reproduced at her maximum biological capacity.

    a. Birth rate - fertility rate

    b. Fertility rate - birth rate

    c. Fertility - fecundity

    d. Fecundity - fertility

3.   The primary cause of world population growth in recent years is a/an:

    a. increase in the birth rate.

    b. decline in the death rate.

    c. decline in all infectious diseases.

    d. increase in post baby boom birth rates.

4.   The average lifetime in years of people born in a specific year is known as:

    a. life expectancy.

    b. the crude mortality rate.

    c. the longevity table.

    d. age specific death rates.

5.   _____ is the movement of people out of a geographic area to take up residency elsewhere.

    a. Immigration

    b. Emigration

    c. Transmigration

    d. Ex-migration

6.   According to Thomas Malthus's perspective on population:

    a. the population would increase in a geometric progression while the food supply would increase in an arithmetic progression.

    b. the population would increase in an arithmetic progression while the population would increase in a geometric progression.

    c. the food supply is not threatened by overpopulation because technology makes it possible to produce the food and other goods needed to meet the demands of a growing population.

    d. societies move through a process of demographic transition.

7.   According to Karl Marx and Friedrich Engels's perspective on population:

    a. the population would increase in a geometric progression while the food supply would increase in an arithmetic progression.

    b. the population would increase in an arithmetic progression while the food supply would increase in a geometric progression.

    c. the food supply is not threatened by overpopulation because technology makes it possible to produce the food and other goods needed to meet the demands of a growing population.

    d. societies move through a process of demographic transition.

Chapter 19

8. According to the demographic transition theory, significant population growth occurs because birth rates are relatively high while death rates decline in the stage of economic development.
    a. preindustrial
    b. early industrial
    c. advanced industrial
    d. postindustrial

9. All of the following statements regarding preindustrial cities are true, **except**:
    a. the largest preindustrial city was Rome.
    b. preindustrial cities were limited in size because of crowded housing conditions and a lack of adequate sewage facilities.
    c. food supplies were limited in preindustrial cities.
    d. preindustrial cities lacked a sense of community.

10. The *Gemeinschaft* and *Gesellschaft* typology originated with:
    a. Emile Durkheim.
    b. Gideon Sjoberg.
    c. Max Weber.
    d. Ferdinand Tonnies.

11. _____ refers to one or more central cities and their surrounding suburbs that dominate the economic and cultural life of a region.
    a. Urban sprawl
    b. Megalopolis
    c. Metropolis
    d. Urbanization

12. Postindustrial cities are characterized by:
    a. "light" industry, information processing services, educational complexes, retail trade centers, and shopping malls.
    b. the growth of the factory system.
    c. agricultural production.
    d. "heavy" industry, such as automobile manufacturing.

13. Ecological models of urban growth are based on a _____ perspective.
    a. functionalist
    b. conflict
    c. neo Marxist
    d. interactionist

14. All of the following are ecological models of urban growth, except the:
    a. concentric zone model.
    b. sector model.
    c. urban sprawl model.
    d. multiple nuclei model.

15. An upper-middle class doctor who moves her family from the suburbs into the central city to renovate an older home is an example of:

    a. succession.

    b. gentrification.

    c. ex-suburbanization.

    d. downward immigration.

16. According to political economy models, urban growth is:

    a. influenced by terrain and transportation.

    b. based on the clustering of people who share similar characteristics.

    c. linked with peaks and valleys in the economic cycle.

    d. influenced by capital investment decisions, power and resource inequality, and government subsidy programs.

17. _____ refers to the tendency of some neighborhoods, cities, or regions to grow and prosper while others stagnate and decline.

    a. Invasion

    b. Succession

    c. Gentrification

    d. Uneven development

18. The United States, Japan, and Germany are _____ nations.

    a. core

    b. peripheral

    c. semiperipheral

    d. globalized

19. Sociologist _____ has argued that urbanism is a "way of life."

    a. Herbert Gans

    b. Georg Simmel

    c. Louis Wirth

    d. Elizabeth Wilson

20. According to sociologists, edge cities:

    a. initially develop as industrial parks.

    b. drain taxes from central cities and older suburbs.

    c. have existed since World War II.

    d. always correspond to municipal boundaries.

TRUE FALSE QUESTIONS

1. Demographers analyze fertility, mortality, and migration rates.
    True or False

2. The world's population is increasing by 76 million people per year.
    True or False

3. In most areas of the world, women are having more children.
    True or False

4. The primary cause of world population growth in recent years has been a decline in mortality.
    True or False

5. Pull factors of migration include political unrest and war.
    True or False

6. Sex ratio is the number of females per 100 males in a given population.
    True or False

7. Population pyramids are graphic representations of the distribution of a population by sex and age.
    True or False

8. According to the Marxist perspective, overpopulation occurs because capitalists desire to have a surplus of workers so as to suppress wages and increase workers' productivity.
    True or False

9. About 50 percent of the world's. population lives in cities.
    True or False

10. The sector model views the city as a series of circular areas or zones, each characterized by a different type of land use that developed from a central core.
    True or False

11. According to conflict theorists, cities grow and decline by chance.
    True or False

12. According to feminist theorists, public patriarchy may be perpetuated by cities through policies that limit women's access to paid work and public transportation.
    True or False

13. Interactionists examine the experience of urban life rather than the political economy of the city.
    True or False

14. Herbert Gans has suggested that almost all city dwellers live in urban areas by choice.
    True or False

15. Nationally, most suburbs are predominantly white.
    True or False

FILL IN THE BLANK QUESTIONS

1. The biological and social characteristics of a population is known as the _____ .

2. A graphic representation of a population by sex and age is defined as a _____ .

3. According to _____ limits to fertility are defined as _____ checks.

4. The point at which no population increases occurs from year to year is defined as _____ .

5. According to Lynn Appleton, different kinds of cities have different _____ which are prevailing ideologies of how men and women should think.

6. According to the sociologist Herbert Gans, _____ are students, artists, entertainers, and professionals who choose to live in the city.

7. The _____ model of urban development cities have numerous centers of development.

8. According to _____ urban living could have a liberating effect on people because they have opportunities for individualism and autonomy.

9. _____ is the movement of people into a geographic area to take up residency.

10. Things that attract people to move into another country are known as _____ factors.

SHORT ANSWER/ESSAY QUESTIONS

1. What is demography and how are people affected by demographic changes?

2. What is the Malthusian perspective? Do the views of Karl Marx support this? Explain.

3. Explain the three functionalist models of urban growth.

4. What are the stages in the demographic transition theory?

5. How have recent acts of global terrorism affect U.S.A. cities and other cities about the world?

STUDENT CLASS PROJECTS AND ACTIVITIES

1. Utilizing the most current U.S. Census data, construct a population pyramid of the United States, your home state, and the city in which you live or reside, or of any city in the United States. Provide the pyramids, interpretations of the statistics, a summary of the data, a conclusion from each pyramid constructed, and bibliographical references. Submit your project to your instructor at the appropriate time.

2. Construct a demographic analysis of the state in which your college or university is located and compare this with an analysis of the entire United States. Present data on the size of the population, the numbers and percentage of increase or decrease from the past twenty years, the birth rate, the death rate, sex ratio, infant mortality, cause of death, and life expectancy. Provide a summary of the data, a conclusion, and an evaluation of this project. Submit your project at the appropriate time to your instructor.

3. Select and submit 10 articles from various sources on any topic covered in this chapter Population and Urbanization. Because this is a topic of interest and concern, there are many sources of information on this subject. You are to provide a copy of each article with your paper and you must: (1) provide the title of the article; (2) provide the data and source of the article; (3) provide a summary of the article; (4) provide two or three issues that each article raises; (5) provide at least two to three questions per each article that are generated from reading the article; (6) provide a personal conclusion and evaluation of this project. Submit your paper to your instructor at the appropriate time, following any additional instructions you may have received.

4. Construct a plan of a model city. In the plan, provide for all necessary public facilities, such as: an efficient transportation system, an efficient governmental system, the most efficient use of land, provision for industrial and commercial bases, provision for education, medical, recreational, and religious facilities, provision for optimum housing , promotions for attracting an equitable balance of ethnic, age, and income groups, and provision for long-range planning for optimum population size and city size. Include any other amenities in the planning of this optimum model city. Submit this project to your instructor at the appropriate time.

INTERNET ACTIVITIES

1. Explore the HUD site and learn about the history of the government's involvement in the life of cities. The mission of the *Department of Housing and Urban Development* is to provide "a decent, safe, and sanitary home and suitable living environment for every American." www.hud.gov/

2. If you are interested in more detailed information on the population crisis in Africa you should access the following site. Demographic information collected by the *World Health Organization*, the *United Nations* and the U.S. Census Bureau are available.

    a. www.un.org/esa/africa/

    b. www.afro.who.int/

3. Surf this site to learn about world population trends. It is possible from this site to obtain statistical reports, United Nations documents, wall charts, and records of population policies of governments and world organizations. www.un.org/popin/

4. *Population.com* is a huge resource for studies on population, **migration** and urbanization. This site has an extensive report as well as charts on population trends around the world. You can work to apply some of the concepts you have learned in this chapter to a specific region of the globe with a distinct history and culture. www.population.com/

5. This is the homepage for the *National Urban League*. The Urban League movement was founded in 1910. The National Urban League, headquartered in New York City, spearheads this nonprofit, nonpartisan, community-based movement. The heart of the Urban League movement is the professionally staffed Urban League affiliates in over 100 cities in 34 states and the District of Columbia. Search through the site and discover what kinds of issues urban leaders are facing. www.nul.org/

INFOTRAC EXERCISES

1. Investigate **global population** from a variety of perspectives. Determine the key issues based on these articles.

2. A key component in understanding **demographic transitions** is the **sex ratio** of a society. You will need to weed out articles about fig wasps and turtles, but there are a number of very informative reports and research articles on this phenomenon. Interesting comparisons can be made between biological studies of animals and those about humans' social behavior.

3. Conduct a keyword search for **zero population growth.** Find the article entitled: *Allowing fertility decline: 200 years after Malthus's essay on population.* The economic opportunity model in contrast to the **demographic transition** model is presented as a way to reduce population growth. Analyze this new alternative in light of what you have learned from reading chapter 15.

4. Search InfoTrac for articles about **urbanization**. There are a number of interesting articles that take this process into a new direction.

    a. How progress ate America

    b. The Urbanization of opera: Music theater in Paris in the nineteenth century

    c. You can't keep a good myth down

    d. Urbanization and the decline of witchcraft: an examination of London

    e. Relationships between health services, socioeconomic variables and inadequate weight gain among Brazilian children

    f. Asphalt Jungle: A global land rush is gobbling up the space and resources needed for agriculture and wildlife. Only the cockroaches are thrilled.

Solutions

MULTIPLE CHOICE QUESTIONS

1. D p. 629

2. C p. 628

3. B p. 631

4. A p. 630

5. B p. 632

6. A p. 635

7. C p. 635

8. B p. 636

9. D p. 639

10. D p. 639

11. C p. 640

12. A p. 640

13. A p. 643

14. C p. 642-643

15. B p. 643

16. D p. 644

17. D p. 645

18. A p. 648

19. C p. 646

20. B p. 651

TRUE FALSE QUESTIONS

1. T p. 628

2. T p. 628

3. F p. 629

4. T p. 630

5. F p. 632

6. F p. 633

7. T p. 633

8. T p. 635

9. T p. 638

10. F p. 643

11. F p. 644

12. T p. 645

13. T p. 646

14. F p. 646

15. T p. 651

FILL IN THE BLANK QUESTIONS

1. population composition

2. population pyramid

3. Thomas Malthus, preventative

4. zero population growth

5. gender regimes

6. cosmopolites

7. multiple nuclei

8. Georg Simmel

9. Immigration

10. pull

Chapter 20

COLLECTIVE BEHAVIOR, SOCIAL MOVEMENTS AND SOCIAL CHANGE

BRIEF CHAPTER OUTLINE

Collective Behavior
- Conditions for Collective Behavior
- Dynamics of Collective Behavior
- Distinctions Regarding Collective Behavior
- Types of Crowd Behavior
- Explanations of Crowd Behavior
- Mass Behavior

Social Movements
- Types of Social Movements
- Stages in Social Movements

Social Movement Theories
- Relative Deprivation Theory
- Value-Added Theory
- Resource Mobilization Theory
- Social Constructionist Theory: Frame Analysis
- New Social Movement Theory

Social Change In The Future
- The Physical Environment and Change
- Population and Change
- Technology and Change
- Social Institutions and Change
- A Few Final Thoughts

CHAPTER SUMMARY

Social change is the alteration, modification, or transformation of public policy, culture, or social institutions over time. Such change usually is brought about by **collective behavior** -- voluntary, often spontaneous activity that is engaged in by a large number of people and typically violates dominant group norms and values. A **crowd** is a relatively large number of people who are in one another's immediate vicinity. Five categories of crowds have been identified: (1) casual crowds are relatively large gatherings of people who happen to be in the same place at the same time; (2) conventional crowds are comprised of people who specifically come together for a scheduled event and thus share a common focus; (3) expressive crowds provide opportunities for the expression of some strong emotion; (4) acting crowds are collectivities so intensely focused on a specific purpose or object that they may erupt into violent or destructive behavior; and (5) protest crowds are gatherings of people who engage in activities intended to achieve specific political goals. Protest crowds sometime participate in **civil disobedience** -- nonviolent action that seeks to change a policy or law by refusing to comply with it. Explanations of crowd behavior include contagion theory, social unrest and circular reaction, convergence theory, and emergent norm theory. Examples of **mass behavior** -- collective behavior that takes place when people respond to the same event in much the same way -- include rumors, gossip, mass hysteria, fads, fashions, and public opinion. The major types of **social movements** -- organized groups that act consciously to promote or resist change through collective action -- are reform movements, revolutionary movements, religious movements, alternative movements, and resistance movements. Sociological theories explaining social movements include relative deprivation theory, value added theory, resource mobilization theory, and recent emerging perspectives. Social change produces many challenges that remain to be resolved: environmental problems, changes in the demographics of the population, and new technology that benefits some -- but not all -- people. As we head into the future, we must use our sociological imaginations to help resolve these problems.

LEARNING OBJECTIVES

After reading Chapter 20, you should be able to:

1. Define collective behavior and describe the conditions necessary for such behavior to occur.

2. Distinguish between crowds and masses and identify casual, conventional, expressive, acting, and protest crowds.

3. Discuss the key elements of these four explanations of collective behavior: contagion theory, social unrest and circular reaction, convergence theory, and emergent norm theory.

4. Define mass behavior and describe the most frequent types of this behavior.

5. Describe social movements and note when and where they are most likely to develop.

6. Differentiate among the five major types of social movements based on their goals and the amount of change they seek to produce.

7. Identify the stages in social movements and explain why social movements may be an important source of social change.

8. Compare relative deprivation theory and value added theory as explanations of why people join social movements.

9. State the key assumptions of resource mobilization theory.

10. Explain the basis and the assumptions of social constructionist theory and explain how problems are framed from this perspective.

11. Describe "new social movements" and give examples of issues of concern to participants in these movements.

12. Describe the effects of physical environment, population trends, technological development, and social institutions on social change.

KEY TERMS

(defined at page number shown and in glossary)

civil disobedience 665
collective behavior 660
crowd 663
environmental racism 677
gossip 668
mass 663
mass behavior 667
mob 664

panic 665
propaganda 670
public opinion 669
riot 664
rumors 667
social change 659
social movement 671

KEY PEOPLE

(identified at page number shown)

Herbert Blumer 664
Pierre Bourdieu 669
Lory Britt 672
Steven M. Buechler 660
Stella M. Capek 677
Rachel Carson 660
Steven E. Clayman 666
Riley E. Dunlap 671
Kai Erikson 672
William A. Gamson 677
Lois Gibbs 662

Gustave Le Bon 665
John Lofland 663
Clark McPhail and Ronald T. Wohlstein 660
William Ogburn 681
Robert E. Park 665
Georg Simmel 669
Neal Smelser 674
Charles Tilly 675
Ralph H. Turner and Lewis M. Killian 663
Thorstein Veblen 669

CHAPTER OUTLINE

I.   COLLECTIVE BEHAVIOR

    A.   **Social change** is the alteration, modification, or transformation of public policy, culture, or social institutions over time; such change usually is brought about by **collective behavior** -- relatively spontaneous, unstructured activity that typically violates established social norms.

    B.   Conditions for Collective Behavior

        1.   Collective behavior occurs as a result of some common influence or stimuli that produces a response from a collectivity -- a relatively large number of people who mutually transcend, bypass, or subvert established institutional patterns and structures.

2.   Major factors that contribute to the likelihood that collective behavior will occur are:

    a.   Structural factors that increase the chances of people responding in a particular way;

    b.   Timing;

    c.   A breakdown in social control mechanisms and a corresponding feeling of normlessness;

    d.   A common stimulus, for example the publication of the stimulating book, *Silent Spring*.

C.   Dynamics of Collective Behavior

    1.   People may engage in collective behavior when they find that their problems are not being solved through official channels; as the problem appears to grow worse, organizational responses become more defensive and obscure.

    2.   People's attitudes are not always reflected in their political and social behavior

    3.   People act collectively in ways they would not act singly due to:

        a.   The noise and activity around them.

        b.   A belief that it is the only way to fight those with greater power and resources.

D.   Distinctions Regarding Collective Behavior

    1.   People engaging in collective behavior may be a:

        a.   **Crowd** -- a relatively large number of people who are in one another's immediate face to face presence; or

        b.   **Mass** -- a number of people who share an interest in a specific idea or issue but who are not in one another's immediate physical vicinity.

    2.   Collective behavior also may be distinguished by the dominant emotion expressed (e.g., fear, hostility, joy, grief, disgust, surprise, or shame).

E.   Types of Crowd Behavior

    1.   **Herbert Blumer** divided crowds into four categories:

        a.   Casual crowds -- relatively large gatherings of people who happen to be in the same place at the same time; if they interact at all, it is only briefly.

        b.   Conventional crowds -- people who specifically come together for a scheduled event and thus share a common focus.

        c.   Expressive crowds -- people releasing their pent up emotions in conjunction with others who experience similar emotions.

        d.   Acting crowds -- collectivities so intensely focused on a specific purpose or object that they may erupt into violent or destructive behavior. Examples

            i.   A **mob** -- a highly emotional crowd whose members engage in, or are ready to engage in, violence against a specific target which may be a person, a category of people, or physical property.

            ii.   A **riot** -- violent crowd behavior fueled by deep seated emotions but not directed at a specific target.

        iii.   A **panic** -- a form of crowd behavior that occurs when a large number of people react with strong emotions and self destructive behavior to a real or perceived threat.

    2.   To these four types of crowds, Clark McPhail and Ronald T. Wohlstein added *protest crowds* -- crowds that engage in activities intended to achieve specific political goals.

        a.   Protest crowds sometimes take the form of **civil disobedience** -- nonviolent action that seeks to change a policy or law by refusing to comply with it.

        b.   At the grassroots level, protests often are seen as the only way to call attention to problems or demand social change.

F.   Explanations of Crowd Behavior

    1.   According to contagion theory, people are more likely to engage in antisocial behavior in a crowd because they are anonymous and feel invulnerable; Gustave Le Bon argued that feelings of fear and hate are contagious in crowds because people experience a decline in personal responsibility.

    2.   According to **Robert Park**, social unrest is transmitted by a process of *circular reaction* -- the interactive communication between persons in such a way that the discontent of one person is communicated to another who, in turn, reflects the discontent back to the first person.

    3.   *Convergence* theory focuses on the shared emotions, goals, and beliefs many people bring to crowd behavior.

        a.   From this perspective, people with similar attributes find a collectivity of like minded persons with whom they can release their underlying personal tendencies.

        b.   Although people may reveal their "true selves" in crowds, their behavior is not irrational; it is highly predictable to those who share similar emotions or beliefs.

    4.   According to Ralph Turner's and Lewis Killian's *emergent norm theory*, crowds develop their own definition of *the situation and establish* norms for behavior that fits the occasion.

        a.   Emergent norms occur when people define a new situation as highly unusual or see a long standing situation in a new light.

        b.   Emergent norm theory points out that crowds are not irrational; new norms are developed in a rational way to fit the needs of the immediate situation.

G.   Mass Behavior

    1.   **Mass behavior** is collective behavior that takes place when people (who often are geographically separated from one anther) respond to the same event in much the same way. The most frequent types of mass behavior are:

    2.   **Rumors** -- unsubstantiated reports on an issue or subject -- and **gossip** -- rumors about the personal lives of individuals.

    3.   *Mass hysteria* is a form of dispersed collective behavior that occurs when a large number of people react with strong emotions and self destructive behavior to a real

or perceived threat; many sociologists believe this behavior is best described as a panic with a dispersed audience.

4. *Fads and Fashions*

   a. A *fad* is a temporary but widely copied activity enthusiastically followed by large numbers of people.

   b. *Fashion* is a currently valued style of behavior, thinking or appearance. Fashion also applies to art, music, drama, literature, architecture, interior design, and automobiles, among other things.

5. **Public opinion** consists of the attitudes and beliefs communicated by ordinary citizens to decision makers (as measured through polls and surveys based on interviews and questionnaires).

   a. Even on a single topic, public opinion will vary widely based on characteristics such as race, ethnicity, religion, region of the country, urban or rural residence, social class, education level, gender, and age.

   b. As the masses attempt to influence elites and visa versa, a two way process occurs with the dissemination of **propaganda** -- information provided by individuals or groups that have a vested interest in furthering their own cause or damaging an opposing one.

II. SOCIAL MOVEMENTS

A. A **social movement** is an organized group that acts consciously to promote or resist change through collective action.

B. Types of Social Movements

   1. *Reform* movements seek to improve society by changing some specific aspect of the social structure.

   2. *Revolutionary* movements seek to bring about a total change in society. **Terrorism** is the calculated unlawful use of physical force or threats of violence against persons or property in order to intimidate or coerce a government, organization, or individual for the purpose of gaining some political, religious, economic or social objective.

   3. *Religious* movements seek to produce radical change in individuals and typically are based on spiritual or supernatural belief systems.

   4. *Alternative* movements seek limited change in some aspect of people's behavior (e.g., a movement that attempts to get people to abstain from drinking alcoholic beverages).

   5. *Resistance* movements seek to prevent or to undo change that already has occurred.

C. Stages in Social Movements

   1. In the *preliminary* stage, widespread unrest is present as people begin to become aware of a threatening problem. Leaders emerge to agitate others into taking action.

   2. In the *coalescence* stage, people begin to organize and start making the threat known to the public. Some movements become formally organized at local and regional levels.

   3. In the *institutionalization* stage, an organizational structure develops, and a paid staff (rather than volunteers) begins to lead the group.

III. SOCIAL MOVEMENT THEORY

A. *Relative deprivation* theory asserts that people who suffer relative deprivation are likely to feel that a change is necessary and to join a social movement in order to bring about that change.

B. According to **Neal Smelser**'s *value added theory*, six conditions are necessary and sufficient to produce social movements when they combine or interact in a particular situation:

1. Structural conduciveness

2. Structural strain

3. Spread of a generalized belief

4. Precipitating factors

5. Mobilization for action

6. Social control factors

C. *Resource mobilization* theory focuses on the ability of a social movement to acquire resources (money, time and skills, access to the media, etc.) and mobilize people to advance the cause.

D. Social Constructionist theory is based on the assumption that social movements are interactive, symbolically defined, and a negotiated process.

1. This process involves participants, opponents, and bystanders.

2. Research based on this perspective often investigates how problems are framed and what names they are given.

3. Distinct frame alignment processes occur in social movements:

a. frame bridging;

b. frame amplification;

c. frame extension; and

d. frame transformation.

E. New social movement theory looks at a diverse array of collective actions and the manner in which those actions are based in politics, ideology, and culture.

1. It incorporates sources of identity, including race, class, gender, and sexuality as sources of collective action and social movement.

2. Examples of already existing "new social movements" include ecofeminism and environmental justice movements.

a. According to ecofeminists, patriarchy is a root cause of environmental problems because it contributes to a belief that nature is to be possessed and dominated, rather than treated as a partner.

b. Environmental justice movements focus on the issue of **environmental racism** -- the belief that a disproportionate number of hazardous facilities (including industries such as waste disposal/treatment and chemical plants) are placed in low income areas populated primarily by people of color.

IV. SOCIAL CHANGE IN THE FUTURE

    A.   The Physical Environment and Change: Changes in the physical environment often produce changes in the lives of people; in turn, people can make dramatic changes in the physical environment, over which we have only limited control.

    B.   Population and Change: Changes in population size, distribution, and composition affect the culture and social structure of a society and change the relationships among nations.

    C.   Technology and Change: Advances in communication, transportation, science, and medicine have made significant changes in people's lives, especially in developed nations; however, these changes also have created the potential for new disasters, ranging from global warfare to localized technological disasters at toxic waste sites.

    D.   Social Institutions and Change: During the past twentieth century, many changes occurred in the family, religion, education, the economy, and the political system; at the beginning of the new century, the U.S. government seemed less able to respond to the needs and problems of the country.

    E.   Changes in physical environment, population, technology, and social institutions operate together in a complex relationship, sometimes producing consequences we must examine by using our sociological imagination.

    F.   A few final thoughts: one purpose of this text is to facilitate understanding of different viewpoints in order to resolve social issues, thereby, producing a better way of life in this country and worldwide.

PRACTICE TESTS

MULTIPLE CHOICE QUESTIONS

Select the response that best answers the question or completes the statement:

1.   All of the following are factors that contribute to the likelihood that collective behavior will occur, **except**:

    a.   the presence of deviant behavior.

    b.   structural factors that increase the chances of people responding in a particular way.

    c.   timing.

    d.   a breakdown in social control mechanisms and a corresponding feeling of normlessness.

2.   A _____ is a number of people who share an interest in a specific issue but are not in close proximity to each other.

    a.   crowd

    b.   mass

    c.   riot

    d.   mob

3. Casual crowds are:

   a. comprised of people who specifically come together for a scheduled event and thus share a common focus.

   b. situations that provide an opportunity for the expression of some strong emotion.

   c. comprised of people who happen to be in the same place at the same time.

   d. comprised of people who are so intensely focused on a specific purpose or object that they may erupt into violent or destructive behavior.

4. Revelers assembled at Mardi Gras or on New Year's Eve at Times Square in New York are an example of:

   a. protest crowds.

   b. expressive and acting crowds.

   c. conventional crowds.

   d. panics.

5. When the residents of Love Canal burned both the governor and the health commission in effigy, they were engaging in a/an:

   a. acting crowd.

   b. casual crowd.

   c. conventional crowd.

   d. panic.

6. Convergence theory focuses on:

   a. the social-psychological aspects of collective behavior, including how moods, attitudes, and behavior are communicated.

   b. how social unrest is transmitted by a process of circular reaction.

   c. the importance of social norms in shaping crowd behavior.

   d. the shared emotions, goals, and beliefs many people bring to crowd behavior.

7. All of the following statements regarding the emergent norm theory are true, **except**:

   a. Emergent norm theory is based on the symbolic interactionist perspective.

   b. Sociologists using the emergent norm approach seek to determine how individuals in a given collectivity develop an understanding of what is going on, how they construe these activities, and what types of norms are involved.

   c. Emergent norm theory points out that crowds sometimes are irrational.

   d. Emergent norm theory originated with sociologists Ralph Turner and Lewis Killian.

8. Rumors, gossip, fashions, and fads are examples of _____ behavior.

   a. mob

   b. mass

   c. irrational

   d. casual

9. A form of dispersed collective behavior that occurs when a large number of people react with strong emotions and self-destructive behavior to a real or perceived threat is known as:

    a. mob behavior.

    b. mass behavior.

    c. mass hysteria.

    d. contagious behavior.

10. "Streaking" -- students taking off their clothes and running naked in public -- in the 1970s is an example of a:

    a. panic.

    b. trend.

    c. fashion.

    d. fad.

11. According to the text, _____ is information provided by individuals or groups that have a vested interest in furthering their own cause or damaging an opposing one.

    a. propaganda

    b. public opinion

    c. political rhetoric

    d. a press release

12. Which of the following statements regarding social movements is true?

    a. Social movements are more likely to develop in preindustrial societies where there is an acceptance of traditional beliefs and practices.

    b. Social movements have become institutionalized and are a part of the political mainstream.

    c. Social movements make democracy less accessible to excluded groups.

    d. Social movements offer "outsiders" an opportunity to have their voices heard.

13. All of the following are types of social movements, except: _____ movements.

    a. alternative

    b. dissident

    c. religious

    d. revolutionary

14. According to relative deprivation theory:

    a. people who are satisfied with their present condition are more likely to seek social change.

    b. certain conditions are necessary for the development of a social movement.

    c. people who feel that they have been deprived of their "fair share" are more likely to feel that change is necessary and to join a social movement.

    d. some people bring more resources to a social movement than others.

15. _____ theory is based on the assumption that six conditions, including structural conduciveness and structural strain, must be present for the development of a social movement.
    a. Value added
    b. Relative deprivation
    c. Resource mobilization
    d. Emergent norm

16. _____ theory focuses on the ability of members of a social movement to acquire resources and mobilize people in order to advance their cause.
    a. Value added
    b. Relative deprivation
    c. Resource mobilization
    d. Emergent norm

17. _____ is a social movement based on the belief that patriarchy is a root cause of environmental problems.
    a. Ecology Today
    b. Conflict Ecologists
    c. Environmental Justice
    d. Ecofeminism

18. In the _____ stage of a social movement, people begin to organize and to publicize the problem.
    a. preliminary
    b. coalescence
    c. institutionalization
    d. deinstitutionalization

19. The belief that a disproportionate number of hazardous facilities are placed in low income areas populated by people of color is known as:
    a. environmental racism.
    b. environmental justice.
    c. reverse environmentalism.
    d. racial pollution.

20. All of the following statements regarding natural disasters are true, **except**:
    a. Major natural disasters can dramatically change the lives of people.
    b. Trauma that people experience from disasters may outweigh the actual loss of physical property.
    c. Natural disasters are not affected by human decisions.
    d. Disasters may become divisive elements that tear communities apart.

TRUE FALSE QUESTIONS

1. Collective behavior lacks an official division of labor, hierarchy of authority, and established rules and procedures.
   True or False

2. People are more likely to act as a collectivity when they believe it is the only way to fight those with greater power and resources.
   True or False

3. People gathered for religious services and graduation ceremonies are examples of casual crowds.
   True or False

4. Panics often arise when people believe that they are in control of a situation.
   True or False

5. Protest crowds engage in activities intended to achieve specific political goals.
   True or False

6. Sociologist Robert E. Park was the first U.S. sociologist to investigate crowd behavior.
   True or False

7. According to Clayman, people like to "boo" a speech independently.
   True or False

8. For mass behavior to occur, people must be in close proximity geographically.
   True or False

9. Public opinion does not always translate into action by decision makers in government and industry or by individuals.
   True or False

10. Grassroots environmental movements are an example of reform movements.
    True or False

11. The 2001 terrorist attacks in New York City and Washington D.C. proved that revolutionary terrorists can originate from outside the country.
    True or False

12. Revolutionary movements also are referred to as expressive movements.
    True or False

13. Movements based on relative deprivation are most likely to occur when people have unfulfilled rising expectations.
    True or False

14. Social construction theory is based on conflict theory.
    True or False

15. One purpose of this text is to expose the readers to different view points.
    True or False

FILL IN THE BLANK QUESTIONS

1. The publication of *Silent Spring* in 1962 by biologist _____ is credited with triggering collective behavior directed at demanding a _____ .

2. The person most connected to the grassroots campaign of exposing sites of the chemical dump at Love Canal is _____ .

3. Nonviolent action that seeks to change a policy or law by refusing to comply with it is known as _____ .

4. _____ are unsubstantiated reports on an issue or subject.

5. The radio dramatization, The War of the Worlds, produced a type of _____ behavior defined as mass _____ .

6. A _____ is a temporary but widely copied activity enthusiastically followed by large numbers of people.

7. The attitudes and beliefs communicated by ordinary citizens to decision makers is defined as _____ .

8. Information provided by individuals or groups that have a vested interest in furthering their own course or damaging an opposing one is defined as _____ .

9. The most common type of crowd behavior wherein people seek to escape from a perceived danger is known as _____ .

10. Rumors about the personal lives of individuals is defined as _____ .

SHORT ANSWER/ESSAY QUESTIONS

1. What is collective behavior and what causes people to engage in collective behavior?

2. What are some types of crowd behavior? What causes crowd behavior? How could behavior influence individual behavior?

3. What are the five major theories that explain social movements? Which do you think is most applicable to solving future social problems? Why?

4. What is a social movement? What are the major types of social movements?

5. Why do people engage in social movements? Are social movements affective avenues for social change? Explain.

STUDENT CLASS PROJECTS AND ACTIVITIES

1. The uprising against socialism in the Soviet Union in 1991 is an example of a revolutionary movement; it sought, and apparently produced an entire restructuring of the Soviet political and economic system by overthrowing the existing social order and creating a new one. This could be considered the second of the revolutions that have occurred in this country since the Russian Revolution of 1917. Choose one of these two revolutions; trace the development of the movement, including the conditions necessary for the development of a social movement according to Smelser as mentioned in the text. In your paper, provide examples of the six conditions of the revolution and critique the success of the movement. Submit your paper to your instructor at the appropriate time, following any additional instructions you have been given.

2. Collect at least 10 articles dealing with some form of collective behavior discussed in the text. The articles could focus on fads, fashions, mobs, the public, or specific types of social movements. Provide a copy of each article in your paper. You are to: (1) summarize each article; (2) explain the significance (if any) of the article; (3) write a personal reaction to each article; (4) provide a conclusion and personal evaluation of the project; and (5) provide a bibliographic reference for each article selected. You should submit your paper to your instructor at the appropriate time, following any additional instructions given to you.

3. Write a paper on the topic of the impact of artificial intelligence in our society today and upon the societies for tomorrow. Provide at least three bibliographical references in your paper. Submit your paper to your instructor at the appropriate time, following any additional instructions you may have been given.

INTERNET ACTIVITIES

1. To learn about international terrorist groups and guerilla groups go to the following sites and write up a brief summary of the major terrorist organizations functioning today. Be sure to focus on the revolutionary aspects of each. Follow links on each site.

    a. www.foreignpolicy-infocus.org/briefs/vol3/v3n38terr_body.html

    b. www.state.gov/s/ct/

    c. www.state.gov/s/ct/rls/pgtrpt/2000/2450.htm

    d. www.infoplease.com/spot/terrorism1.html

    e. www.terrorism.net/

2. **Civil disobedience** is a form of **collective behavior**. This web site contains a history of **civil disobedience** in America as well as a training manual for those wishing to organize their own social movement. www.actupny.org/documents/CDdocuments/CDindex.html

3. *PETA* (People for the Ethical Treatment of Animals) represents an animal rights activist movement. Members of PETA often engage in tactics that border on violent, and sometimes can be considered to be violent as they seek to eliminate cruelty to animals. Look at the cruelty free companies that do not use animals in testing their products. www.peta-online.org

4. Environmental terrorism is one of the topics covered in this chapter. Examine the following web sites that give conflicting evidence to support their claims.
    a. http://users.aol.com/DaveMcCall/terror.htm
    b. www.greenpeace.org/
    c. www.sierraclub.org/

5. These are just a few of the sites on the Internet dealing with riots. Conduct a more extensive search for historical accounts and news stories of riots here in the U.S. and around the world.
    a. http://detnews.com/history/riot/riot.htm
    b. www.chipublib.org/004chicago/disasters/riots_1966to1977.html
    c. www.cnn.com/WORLD/asiapcf/9903/21/indonesia.borneo/
    d. www.cato.org/pubs/journal/cj14n1-13.html

INFOTRAC EXERCISES

1. Search for references on InfoTrac about **environmental movements**. Bring to class an article or brief report. Focus attention on the social aspects of these movements.

2. There are periodical references on the "social aspects" of **collective behavior**. Read one and then answer this question, *How can this article add to my knowledge about collective behavior?*

3. Search for the word **propaganda**. There are a number of categories such as "propaganda in television," "communist propaganda" and "war propaganda". Explore the uses of this category of information.

4. Look up the concept **urban legend**. InfoTrac has a number of periodical references to this phenomenon. Bring an example to class. How do urban legends fit into the study of **collective behavior**?

Solutions

MULTIPLE CHOICE QUESTIONS

1. A p. 660

2. B p. 663

3. C p. 664

4. B p. 664

5. A p. 664

6. D p. 666

7. C p. 666-667

8. B p. 667

9. C p. 668

10. D p. 669

11. A p. 670

12. D p. 671

13. B p. 672-673

14. C p. 674

15. A p. 674-675

16. C p. 675

17. D p. 677

18. B p. 673

19. A p. 677

20. C p. 679

TRUE FALSE QUESTIONS

1. T p. 660

2. T p. 663

3. F p. 664

4. F p. 665

5. T p. 665

6. T p. 665

7. F p. 666

8. F p. 667

9. T p. 669

10. T p. 672

11. T p. 673

12. F p. 673

13. T p. 674

14. F p. 676

15. T p. 683

FILL IN THE BLANK QUESTIONS

1. Rachel Carson, clean environment

2. Lois Gibbs

3. civil disobedience

4. Rumors

5. mass, hysteria

6. fad

7. public opinion

8. propoganda

9. panic

10. gossip